Professional Windows PowerShell™ Programming

Professional Windows PowerShell™ Programming

Snap-ins, Cmdlets, Hosts, and Providers

Arul Kumaravel
Jon White
Michael Naixin Li
Scott Happell
Guohui Xie
Krishna C. Vutukuri

WILEY

Wiley Publishing, Inc.

Windows PowerShell™ Programming: Snap-ins, Cmdlets, Hosts, and Providers

Published by
Wiley Publishing, Inc.
10475 Crosspoint Boulevard
Indianapolis, IN 46256
www.wiley.com

Published simultaneously in Canada

ISBN: 978-0-470-17393-0

Manufactured in the United States of America

10 9 8 7 6 5 4 3 2 1

Library of Congress Cataloging-in-Publication Data

About the Author

Arul Kumaravel is currently the Development Manager of the Windows PowerShell team. He has worked with this team since its early days and led the team in shipping of version 1 of the product, and is presently leading the development of next version of PowerShell. Fascinated by computers from an early age, when he first learned programming using BASIC, he went on to get his Master of Science degree in Computer Science from both the College of Engineering, Madras, India, and the University of Iowa. As a Microsoft intern, he wrote the first JavaScript/VBScript debugger for Internet Explorer 3, and was impressed by the potential to make a difference in millions of people's lives by working for Microsoft. He has been working at Microsoft for the past 11 years in various groups, shipping multiple versions of products, including Internet Explorer, the Windows operating system, and Content Management Server, and has even dabbled with Software as a Service with small business online services. More recently, attracted by the business side of technology, Arul has taken on the arduous task of pursuing his M.B.A. at the Wharton Business School. He can be reached at `arulk@hotmail.com`.

Jon White is a software engineer who lives and works in the idyllic surroundings of Seattle's eastern suburbs. An original member of the PowerShell team at Microsoft, his professional career started in the Administrative Tools group in Windows Server. As a hobbyist, Jon learned programming in his early teens after his father bought an 8088-based PC clone at a second-hand shop. The PC came with MS-DOS 2.0, which featured `debug.exe` with a 16-bit disassembler, but no assembler. As a result, Jon's first dive into programming was disassembling long tables of bytes to create a reverse-lookup dictionary for manually converting assembly programs into executable binary code. Coincidentally, later in life he filed the bug which removed `debug.exe` from 64-bit Windows. As a member of the PowerShell team, he wrote the language's first production script, when he converted the team's test harness from Perl to PowerShell script in 2004. When he's not working (or writing about work) he's either sailing or playing with fire in the backyard. You can contact him at `jwh@microsoft.com`.

Michael Naixin Li is the Senior Test Lead working on the Windows PowerShell team and currently oversees the testing of Windows PowerShell 2.0. Before Windows PowerShell, Michael worked on various major projects at Microsoft, including the development of MSN 1.x and 2.x, quality management for the COM Services component in Windows 2000, NetDocs Web Client Access, Web Services in Hailstorm, and Software Licensing Service in Windows Vista. Before joining Microsoft, Michael was an assistant professor at Shanghai University of Science and Technology (now called Shanghai University). He holds a Ph.D. in Computer Science from Colorado State University.

Scott Happell has been working as a software engineer and tester for 10 years. Three of those years have been on the Windows PowerShell team, which was what brought him to Microsoft from New Jersey, where he worked at an Internet startup that went belly-up. Scott recently left Microsoft to become a recording engineer/rock star and is trying to find cool ways to use PowerShell to help him create music.

George Xie was a Senior Developer in the Windows PowerShell team for three years, mainly focusing in the area of snap-in model and scripting language. Recently George joined Windows Mobile organization for the Mobile Device Management product. Before joining Microsoft, George worked for Siebel Systems Inc. for several years.

Krishna Chythanya Vutukuri is a Software Developer working on the Windows PowerShell team. Before Windows PowerShell, Krishna worked on various projects at Microsoft, which included the development of Windows Presentation Foundation. Before joining Microsoft, Krishna held various product development positions at Hewlett-Packard India Software Operations and Wipro Technologies. He holds a M.Sc (Tech.) in Information Systems from Birla Institute of Technology and Science, Pilani, India.

Credits

Executive Editor
Chris Webb

Development Editor
Howard Jones

Technical Editor
Marco Shaw

Production Editor
Rachel McConlogue

Copy Editor
Luann Rouff

Editorial Manager
Mary Beth Wakefield

Production Manager
Tim Tate

Vice President and Executive Group Publisher
Richard Swadley

Vice President and Executive Publisher
Joseph B. Wikert

Project Coordinator, Cover
Lynsey Osborn

Contents

Preface

Welcome to *Professional Windows PowerShell Programming*.

Way back in 2003, I attended a talk at a conference center at Microsoft by some engineers from the Microsoft Management Console team who were giving a demonstration of a prototype enhancement to MMC. The prototype was one of the early murmurs of Microsoft's response to the deluge of customer feedback they'd received about the Windows administrative user experience after the delivery of their first truly Internet-focused server operating system, Windows 2000 Server. The feedback wasn't all good.

Windows 2000 Server started its long evolution as a text-based file manager for DOS. During the bulk of its development, there was simply no idea that anyone would use it for anything other than checking their mail and organizing a 20-megabyte hard disk. As a result, the management story for Windows 2000 Server was provided in The Windows Way, which was a rich interactive experience, a full set of native and COM APIs, and no bridge between the two. In Linux, you could write a shell script to configure your mail and DNS servers; in Windows, you had to either do it manually or learn C++ and COM.

The incorporation of Visual Basic Script and JavaScript into Windows served this niche to a certain extent, but never really brought parity between the GUI experience and the command-line experience. Since these scripting languages interact with the operating system through a subset of COM, and a GUI application can use all of COM, call the Win32 API, and (in the case of certain programs such as Task Manager) call directly into the native kernel API, the capabilities of Windows scripts were always eclipsed by what was provided in the GUI.

But back to the demo: People filed into the room, a pair of engineers behind the podium broke the ice by joking about the PA system, the lights dimmed, and they started the show. The new MMC prototype, they revealed, was a GUI that used a command-line engine as its API layer. Every node expansion became a query, every "OK" click became a command, and every action taken by the GUI operator was displayed as script at the bottom of the screen with 100% fidelity. Old engineers shifted nervously in their seats, senior managers sat entranced with dollar signs in their eyes, and the caterer, noticing the direction of everyone's eyes, palmed an hors d'oeuvre and went outside to smoke a cigarette.

This demo ushered in what, in the following three years, would become Windows PowerShell. Version 1, available for download on the web and as an optional component on Windows Server 2008, provides a rich programming environment for users of every stripe, and for the first time gives Windows users a consistent glide path from the command-line experience all the way to COM and beyond.

This book is intended for the PowerShell snap-in and host developer audience, and introduces the reader to PowerShell programming from the API level. Written by members of the PowerShell v1.0 team, it covers development of cmdlets, providers, snap-ins, hosting applications, and custom host implementations in greater depth than the SDK documentation.

Enjoy.

Introduction

Conventions

To help you get the most from the text and keep track of what's happening, we've used a number of conventions throughout the book.

> **Boxes like this one hold important, not-to-be-forgotten information that is directly relevant to the surrounding text.**
>
> *Notes to the current discussion are offset and placed in italics like this.*

As for styles in the text:

- *We highlight* new terms and important words when we introduce them.
- We show keyboard strokes like this: Ctrl+A.
- Filenames, URLs, and code within the text appear like so: `persistence.properties`.
- We present code in two different ways:

```
We use a monofont type with no highlighting for most code examples.
```

```
We use gray highlighting to emphasize code that's particularly important
in the present context.
```

Source Code

As you work through the examples in this book, you may choose either to type in all the code manually or to use the source code files that accompany the book. All of the source code used in this book is available for download at `www.wrox.com`. Once at the site, simply locate the book's title (either by using the Search box or by using one of the title lists) and click the Download Code link on the book's detail page to obtain all the source code for the book. Because many books have similar titles, you may find it easiest to search by ISBN; this book's ISBN is 978-0-470-17393-0.

Once you download the code, just decompress it with your favorite compression tool. Alternatively, you can go to the main Wrox code download page at `www.wrox.com/dynamic/books/download.aspx` to see the code available for this book and all other Wrox books.

Errata

We make every effort to ensure that there are no errors in the text or in the code. However, no one is perfect, and mistakes do occur. If you find an error in one of our books, such as a spelling mistake or a faulty piece of code, we would be very grateful for your feedback. By sending in errata, you may save another reader hours of frustration, and at the same time you will be helping us provide even higher quality information.

To find the errata page for this book, go to `www.wrox.com` and locate the title using the Search box or one of the title lists. Then, on the book details page, click the Book Errata link. On this page you can view all errata that has been submitted for this book and posted by Wrox editors. A complete book list, including links to each book's errata, is also available at `www.wrox.com/misc-pages/booklist.shtml`.

If you don't spot "your" error on the Book Errata page, go to `www.wrox.com/contact/techsupport.shtml` and complete the form there to send us the error you have found. We'll check the information and, if appropriate, post a message to the book's errata page and fix the problem in subsequent editions of the book.

p2p.wrox.com

For author and peer discussion, join the P2P forums at `p2p.wrox.com`. The forums are a Web-based system for you to post messages relating to Wrox books and related technologies and to interact with other readers and technology users. The forums offer a subscription feature to e-mail you topics of interest of your choosing when new posts are made to the forums. Wrox authors, editors, other industry experts, and your fellow readers are present on these forums.

At `http://p2p.wrox.com` you will find a number of different forums that will help you not only as you read this book, but also as you develop your own applications. To join the forums, just follow these steps:

1. Go to `p2p.wrox.com` and click the Register link.
2. Read the terms of use and click Agree.
3. Complete the required information to join as well as any optional information you wish to provide and click Submit.
4. You will receive an e-mail with information describing how to verify your account and complete the joining process.

You can read messages in the forums without joining P2P but in order to post your own messages, you must join.

Once you join, you can post new messages and respond to messages other users post. You can read messages at any time on the Web. If you would like to have new messages from a particular forum e-mailed to you, click the Subscribe to this Forum icon by the forum name in the forum listing.

For more information about how to use the Wrox P2P, be sure to read the P2P FAQs for answers to questions about how the forum software works as well as many common questions specific to P2P and Wrox books. To read the FAQs, click the FAQ link on any P2P page.

1

Introduction to PowerShell

Welcome to Windows PowerShell, the new object-based command-line interface shell and scripting language built on top of .NET. PowerShell provides improved control and automation of IT administration tasks for the Windows platform. It is designed to make IT professionals and developers more productive.

Several books that introduce end-user IT professionals to Windows PowerShell are already available, but PowerShell development from the perspective of cmdlet, provider, and host developers has gone largely unmentioned. This book attempts to fill that gap by introducing the reader to the concepts, components, and development techniques behind building software packages that leverage Windows PowerShell. This book is written for developers who want to extend the functionality of Windows PowerShell and extend their applications using PowerShell.

Traditionally, when developers write a command-line utility, they have to write code for parsing the parameters, binding the argument values to parameters during runtime. In addition, they have to write code for formatting the output generated by the command. Windows PowerShell makes that easy by providing a runtime engine with its own parser. It also provides functionality that enables developers to add custom formatting when their objects are displayed. By performing the common tasks associated with writing command-line utilities, Windows PowerShell enables developers to focus on the business logic of their application, rather than spend development time solving universal problems.

Windows PowerShell Design Principles

Windows PowerShell was designed in response to years of customer feedback about the administrative experience on Microsoft Windows. Early on, many users asked why some of the traditional Unix shells weren't licensed and included in Windows, and it became apparent that the right answer was to produce a whole new kind of shell that would leave these legacy technologies behind. This thinking was distilled into four guiding principles that provided the foundation for PowerShell's design effort.

Preserve the Customer's Existing Investment

When a new technology is rolled out, it takes time for the technology to be adopted. Moreover, customers are likely to have already invested a lot in existing technologies. It's unreasonable to expect people to throw out their existing investments, which is why PowerShell was designed from the ground up to be compatible with existing Windows Management technologies.

In fact, PowerShell runs existing commands and scripts seamlessly. You can make use of PowerShell's integration with COM, WMI, and ADSI technologies alongside its tight integration with .NET. Indeed, PowerShell is the only technology that enables you to create and work with objects from these various technologies in one environment. You can see examples of this and other design principles in a quick tour of PowerShell later in the chapter.

Provide a Powerful, Object-Oriented Shell

`CMD.exe` and other traditional shells are text-based, meaning that the commands in these shells take text as input and produce text as output. Even if these commands convert the text internally into objects, when they produce output they convert it back to text. In traditional shells, when you want to put together simple commands in the pipeline, a lot of text processing is done between commands to produce desired output. Tools such as SED, AWK, and Perl became popular among command-line scripters because of their powerful text-processing capabilities.

PowerShell is built on top of .NET and is an object-based shell and scripting language. When you pipe commands, PowerShell passes objects between commands in the pipeline. This enables objects to be manipulated directly and to be passed to other tools. PowerShell's tight integration with .NET brings the functionality and consistency of .NET to IT professionals without requiring them to master a high-level programming language such as C# or VB.NET.

Extensibility, Extensibility, Extensibility

This design principle aims to make the IT administrator more productive by providing greater control over the Windows environment and accelerating the automation of system administration. Administrators can start PowerShell and use it immediately without having to learn anything because it runs existing commands and scripts, and is therefore easy to adopt. It is an easy to use shell and language for administrators.

All commands in PowerShell are called *cmdlets* (pronounced "commandlet"), and they use verb-noun syntax — for example, `Start-Service`, `Stop-Service` or `Get-Process`, `Get-WMIObject`, and so on. The intuitive nature of verb-noun syntax makes learning commands easy for administrators. PowerShell includes more than 100 commands and utilities that are admin focused. In addition, PowerShell provides a powerful scripting language that supports a wide range of scripting styles, from simple to sophisticated. This enables administrators to write simple scripts and learn the language as they go. With this combined functionality and ease of use, PowerShell provides a powerful environment for administrators to perform their daily tasks.

Tear Down the Barriers to Development

Another design principle of PowerShell is to make it easy for developers to create command-line tools and utilities. It provides common argument parsing code, parameter binding code that enables developers to write code only for the admin functionality they are providing. The PowerShell development model separates the processing of objects from formatting and outputting. PowerShell provides a set of cmdlets for manipulating objects, formatting objects, and outputting objects. This eliminates the need for developers to write this code. PowerShell leverages the power of .NET, which enables developers to take advantage of the vast library of this framework. It provides common functionality for logging, error handling, and debugging and tracing capabilities.

A Quick Tour of Windows PowerShell

This section presents a quick tour of Windows PowerShell. We'll start with a brief look at installing the program, and then move right into a discussion of cmdlets.

You start Windows PowerShell either by clicking the Windows PowerShell shortcut link or by typing **PowerShell** in the Run dialog box (see Figure 1-1).

Figure 1-1: Click the shortcut link and you'll get the prompt shown here.

Cmdlets

Windows PowerShell enables access to several types of commands, including functions, filters, scripts, aliases, cmdlets, and executables (applications). PowerShell's native command type is the cmdlet. A *cmdlet* is a simple command used for interacting with any management entity, including the operating system. You can think of a cmdlet as equivalent to a built-in command in another shell. The traditional shell generally processes commands as separate executables, but a cmdlet is an instance of a .NET class, and runs within PowerShell's process.

Windows PowerShell provides a rich set of cmdlets, including several that enhance the discoverability of the shell's features. We begin our tour of Windows PowerShell by learning about a few cmdlets that will help you get started in this environment. The first cmdlet you need to know about is `get-help`:

```
PS C:\> get-help
TOPIC
    Get-Help


SHORT DESCRIPTION
    Displays help about PowerShell cmdlets and concepts.


LONG DESCRIPTION


SYNTAX
    get-help {<CmdletName> | <TopicName>}
    help {<CmdletName> | <TopicName>}
    <CmdletName> -?


    "Get-help" and "-?" display help on one page.
    "Help" displays help on multiple pages.

    Examples:
      get-help get-process   : Displays help about the get-process cmdlet.
      get-help about-signing : Displays help about the signing concept.
      help where-object      : Displays help about the where-object cmdlet.
      help about_foreach     : Displays help about foreach loops in PowerShell.
      match-string -?        : Displays help about the match-string cmdlet.


    You can use wildcard characters in the help commands (not with -?).
    If multiple help topics match, PowerShell displays a list of matching
    topics. If only one help topic matches, PowerShell displays the topic.


    Examples:
      get-help *      : Displays all help topics.
      get-help get-*  : Displays topics that begin with get-.
      help *object*   : Displays topics with "object" in the name.
      get-help about* : Displays all conceptual topics.




    For information about wildcards, type:
      get-help about_wildcard



REMARKS
```

```
    To learn about PowerShell, read the following help topics:
      get-command  : Displays a list of cmdlets.
      about_object : Explains the use of objects in PowerShell.
      get-member   : Displays the properties of an object.


    Conceptual help files are named "about_<topic>", such as:
      about_regular_expression.

    The help commands also display the aliases on the system.
    For information about aliases, type:

      get-help about_alias


PS C:\>
```

As you can see, get-help provides information about how to get help on PowerShell cmdlets and concepts. This is all well and good, but you also need to be able to determine what commands are available for use. The get-command cmdlet helps you with that:

```
PS C:\> get-command

CommandType     Name                          Definition
-----------     ----                          ----------
Cmdlet          Add-Content                   Add-Content [-P
Cmdlet          Add-History                   Add-History [[-
Cmdlet          Add-Member                    Add-Member [-Me
Cmdlet          Add-PSSnapin                  Add-PSSnapin [-
Cmdlet          Clear-Content                 Clear-Content [
Cmdlet          Clear-Item                    Clear-Item [-Pa
Cmdlet          Clear-ItemProperty            Clear-ItemPrope
Cmdlet          Clear-Variable                Clear-Variable
Cmdlet          Compare-Object                Compare-Object
Cmdlet          ConvertFrom-SecureString      ConvertFrom-Sec
Cmdlet          Convert-Path                  Convert-Path [-
Cmdlet          ConvertTo-Html                ConvertTo-Html
Cmdlet          ConvertTo-SecureString        ConvertTo-Secur
Cmdlet          Copy-Item                     Copy-Item [-Pat

...
```

As shown in the preceding output, get-command returns all the available commands. You can also find cmdlets with a specific verb or noun:

```
PS C:\> get-command -verb get

CommandType     Name                          Definition
-----------     ----                          ----------
Cmdlet          Get-Acl                       Get-Acl [[-Path]
Cmdlet          Get-Alias                     Get-Alias [[-Nam
Cmdlet          Get-AuthenticodeSignature     Get-Authenticode
Cmdlet          Get-ChildItem                 Get-ChildItem [[
Cmdlet          Get-Command                   Get-Command [[-A
```

```
Cmdlet          Get-Content                    Get-Content [-Pa
Cmdlet          Get-Credential                 Get-Credential [
Cmdlet          Get-Culture                    Get-Culture [-Ve
Cmdlet          Get-Date                       Get-Date [[-Date
Cmdlet          Get-EventLog                   Get-EventLog [-L
Cmdlet          Get-ExecutionPolicy            Get-ExecutionPol
Cmdlet          Get-Help                       Get-Help [[-Name
Cmdlet          Get-History                    Get-History [[-I
Cmdlet          Get-Host                       Get-Host [-Verbo
Cmdlet          Get-Item                       Get-Item [-Path]
Cmdlet          Get-ItemProperty               Get-ItemProperty
Cmdlet          Get-Location                   Get-Location [-P
Cmdlet          Get-Member                     Get-Member [[-Na
Cmdlet          Get-PfxCertificate             Get-PfxCertifica
Cmdlet          Get-Process                    Get-Process [[-N
Cmdlet          Get-PSDrive                    Get-PSDrive [[-N
Cmdlet          Get-PSProvider                 Get-PSProvider [
Cmdlet          Get-PSSnapin                   Get-PSSnapin [[-
Cmdlet          Get-Runspace                   Get-Runspace [[-
Cmdlet          Get-Service                    Get-Service [[-N
Cmdlet          Get-TraceSource                Get-TraceSource
Cmdlet          Get-UICulture                  Get-UICulture [-
Cmdlet          Get-Unique                     Get-Unique [-Inp
Cmdlet          Get-Variable                   Get-Variable [[-
Cmdlet          Get-WmiObject                  Get-WmiObject [-
```

When commands are executed, their output is returned to the shell in the form of .NET objects. (In the case of native commands, the text output of the command is converted to .NET string objects before being returned.) These objects can be directly queried and manipulated by using the object's properties and methods. Fortunately, you don't have to know the properties and methods of each object in order to manipulate it. If you're unfamiliar with an object's type, you can use the `get-member` cmdlet to examine its members:

```
PS C:\> "Hello" | get-member

   TypeName: System.String

Name                MemberType         Definition
----                ----------         ----------
Clone               Method             System.Object Clone()
CompareTo           Method             System.Int32 CompareTo(Object value),...
Contains            Method             System.Boolean Contains(String value)
CopyTo              Method             System.Void CopyTo(Int32 sourceIndex,...
EndsWith            Method             System.Boolean EndsWith(String value)...
Equals              Method             System.Boolean Equals(Object obj), Sy...
GetEnumerator       Method             System.CharEnumerator GetEnumerator()
GetHashCode         Method             System.Int32 GetHashCode()
GetType             Method             System.Type GetType()
GetTypeCode         Method             System.TypeCode GetTypeCode()
get_Chars           Method             System.Char get_Chars(Int32 index)
get_Length          Method             System.Int32 get_Length()
IndexOf             Method             System.Int32 IndexOf(Char value, Int3...
```

```
IndexOfAny         Method                System.Int32 IndexOfAny(Char[] anyOf,...
Insert             Method                System.String Insert(Int32 startIndex...
IsNormalized       Method                System.Boolean IsNormalized(), System...
LastIndexOf        Method                System.Int32 LastIndexOf(Char value, ...
LastIndexOfAny     Method                System.Int32 LastIndexOfAny(Char[] an...
Normalize          Method                System.String Normalize(), System.Str...
PadLeft            Method                System.String PadLeft(Int32 totalWidt...
PadRight           Method                System.String PadRight(Int32 totalWid...
Remove             Method                System.String Remove(Int32 startIndex...
Replace            Method                System.String Replace(Char oldChar, C...
Split              Method                System.String[] Split(Params Char[] s...
StartsWith         Method                System.Boolean StartsWith(String valu...
Substring          Method                System.String Substring(Int32 startIn...
ToCharArray        Method                System.Char[] ToCharArray(), System.C...
ToLower            Method                System.String ToLower(), System.Strin...
ToLowerInvariant   Method                System.String ToLowerInvariant()
ToString           Method                System.String ToString(), System.Stri...
ToUpper            Method                System.String ToUpper(), System.Strin...
ToUpperInvariant   Method                System.String ToUpperInvariant()
Trim               Method                System.String Trim(Params Char[] trim...
TrimEnd            Method                System.String TrimEnd(Params Char[] t...
TrimStart          Method                System.String TrimStart(Params Char[]...
Chars              ParameterizedProperty System.Char Chars(Int32 index) {get;}
Length             Property              System.Int32 Length {get;}
```

Windows PowerShell also enables you to execute existing native operating system commands and scripts. The following example executes the ipconfig.exe command to find out about network settings:

```
PS C:\> ipconfig
Windows IP Configuration
Wireless LAN adapter Wireless Network Connection:
   Connection-specific DNS Suffix  . : ARULHOMELAN
   Link-local IPv6 Address . . . . . : fe80::c4e0:69b3:5d35:9b4b%9
   IPv4 Address. . . . . . . . . . . : 192.168.1.13
   Subnet Mask . . . . . . . . . . . : 255.255.255.0
   Default Gateway . . . . . . . . . : 192.168.1.1
```

In a traditional shell, when you want to get the IP address output by the `IPConfig.exe` utility, you have to perform text parsing. For example, you might do something like get the ninth line of text from the output and then get the characters starting from the thirty-ninth character until the end of the line to get the IP address. PowerShell enables you to perform this style of traditional text processing, as shown here:

```
PS C:\Users\arulk> $a = ipconfig
PS C:\Users\arulk> $a[8]
   IPv4 Address. . . . . . . . . . . : 192.168.1.13
PS C:\Users\arulk> $a[10].Substring(39)
192.168.1.13
```

However, this kind of text processing is very brittle and error prone. If the output of `IPconfig.exe` changes, then the preceding script breaks. For example, because PowerShell converts to text output by exes and scripts as `String` objects, it is possible to achieve better text processing. In the preceding example, we are looking for the line that contains IP in the text:

```
PS C:\> $match = @($a | select-string "IP")
PS C:\> $ipstring = $match[0].line
PS C:\> $ipstring
   IPv4 Address. . . . . . . . . . . : 192.168.1.13
PS C:\> $index = $ipstring.indexof(": ")
PS C:\> $ipstring.Substring($index+2)
PS C:\> $ipaddress = [net.ipaddress]$ipstring.Substring($index+2)
PS C:\> $ipaddress
```

In the preceding script, the first line searches for the string IP in the result variable `$a`. `@(...)` and converts the result of execution into an array. The reason we do this is because we will get multiple lines that match the IP in computers that have multiple network adapters. We are going to find out the `ipaddress` in the first adapter. The result returned by `select-string` is a `MatchInfo` object. This object contains a member `Line` that specifies the actual matching line. (I know this because I used `get-member` to find out.) This string contains the IP address after the characters `": "`. Because the `Line` property is a `String` object, you use the `String` object's `IndexOf` method (again, I used `get-member`) to determine the location where the IP address starts. You then use `Substring` with an index of `+ 2` (for `": "` characters) to get the IP address string. Next, you convert the IP address string into the .NET `IPAddress` object, which provides more type safety. As you can see, Windows PowerShell provides great functionality for doing traditional text processing.

Next, let's look at the COM support in PowerShell:

```
PS C:\> $ie = new-object -com internetexplorer.application
PS C:\> $ie.Navigate2("http://blogs.msdn.com/powershell")
PS C:\> $ie.visible = $true
PS C:\> $ie.Quit()
```

You can create COM objects using the `new-object` cmdlet, with the `-com` parameter specifying the programmatic ID of the COM class. In the preceding example, we create an Internet Explorer object and navigate to the blog of the Windows PowerShell team. As before, you can use `get-member` to find out all the properties and methods a COM object supports. Do you see a pattern here?

In addition to COM, PowerShell also has great support for WMI.:

```
PS C:\Users\arulk> $a = get-wmiobject win32_bios
PS C:\Users\arulk> $a


SMBIOSBIOSVersion : Version 1.50
Manufacturer      : TOSHIBA
Name              : v1.50V
SerialNumber      : 76047600H
Version           : TOSHIB - 970814
```

Using `get-wmiobject`, you can create any WMI object. The preceding example creates an instance of a `Win32_Bios` object.

Now that you've seen some of PowerShell's capabilities firsthand, let's take a look at what goes on under the hood while you're providing this functionality to the shell's user.

High-Level Architecture of Windows PowerShell

PowerShell has a modular architecture consisting of a central execution engine, a set of extensible cmdlets and providers, and a customizable user interface. PowerShell ships with numerous default implementations of the cmdlets, providers, and the user interface, and several third-party implementations are provided by other groups at Microsoft and by external companies.

The following sections provide details about each of the architectural elements illustrated in Figure 1-2.

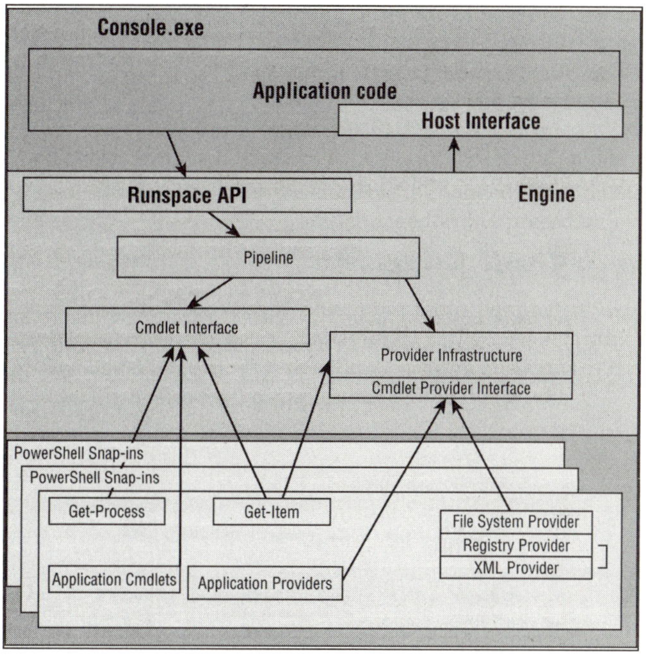

Figure 1-2: The high-level architecture of Windows PowerShell

Host Application

The Windows PowerShell engine is designed to be hostable in different application environments. In order to make use of PowerShell functionality, it needs to be hosted in an application that implements the Windows PowerShell host interface. The host interface is a set of interfaces that provides functionality enabling the engine to interact with the user. This includes but is not limited to the following:

- Getting input from users
- Reporting progress information
- Output and error reporting

The hosting application can be a console application, a windows application, or a Web application. Windows PowerShell includes a default hosting application called `PowerShell.exe`, which is console based. If you're like most developers, you'll rarely need to write your own host implementation. Instead, you'll make use of PowerShell's host interface to interact with the engine. You only need to write a hosting application when you have application requirements for an interface that is richer than the interface provided by the default hosting application. Writing a hosting application involves implementing Windows PowerShell host interfaces and using the Windows PowerShell Runspace and Pipeline APIs to invoke commands. Together, these two interfaces enable communication between the application and the Windows PowerShell engine. You'll learn the details about writing a hosting application in Chapter 7.

Windows PowerShell Engine

The Windows PowerShell engine contains the core execution functionality and provides the execution environment for cmdlets, providers, functions, filters, scripts, and external executables. The engine exposes the functionality through the `Runspace` interface, which is used by the hosting application to interact with the engine. At a high level, the engine consists of a runspace, which is like an instance of the engine, and one or more *pipelines*, which are instances of command lines. These pipeline components interact with the cmdlets through the `cmdlet` interface. All cmdlets need to implement this interface to participate in the pipeline. Similarly, the pipeline interacts with the providers through a well-defined set of provider interfaces. We will delve into more details about the engine as we progress in the book.

Windows PowerShell Snap-ins

Windows PowerShell provides an extensible architecture for adding functionality to the shell by means of snap-ins. A *snap-in* is a .NET assembly or set of assemblies that contains cmdlets, providers, type extensions, and format metadata. All the commands and providers that ship as part of the Windows PowerShell product are implemented as a set of five snap-ins. You can view the list of snap-ins using the `get-pssnapin` cmdlet:

```
PS C:\> get-pssnapin

Name        : Microsoft.PowerShell.Core
PSVersion   : 1.0
Description : This Windows PowerShell snap-in contains Windows PowerShell manage-
ment cmdlets used to manage components of Windows PowerShell.

Name        : Microsoft.PowerShell.Host
PSVersion   : 1.0
Description : This Windows PowerShell snap-in contains cmdlets used by the Win-
dows PowerShell host.

Name        : Microsoft.PowerShell.Management
PSVersion   : 1.0
Description : This Windows PowerShell snap-in contains management cmdlets used to man-
age Windows components.

Name        : Microsoft.PowerShell.Security
PSVersion   : 1.0
Description : This Windows PowerShell snap-in contains cmdlets to manage Windows Pow-
erShell security.

Name        : Microsoft.PowerShell.Utility
```

```
PSVersion   : 1.0
Description : This Windows PowerShell snap-in contains utility Cmdlets used to  manip-
ulate data.
```

Summary

This chapter introduced you to some basic cmdlets to help with discoverability. It also described the high-level architecture of PowerShell. From here, we'll move on to the first step beyond the cmdlet level: learning how to develop a custom snap-in package. The techniques in the following chapter lay the foundation for creating your own cmdlets and providers. You'll also learn about PowerShell's model for distributing and deploying the code you write.

2

Extending Windows PowerShell

As you saw in Chapter 1, Windows PowerShell provides an extensible architecture that allows new functionality to be added to the shell. This new functionality can be in the form of cmdlets, providers, type extensions, format metadata, and so on. A Windows PowerShell snap-in is a .NET assembly that contains cmdlets, providers, and so on. Windows PowerShell comes with a set of basic snap-ins that offer all the basic cmdlets and providers built into the shell. You write a snap-in when you want your cmdlets or providers to be part of the default Windows PowerShell. When a snap-in is loaded in Windows PowerShell, all cmdlets and providers in the snap-in are made available to the user. This model allows administrators to customize the shell by adding or removing snap-ins to achieve precise sets of providers and cmdlets.[1]

This chapter first introduces the two types of PowerShell snap-ins and describes when to use each one. It then shows you step by step how to author, register, and use both types of snap-ins. To make it more meaningful, the code examples also show the minimum coding needed for authoring cmdlets.

Note that all code examples in this chapter and the rest of the book are written in C#.

Types of PowerShell Snap-ins

Any .NET assembly becomes a Windows PowerShell snap-in when the assembly implements a snap-in installer class. Windows PowerShell supports two distinct types of snap-in installer classes. The default recommended type is `PSSnapin`, which registers all cmdlets and providers in a single contained assembly. The second type is `CustomPSSnapin`, which enables developers to specify the list of cmdlets and providers from either a single or multiple assemblies.

Through examples, we first show you how to create and use a standard PowerShell snap-in, and then we explain when you need to use a custom PowerShell snap-in and how to implement and use it.

[1]Note, however, that PowerShell built-in snap-ins, such as Microsoft.PowerShell.Host, cannot be removed.

Creating a Standard PowerShell Snap-in

You can extend Windows PowerShell by writing your own cmdlets and providers. Before you can use those cmdlets and providers with PowerShell, however, you need to register them as PowerShell snap-ins. Chapters 4 and 5 describe in detail how to write cmdlets and providers. This section explains how to author and use your PowerShell snap-in.

Several steps are involved in developing and using a standard PowerShell snap-in. First, you need to write some code for your snap-in and compile the code into a .NET assembly. Second, you need to register the assembly as a snap-in with the PowerShell platform. Registering a snap-in only tells PowerShell where a snap-in is. Before you can use the cmdlets or providers in your snap-in, you need to load the snap-in into a PowerShell session. After a snap-in is loaded, you can use cmdlets or providers in your snap-in just like other built-in native cmdlets and providers. To avoid the need to manually load a snap-in every time you start Windows PowerShell, you can save your loaded snap-ins into a configuration file for use later, or you can explicitly load a snap-in from your PowerShell profile script. The following sections explain in further detail each of the aforementioned steps.

Writing a PowerShell Snap-in

If you want to create a snap-in to register all the cmdlets and providers in a single assembly, then you should create your own snap-in class, inheriting from the `PSSnapIn` class, and add a `RunInstaller` attribute to the class, as illustrated in the following sample code:

```
// Save this to a file using filename: PSBook-2-1.cs

using System;
using System.Management.Automation;
using System.ComponentModel;
namespace PSBook.Chapter2
{
    [RunInstaller(true)]
    public class PSBookChapter2MySnapIn : PSSnapIn
    {
        // Name for the PowerShell snap-in.
        public override string Name
        {
            get
            {
                return "Wiley.PSProfessional.Chapter2";
            }
        }

        // Vendor information for the PowerShell snap-in.
        public override string Vendor
        {
            get
            {
                return "Wiley";
            }
        }
```

```
            // Description of the PowerShell snap-in
            public override string Description
            {
                get
                {
                    return "This is a sample PowerShell snap-in";
                }
            }
        }

        // Code to implement cmdlet Write-Hi
        [Cmdlet(VerbsCommunications.Write, "Hi")]
        public class SayHi : Cmdlet
        {
            protected override void ProcessRecord()
            {
              WriteObject("Hi, World!");
            }
        }

        // Code to implement cmdlet Write-Hello
        [Cmdlet(VerbsCommunications.Write, "Hello")]
        public class SayHello : Cmdlet
        {
            protected override void ProcessRecord()
            {
               WriteObject("Hello, World!");
            }
        }
    }
```

`System.Management.Automation` comes with the PowerShell SDK, which can be downloaded from the Web. `System.Management.Automation` is also available on all systems on which Windows PowerShell is installed; on my machine, it is installed at C:\Windows\assembly\GAC_MSIL\System.Management.Automation\1.0.0.0__31bf3856ad364e35. It inherits from `System.ComponentModel`, which comes with the .NET Framework, which is why it works with the installer in .NET through `installutil.exe`, a tool that .NET provides for installing or uninstalling managed applications on a computer.

For each snap-in, it is required to add a public `Name` property. At snap-in registration time, a Registry key is created using the snap-in name as a key name. The snap-in name is also used to add or remove the snap-in. To avoid potential name collision, we recommend using the following format to specify snap-in names: < *Company* > . < *Product* > . < *Component* > . For example, the built-in PowerShell snap-ins are named as follows:

```
PS E:\PSbook\CodeSample> get-pssnapin | format-list Name
Name : Microsoft.PowerShell.Core
Name : Microsoft.PowerShell.Host
Name : Microsoft.PowerShell.Management
```

```
Name : Microsoft.PowerShell.Security
Name : Microsoft.PowerShell.Utility
```

The other required public property is `Vendor`. In the preceding example, the vendor is `Wiley`. Optionally, you can add a public `Description` property and other properties.

The preceding example also included code for two cmdlets: Write-Hi and Write-Hello. These are included for illustration purposes. For more information on how to write cmdlets, please see Chapter 4. For this simple example, all code is put in a single `.cs` file because it is very simple. In practice, you will likely use a separate file for your snap-in class and other cmdlets and provider classes.

Compile the sample code from Visual Studio or use the following command-line option to create an assembly `PSBook-2-1.dll`:

```
csc /target:library /reference:.\System.Management.Automation.dll PSBook-2-1.cs
```

With that, you have created your first PowerShell snap-in. Note that you need to have the .NET Framework installed in order for this to work. Both `Csc.exe` and `installutil.exe` come with the .NET Framework. `Csc.exe` is a C# compiler. I have the .NET Framework 2.0 installed on my 32-bit machine, and `csc.exe` and `installutil.exe` can be found at the following location:

```
C:\Windows\Microsoft.NET\Framework\v2.0.50727\csc.exe
C:\Windows\Microsoft.NET\Framework\v2.0.50727\installutil.exe
```

On a 64-bit operating system, you can find them at this location:

```
C:\Windows\Microsoft.NET\Framework64\v2.0.50727\csc.exe
C:\Windows\Microsoft.NET\Framework64\v2.0.50727\installutil.exe
```

The path to `csc.exe` on your machine could be different depending on what version of the .NET Framework you install and how your system is configured. If it is not there and you have the .NET Framework installed, you can use the following PowerShell command to find the path:

```
Get-ChildItem -Recurse -path ${env:systemroot} -Include csc.exe
```

In any case, make sure the locations of `csc.exe` and `installutil.exe` are included in your path. In addition, you may need to adjust the relative path to `System.Management.Automation.dll` if it is not in the same folder as the C# files.

In order to use a snap-in, you must register it with PowerShell first. That is described in the next section.

Registering Your PowerShell Snap-in

To register a PowerShell snap-in like the one shown in the preceding section, you can use `installutil.exe`. `InstallUtil.exe` comes with the .NET Framework. You can use the PowerShell command line mentioned earlier to find the path:

```
Get-ChildItem -Recurse -path ${env:systemroot} -Include installutil.exe
```

You must have administrator privileges in order to run `installutil.exe`. On Windows Vista, you can right-click on the Windows PowerShell icon and select Run as Administrator. Here is the command to register the preceding snap-in, assuming `installutil.exe` is in your path:

```
E:\PSbook\CodeSample>installutil PSBook-2-1.dll
Microsoft (R) .NET Framework Installation utility Version 2.0.50727.312
Copyright (c) Microsoft Corporation. All rights reserved.

Running a transacted installation.

Beginning the Install phase of the installation.
See the contents of the log file for the E:\PSbook\CodeSample\PSBook-2-1.dll
assembly's progress.
The file is located at E:\PSbook\CodeSample\PSBook-2-1.InstallLog.
Installing assembly 'E:\PSbook\CodeSample\PSBook-2-1.dll'.
Affected parameters are:
   logtoconsole =
   assemblypath = E:\PSbook\CodeSample\PSBook-2-1.dll
   logfile = E:\PSbook\CodeSample\PSBook-2-1.InstallLog

The Install phase completed successfully, and the Commit phase is beginning.
See the contents of the log file for the E:\PSbook\CodeSample\PSBook-2-1.dll
assembly's progress.
The file is located at E:\PSbook\CodeSample\PSBook-2-1.InstallLog.
Committing assembly 'E:\PSbook\CodeSample\PSBook-2-1.dll'.
Affected parameters are:
   logtoconsole =
   assemblypath = E:\PSbook\CodeSample\PSBook-2-1.dll
   logfile = E:\PSbook\CodeSample\PSBook-2-1.InstallLog

The Commit phase completed successfully.
The transacted install has completed.
```

Depending on the information you implement for the snap-in installer, the following registry information may be created when you register a snap-in:

- A Registry key with *SnapinName*, which was defined in the `PSSnapIn` class, will be created under HKLM\Software\Microsoft\PowerShell\1\PowerShellSnapIns.
- A set of values may be created under this *SnapinName* key.

The following table lists the possible value names, including data types, whether it is optional or required, and a description of each value.

Name	Type	Optional or Required	Description
Application-Base	REG_SZ	Required	Base directory used to load files needed by the PSSnapIn such as type or format files
Assembly-Name	REG_SZ	Required	Strong name of PSSnapIn assembly
Module-Name	REG_SZ	Required	Path to assembly if the PSSnapIn assembly is not stored in GAC
PowerShell-Version	REG_SZ	Required	Version of PowerShell used by this PSSnapIn
Types	REG_MULTI_SZ	Optional	Path of files, which contains type information for this PSSnapIn. It can be an absolute or relative path. A relative path is relative to the `ApplicationBase` directory.
Formats	REG_MULTI_SZ	Optional	Path of files, which contains type information for this PSSnapIn. It can be an absolute or relative path. A relative path is relative to the `ApplicationBase` directory.
Description	REG_SZ	Optional	Non-localized string describing the PSSnapIn. If this information is not provided, an empty string is used as a description of the PSSnapIn.
Description-Indirect	REG_SZ	Optional	Resource pointer to localized PSSnapIn description. This should be in the following format: `ResourceBaseName,ResourceId`. If this information is not provided, a language-neutral description string is used as a description for the PSSnapIn.
Vendor	REG_SZ	Optional	Vendor name for the PSSnapIn. If this information is not provided, an empty string is used as vendor name for the PSSnapIn.
Vendor-Indirect	REG_SZ	Optional	Resource pointer to the localized PSSnapIn vendor name. This should be in the following format: `ResourceBaseName,ResourceId`. If this information is not provided, a language-neutral vendor string is used as vendor of the PSSnapIn.
Version	REG_SZ	Optional	Version for the PSSnapIn
CustomPSS-napInType	REG_SZ	Optional	Name of the class that contains Custom PSSnapIn information

When a snap-in is registered, the DLLs referenced are loaded when used, so make sure you do not register DLLs from a temporary directory; otherwise, when the DLLs are deleted, PowerShell will fail to find and load the DLLs for the snap-in later.

Listing Available PowerShell Snap-ins

You can verify whether a snap-in is registered with Windows PowerShell by listing all the registered PowerShell snap-ins. This can be done using the `Get-PSSnapIn` cmdlet with the `-registered` parameter. The snap-in registered should be shown in the list:

```
PS E:\PSbook\CodeSample> get-pssnapin -registered
Name        : Wiley.PSProfessional.Chapter2
PSVersion   : 1.0
Description : This is a sample PowerShell snap-in
```

Loading a PowerShell Snap-in to a Running Shell

`Installutil.exe` only puts information about a snap-in into the Windows Registry. In order to use cmdlets and providers implemented in a snap-in, you need to load the snap-in into PowerShell, which is done through another PowerShell cmdlet, `Add-PSSnapIn`, as shown below:

```
PS E:\PSbook\CodeSample> add-pssnapin PSBook-Chapter2-SnapIn
```

You can verify that the snap-in is loaded using the cmdlet `Get-PSSnapIn` without the parameter `-registered`:

```
PS E:\PSbook\CodeSample> get-pssnapin
Name        : Wiley.PSProfessional.Chapter2
PSVersion   : 1.0
Description : This is a sample PowerShell snap-in
```

You also can verify that the snap-in assembly is loaded with the following:

```
PS E:\PSbook\CodeSample> (get-process -id $pid).modules | where-object {$_.filename
-like "*PSBook*"}
   Size(K) ModuleName                 FileName
   ------- ----------                 --------
        32 PSBook-2-1.dll             E:\PSbook\CodeSample\PSBook-2-1.dll
```

Just like built-in cmdlets, you can use `get-command` to list them. In Figure 2-1, a wild char is used to list all the cmdlets with the verb "write" and any noun starting with the letter "h". As expected, the two cmdlets we just implemented in the snap-in `Write-Hello` and `Write-Hi` are listed, along with the built-in cmdlet `Write-Host`. Then we invoked the cmdlets `Write-Hi` and `Write-Hello`, just as we would invoke a built-in cmdlet, and they worked as expected. In fact, as you type the cmdlet name, you can use tab-completion. Give that a try and see for yourself.

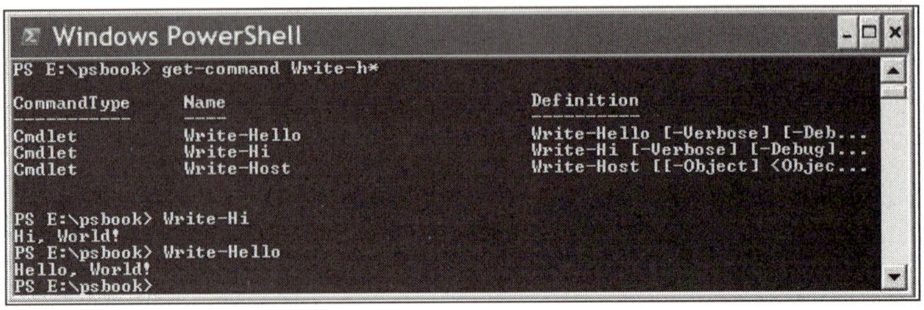

Figure 2-1

Removing a PowerShell Snap-in from a Running Shell

To remove a `PSSnapIn` from Windows PowerShell, use the `Remove-PSSnapin` cmdlet:

```
PS E:\PSbook\CodeSample> Remove-PSSnapin PSBook-Chapter2-SnapIn -passthru

Name        : Wiley.PSProfessional.Chapter2
PSVersion   : 1.0
Description : This is a sample PowerShell snap-in
```

Removing a snap-in disables the shell from further using any cmdlets and providers in the snap-in. After that, you will not see the snap-in listed when running `get-pssnapin`, nor will you see cmdlets or providers listed. However, `remove-pssnapin` does not unload the snap-in assembly from the shell process. You can verify that with the following

```
PS E:\PSbook\CodeSample> (get-process -id $pid).modules | where-object {$_.filename
-like "*PSBook*"}
   Size(K) ModuleName           FileName
   ------- ----------           --------
        32 PSBook-2-1.dll       E:\PSbook\CodeSample\PSBook-2-1.dll
```

As shown in the preceding example, `PSBook-2-1.dll` is still listed as a module in the current shell. You need to close the PowerShell session to unload the snap-in assembly. Otherwise, the assembly is locked and you will not be able to recompile your code after you make changes.

Unregistering a PowerShell Snap-in

To unregister a snap-in from the Registry, run `installutil.exe` with `-u` parameter as shown in the following example (assuming that `installutil.exe` is in your path):

```
PS E:\PSbook\CodeSample> installutil -u PSBook-2-1.dll
Microsoft (R) .NET Framework Installation utility Version 2.0.50727.312
Copyright (c) Microsoft Corporation. All rights reserved.

The uninstall is beginning.
See the contents of the log file for the E:\PSbook\CodeSample\PSBook-2-1.dll
assembly's progress.
```

```
The file is located at E:\PSbook\CodeSample\PSBook-2-1.InstallLog.
Uninstalling assembly 'E:\PSbook\CodeSample\PSBook-2-1.dll'.
Affected parameters are:
   logtoconsole =
   assemblypath = E:\PSbook\CodeSample\PSBook-2-1.dll
   logfile = E:\PSbook\CodeSample\PSBook-2-1.InstallLog

The uninstall has completed.
```

You can verify that by running the following command:

```
PS E:\PSbook\CodeSample> get-pssnapin -registered
```

You should no longer see the snap-in `Wiley.PSProfessional.Chapter2` listed.

In order to unregister a snap-in, you must run the command as Administrator.

Registering a PowerShell Snap-in without Implementing a Snap-in Clas

It is possible to register a `PSSnapin` without implementing a class inherited from `PSSnapIn`. For example, registering `pssnapin` typically happens during setup; if you do not want to invoke any managed code during setup, you may choose to register a `PSSnapin` by directly creating the Registry key and values as mentioned earlier. To demonstrate, try the following steps:

1. Make sure that the snap-in `Wiley.PSProfessional.Chapter2` has been unregistered as mentioned above.
2. Save the following text to file `PSBook-Chapter2-PSSnapin.reg`:[2]

```
Windows Registry Editor Version 5.00

[HKEY_LOCAL_MACHINE\SOFTWARE\Microsoft\PowerShell\1\PowerShellSnapins\
Wiley.PSProfessional.Chapter2]
"PowerShellVersion"="1.0"
"Vendor"="Wiley"
"Description"="This is a sample PowerShell snap-in"
"Version"="0.0.0.0"
"ApplicationBase"="E:\\PSbook\\CodeSample"
"AssemblyName"="PSBook-2-1, Version=0.0.0.0, Culture=neutral,
PublicKeyToken=null"
"ModuleName"="E:\\PSbook\\CodeSample\\PSBook-2-1.dll"
```

3. Double-click the file to add the information to the Registry.
4. Run the command **get-pssnapin –registered**. You should see that the `Wiley.PSProfessional.Chapter2` snap-in is included in the list.

[2]You can use C++ code, Windows Installer XML, or whatever works best for you to add those Registry values.

5. Run the command **add-pssnapin Wiley.PSProfessional.Chapter2**.
6. Run the command **get-pssnapin**. The `Wiley.PSProfessional.Chapter2` snap-in should be included in the loaded snap-in list.

Saving Snap-in Configuration

As you have just seen, you need to use **add-pssnapin** to load the assembly of a snap-in into PowerShell before you can use the cmdlets, providers, and so on, in the snap-in. To avoid typing `add-pssnapin` commands for each snap-in after you start PowerShell, you can save the loaded snap-ins into a configuration file for use later. This can be done using the `Export-Console` cmdlet, as shown in the following example:

```
PS E:\PSbook\CodeSample\PSBook> export-console MyConsole
```

After running the preceding command, the file `MyConsole.psc1` is created in the folder. `MyConsole.psc1` is an XML file that lists all the currently loaded snap-ins. The following code shows a sample configuration XML file:

```
<?xml version="1.0" encoding="utf-8"?>
<PSConsoleFile ConsoleSchemaVersion="1.0">
  <PSVersion>1.0</PSVersion>
  <PSSnapIns>
    <PSSnapIn Name="Wiley.PSProfessional.Chapter2" />
  </PSSnapIns>
</PSConsoleFile>
```

Starting PowerShell with a Saved Snap-in Configuration

To use the console file created earlier, you can start `PowerShell.exe` with the `-psconsolefile` option, as shown here:

```
E:\PSbook\CodeSample\PSBook>powershell -psconsolefile MyConsole.psc1
```

From the shell, using the following command, you can verify that the configuration files are used to create the shell:

```
PS E:\PSbook\CodeSample\PSBook> $consolefilename
E:\PSbook\CodeSample\PSBook\MyConsole.psc1
```

`$consolefilename` is a read-only variable containing the configuration file name used for the PowerShell session. You can also verify that the snap-ins specified in the configuration file (is this case, the `Wiley.PSProfessional.Chapter2` snap-in) are actually loaded using the `get-pssnapin` cmdlet:

```
PS E:\PSbook\CodeSample\PSBook> get-pssnapin
Name        : Wiley.PSProfessional.Chapter2
PSVersion   : 1.0
Description : This is a sample PowerShell snap-in
```

Note that configuration files created by `Export-Console` are for use on the same machine where the files are created. If you want to use the same configuration file for other machines, you need to ensure that the `PSSnapins` specified in the configuration file have been registered on those machines.

Using a Profile to Save a Snap-in Configuration

Another way to avoid manually typing `add-pssnapin` commands in a shell every time you start PowerShell is to add `add-pssnapin` cmdlets to the PowerShell profile. There are four PowerShell profiles from which you can choose to customize Windows PowerShell, depending on where/when you would like to effect the changes. For more details on customizing PowerShell using profiles, see the section "Understanding the Profiles" inside `Getting Started.rtf`, which was installed with Windows PowerShell under the `$pshome` folder.

Creating a Custom PowerShell Snap-in

You need to derive your snap-in class from the `CustomPSSnapIn` class if you want to do any of the following:

- Register a specific list of cmdlets and providers in an assembly
- Register cmdlets and providers from more than one assembly
- Register specific types and formats

The following section describes how to create and use a custom `pssnapin`.

Writing a Custom PowerShell Snap-in

Earlier in this chapter, you learned how to write a standard `pssnapin`. This section extends that example by showing you how to create a custom `pssnapin`. Here, you will create a custom `pssnapin` in such a way that it only exposes one of the cmdlets implemented in the earlier example, and rename the cmdlet from Write-Hello to Say-Hello.

The following code example illustrates how to do that (the filename is `psbook-2-2.cs`):

```
using System;
using System.Diagnostics;
using System.Management.Automation;           //Windows PowerShell namespace
using System.ComponentModel;
using System.Collections.ObjectModel;         // For Collection
using System.Management.Automation.Runspaces;   // Needed for CmdletConfiguration-
Entry
[RunInstaller(true)]
public class PSBookChapter2MyCustomeSnapIn: CustomPSSnapIn
{
    // Specify the cmdlets that belong to this custom PowerShell snap-in.
    private Collection<CmdletConfigurationEntry> cmdlets;
```

```
        public override Collection<CmdletConfigurationEntry> Cmdlets
        {
            get
            {
                if (cmdlets == null)
                {
                   cmdlets = new Collection<CmdletConfigurationEntry>();
               cmdlets.Add(
                  new CmdletConfigurationEntry(
                     "Say-Hello ",          // cmdlet name
                     typeof(SayHello),      // cmdlet class type
                     null                   // help filename for the cmdlet
                  )
               );
                }

                return cmdlets;
            }
    }

        public override string Name
        {
            get { return "Wiley.PSProfessional.Chapter2-Custom"; }
        }

        public override string Vendor
        {
            get { return "Wiley"; }
        }

        public override string Description
        {
            get { return " This is a sample PowerShell custom snap-in"; }
        }

        // Specify the providers that belong to this custom PowerShell snap-in.
        private Collection<ProviderConfigurationEntry> providers;
        public override Collection<ProviderConfigurationEntry> Providers
        {
            get {
            if (providers == null)
                {
                   providers = new Collection< ProviderConfigurationEntry >();
                   return providers;
            }
        }
    }

    // Specify the Types that belong to this custom PowerShell snap-in.
        private Collection< TypeConfigurationEntry > types;
        public override Collection< TypeConfigurationEntry > Types
        {
           get
              {
```

```
            if (types == null)
                {
                    types = new Collection< TypeConfigurationEntry >();
                return types;
            }
        }
    }

    // Specify the Format that belong to this custom PowerShell snap-in.
        private Collection< FormatConfigurationEntry > formats;
        public override Collection< FormatConfigurationEntry > Formats
        {
            get {
            if (formats == null)
                {
                    formats = new Collection< FormatConfigurationEntry >();
return formats;
        }
    }
    }
  }
```

You can redefine the name for cmdlets as you wish. In the preceding code, we renamed the cmdlet `write-hello` to `Say-hello`. Note that the cmdlet name in the original assembly will not be visible. Therefore, if the same cmdlet name is implemented in two different assemblies with different behaviors, then you can use a custom snap-in to give a different name to the cmdlet in each assembly, to avoid name conflicts.

Only those cmdlets that are included in the collection returned by the property `Cmdlets` will be visible in the shell after the snap-in is loaded.

In the preceding code, only skeleton code for providers, types, and formats are included, to illustrate how to add them in a custom snap-in. For details on how to write providers, see Chapter 5. For information about types and format, see Chapter 8.

Using a Custom PowerShell Snap-in

Although writing a custom PowerShell snap-in is a little different from writing a standard PowerShell snap-in, using a custom PowerShell snap-in is the same. Just make sure that the assemblies referenced by your custom PowerShell snap-in are in the same folder as your custom PowerShell snap-in assembly. Here are the steps to follow:

1. Compile the custom snap-in assembly use the following command:

    ```
    Csc /target:library /reference:psbook-2-1.dll
    -reference:.\system.management.automation.dll psbook-2-2.cs
    ```

    The preceding command assumes that `csc.exe` is in your path and that both `psbook-2-1.dll` and `system.management.automation.dll` are in the same folder as the `psbook-2-2.cs` file.

2. Register the snap-in using `installutil.exe`. Note that for a custom snap-in, a special Registry value named `CustomPSSnapInType` is created. In addition, the snap-in class type, `PSBook.PSBookChapter2MySnapIn` in this case, is used as value data:

```
E:\PSbook\CodeSample\PSBook>InstallUtil PSBook-2-2.dll
```

3. Verify that the snap-in has been registered successfully:

```
E:\PSbook\CodeSample\PSBook>get-pssnapin -registered
Name        : Wiley.PSProfessional.Chapter2-Custom
PSVersion   : 1.0
Description : This is a sample PowerShell custom snap-in.
```

4. Use `add-pssnapin` to load the snap-in. If separate assemblies are used by the custom snap-in, make sure those assemblies exist either in the same folders as the snap-in assembly or in the GAC.

```
PS E:\PSbook\CodeSample\PSBook>add-pssnapin
Wiley.PSProfessional.Chapter2-Custom
```

5. Now make sure the standard snap-in registered earlier is not loaded, so you only see cmdlets registered through the custom snap-in. If the standard snap-in is loaded, use the following command to remove it from the current session:

```
Remove-PsSnapin PSBook-Chapter2-SnapIn
```

As you can see in Figure 2-2, you can only use the new cmdlet name as defined in the custom snap-in. The original cmdlet `Write-Hello` is not accessible through the custom snap-in.

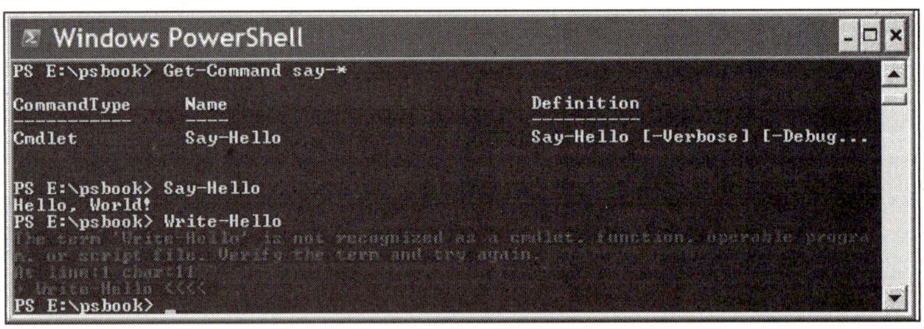

Figure 2-2

6. Just as you can with a standard PowerShell snap-in, you can uninstall a custom PowerShell snap-in using `installutil -u`, and save snap-in configurations to a configuration file using `export-console`.

Earlier in this chapter, you learned that if you want to register all the cmdlets and providers in an assembly, you can do so without implementing any snap-in code by creating registry information.

However, if you want to register a subset of cmdlets or providers from one or more assemblies, you have to implement your custom snap-in, as described in this section. This is because Powershell doesn't save cmdlets or providers mapped in the registry. Instead, it creates the mapping on-the-fly by calling the public properties, such as cmdlets and providers, when a custom snap-in is loaded.

Summary

This chapter introduced you to the `PSSnapin` and `CustomPSSnapin` classes and described the differences between them. You also learned how to write and use both types of PowerShell snap-ins. We demonstrated what Registry information you need to create if you do not want to implement `PSSnapin` classes for registering standard PowerShell snap-ins.

Now that you know how to register your own cmdlets, providers, types, and so on, after introducing extended type systems in the next chapter, we will explore in greater detail how to write cmdlets and providers.

You may have noticed that this chapter didn't cover using parameters, taking input from the pipeline, and creating a help file. Those topics are covered later, in Chapter 4.

3

Understanding the Extended Type System

All languages use a type system to define values and expressions into types. PowerShell is built on top of the .NET Framework and it uses the .NET Framework as its type system. However, the .NET Framework is designed for use with compiled programming languages and is targeted toward developers; it is neither designed for the scripting environment nor suitable for use by scripters. To solve this problem, Windows PowerShell extends the .NET Framework to form an *Extended Type System (ETS)*. The ETS forms the core of the Windows PowerShell language's type system. Specifically, the ETS provides `PSObject`, which is the object created whenever new objects or variables are created in Windows PowerShell. `PSObject` provides the necessary access to the Windows PowerShell type system.

For scripters, `PSObject` provides a uniform interface to the different types of objects that can be created in .NET, COM, WMI, ADSI, and so on. For developers, it provides a mechanism to manipulate the objects and structured data using same syntax as CLR class. In addition to the aforementioned functionality, the ETS provides the capability to extend original objects so that they can better serve in the scripting environment. It provides the foundation of a malleable type system, enabling the script developer to define types dynamically and so that the rest of the PowerShell system knows how to work with that object.

This chapter describes the different components of the Windows PowerShell type system. First we start with `PSObject`, the core of the system. Then we will look at other features, including type extensions, type adapters, type conversion, and how a scripter or a developer can use these different features to dynamically manage an object. Finally, we end the chapter by looking at different built-in type adapters.

PSObject

Every object has properties that hold data, and methods that can be called to manipulate the data. Imagine the capability to create objects of any type, independent of the type of object created; and imagine that you could access it the same way. `PSObject` provides this capability. In this section we begin our exploration of ETS by learning about `PSObject`. `PSObject` is the basis of all object access from the Windows PowerShell's scripting language, and it provides a standard abstraction for the .NET developer (see Figure 3-1).

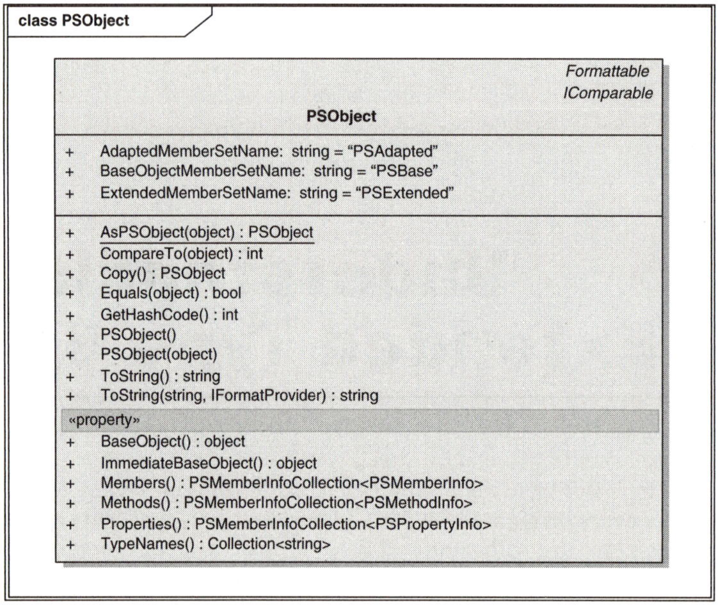

Figure 3-1: The PSObject class

`PSObject` consists of the following members:

- `PSObject(object)`
- `PSObject()`
- `AsPSObject(object)`
- `ImmediateBaseObject()`
- `BaseObject()`
- `Members()`
- `Methods()`
- `Properties()`
- `TypeNames()`

Constructing a PSObject

There are three different ways to create a `PSObject`: `PSObject(object)`, `PSObject()`, and `PSObject.AsPSObject(someobject)`.

PSObject(Object)

The first method to create a `PSObject` is to create the object that needs to be wrapped and then call the `PSObject` constructor that takes the object as its parameter. This constructor creates the `PSObject`, which exposes the underlying object's methods and properties:

C#

```
namespace PSBook.Chapter3
{
    class Sample1
    {
        static void Main(string[] args)
        {
            System.DateTime date = new System.DateTime(2007, 12, 25);
            PSObject psobject = new PSObject(date);
        }
    }
}
```

PS

```
$date = new-object System.datetime 2007,12,25
$psobject = new-object system.management.automation.psobject $date
```

PSObject()

The second method of creating a `PSObject` is to call the constructor with no parameters. This creates a `PSObject` with a `PSCustomObject` as the object being wrapped, as shown in Figure 3-2.

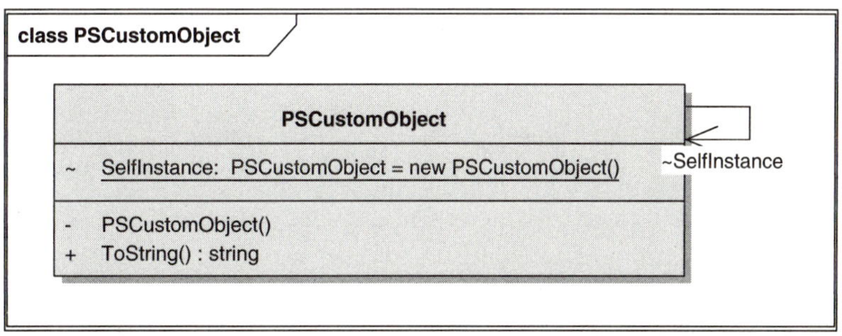

Figure 3-2: A `PSCustomObject` as the object being wrapped

`PSCustomObject` is a simple object that doesn't do much. It is used as a placeholder object to signify that this `PSObject` doesn't wrap any object. You might be wondering why you would create a `PSObject` with no object wrapped. The reason is because PowerShell provides the capability to define your own methods and properties, called *extended members* (described in later section), that can be added to the `PSObject`. This enables `PSObjects` created using this method to act as very powerful type-name property bags.

C#

```
namespace PSBook.Chapter3
{
    class Sample2
```

```
    {
        static void Main(string[] args)
        {
            PSObject psobject = new PSObject();
        }

    }
}
```

PS

```
$psobject = new-object system.management.automation.psobject
```

PSObject.AsPSObject(someObject)

The third method for creating objects is to use the static method `AsPSObject` to create `PSObjects`. This is the most frequently used method to create `PSObjects` internally by Windows PowerShell. This method checks the given object to determine whether it already is a `PSObject`. If it is, then it just returns that `PSObject`; otherwise, it returns a `PSObject` by calling the method `PSObject(someobject)`, described earlier.

C#

```
namespace PSBook.Chapter3
{
    class Sample3
    {
        static void Main(string[] args)
        {
            // Create a CLR datetime object
            System.DateTime  date = new DateTime(2007, 12, 25);
            // Use it to create a PSObject
            PSObject psobject = new PSObject(date);

            // Create a PSObject using AsPSobject method

            //This will return the existing psobject as result
            PSObject psobject2 = PSObject.AsPSObject(psobject);

            //This will create new PSObject that wraps the date object
          //and return that object as result
            PSObject psobject3 = PSObject.AsPSObject(date);
        }
    }
}
```

PS

```
#create CLR Object
$date = new-object system.datetime 2007,12,25

#Create a PSObject using CLR object
$psobject = new-object system.management.automation.psobject  $date

#Create a PSObject using statis AsPSObject Method
```

```
#This will return the passed psobject as result without any modification
$psobject1 = [System.Management.Automation.PSObject]::AsPSObject($psobject)

#This will create a new PSObject and return it as result
$psobject2 = [System.Management.Automation.PSObject]::AsPSObject($date)
```

ImmediateBaseObject and BaseObject

After the `PSObject` is created, the developer might occasionally need to access the object being wrapped by the `PSObject`. `PSObject` provides two properties to do this:

- `BaseObject`: This property returns the object being wrapped by the `PSObject`. If the immediate object being wrapped is another `PSObject`, then this property returns its base object. This continues until it finds an object that is not a `PSObject`. Using this property, you are guaranteed to get the CLR object that is being wrapped.
- `ImmediateBaseObject`: This property returns the object being currently wrapped by the `PSObject`. If the current object being wrapped is a `PSObject`, then it will return that object. This property does not attempt to go beyond the first-level object. You are guaranteed to get the immediate object being wrapped by accessing this property.

Let's look at the code sample that shows how these two properties can be accessed. As before, the first code sample is in C#, and the second code sample is in PowerShell script:

C#

```
namespace PSBook.Chapter3
{
    class Sample4
    {
        static void Main(string[] args)
        {
            // Create a CLR datetime object
            System.DateTime date = new DateTime(2007, 12, 25);
            // Use it to create a PSObject
            PSObject psobject = new PSObject(date);

            // Create a PSObject using the PS object
            PSObject psobject2 = new PSObject(psobject);

            //This will return the psobject that we wrapped.
            Object obj = psobject2.ImmediateBaseObject;

//The next line will output  //System.Management.Automation.PSObject
            Console.WriteLine(obj.GetType().FullName);

            //This will return the DateTime object
     //that we originally wrapped in the PSObject
            obj = psobject2.BaseObject;
            //The next line will output  System.DateTime
            Console.WriteLine(obj.GetType().FullName);
        }
```

```
    }
}
```

PS

```
#create CLR Object
$date = new-object system.datetime 2007,12,25

#Create a PSObject using CLR object
$psobject = new-object system.management.automation.psobject  $date

#Create a PSObject using the created PSObject
$psobject2 = new-object system.management.automation.psobject $psobject

#The next line will return the object we just wrapped
$obj = $psobject2.psobject.ImmediateBaseObject
#Next line will output system.management.automation.psobject
$obj.GetType().FullName

#The next line will return the DateTime object we originally wrappe
#in the PSObject
$obj = $psobject2.psobject.BaseObject
#Next line will output System.DateTime
$obj.GetType().FullName
```

Members

Now that you know how to construct a `PSObject`, let's see how `PSObject` can be used to access the different object types that it can encapsulate. Regardless of the type of object wrapped, all members of the underlying object can be accessed through the `PSObject`. These members are available from a `PSObject` as shown in the preceding `PSObject` definition. They are available using three different collections:

- **Members:** Gets the collection of members contained in this `PSObject`.
- **Methods:** Gets the collection of methods contained in this `PSObject`.
- **Properties:** Gets the collection of properties contained in this `PSObject`.

All member types derive from `PSMemberInfo`, which is summarized in Figure 3-3, and described in the following list:

- `Name` is the name of the member itself.
- `IsInstance` indicates whether this member is an `InstanceMember` or not. If the type is defined only on this instance of the `PSObject`, then it will be true.
- `Value` is the value returned from the particular member. Each member type defines how it deals with value.
- `TypeNameOfValue` is the `TypeName` of the value returned by `Value`.

Each of the Member, Properties, and Methods collections derive from `PSMemberInfoCollection`. We will look into the details of this collection before moving on to types of members.

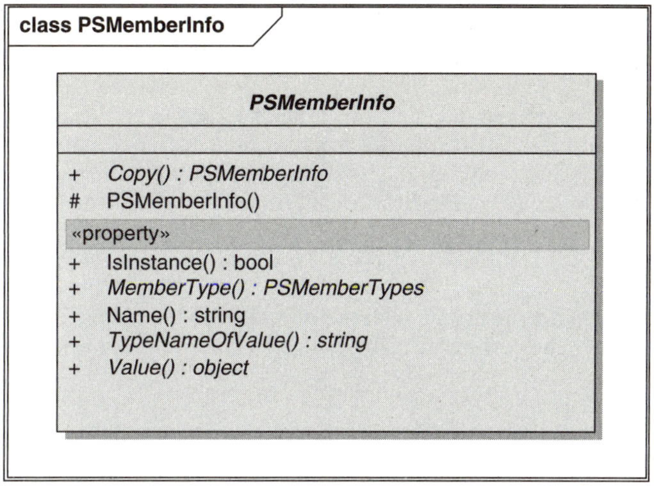

Figure 3-3: `PSMemberInfo`-derived member types

PSMemberInfoCollection

All member collections — Members, Properties, and Methods — are returned as `PSMemberInfoCollection`. It is a collection of objects that are all derived from `PSMemberInfo`. This collection allows for retrieving, adding, and removing members.

`PSMemberInfoCollection` is defined in Figure 3-4, and described in the following list:

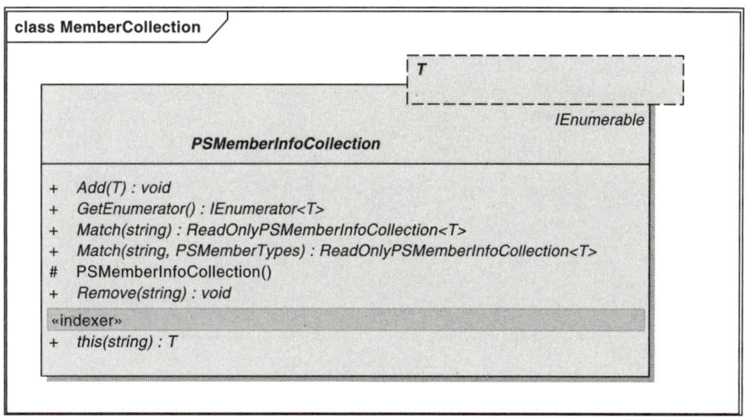

Figure 3-4: `PSMemberInfoCollection`

- `Constructor` takes no arguments and is protected.
- `Add` allows adding members to this collection. It will clone the incoming `PSMemberInfo`. It also prevents the addition of any members with the same names as intrinsic members.
- `Remove` removes the named member from this collection.

- `this` is an indexer on this collection. It takes the name of the member. If the member does not exist, `Null` is returned. This does not handle any wildcard characters — it is a straight case-insensitive match.
- `Match` looks up a member or collection of members based on the `name` parameter. It handles wildcard characters; and because this means it can return > 1 match, it returns a collection. This collection is read-only (see the following section), as adding and removing from the returned collection will not modify the collection in which the match occurred.
- `Match` has an overload that allows a match to be performed only against the specified `PSMemberTypes`.
- `GetEnumerator` implements the interface necessary to make this class `IEnumerable`. This allows a `foreach` loop to be performed using this collection. It returns an `IEnumerator` of the collection members.

Sometimes you will want to return a collection that can be read but not modified. `ReadOnlyPSMember-InfoCollection`, which you will learn about next, is used for this purpose.

ReadOnlyPSMemberInfoCollection

`ReadOnlyPSMemberInfoCollection` is a collection of members (derived from `PSMemberInfo`). It is present on `PSMemberInfoCollection` in order to facilitate the retrieval and counting of members.

`ReadOnlyPSMemberInfoCollection` is defined in Figure 3-5 and described in the following list:

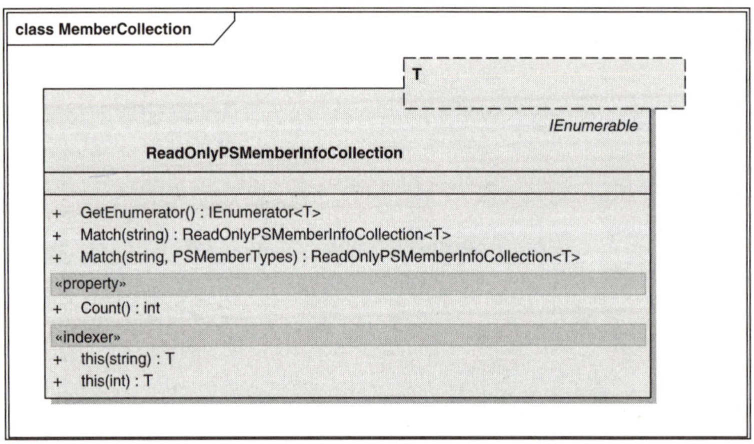

Figure 3-5: **`ReadOnlyPSMemberInfoCollection`**

- `this(string)` is an indexer on this collection. It takes the name of the member to locate. If the member does not exist, then `Null` is returned. This does not handle any wildcard characters — it is a straight case-insensitive match.
- `this(int)` is an indexer on this collection. It takes an integer that is the position in the collection of the desired member. This allows the use of a `for` statement and associated indexer.
- `Match` looks up a member or collection of members based on the `name` parameter. It handles wildcard characters; and because this means it can return > 1 match, it returns a collection. This

collection is read-only, as adding and removing from the returned collection will not modify the collection in which the match occurred.

- `Match` has an overload that allows a match to be performed only against the specified `PSMemberTypes`.
- `Count` indicates the number of elements in this collection.
- `GetEnumerator` implements the interface necessary to make this class `IEnumerable`. This allows a `foreach` loop to be performed using this collection. It returns an `IEnumerator` of the collection members.

Base, Adapted, and Extended Members

Each of the members in the `PSObject` can be classified into one of three types based on the source of the member. This is an important concept that differentiates `PSObject` from other objects with which you may have worked.

- **Base members:** When a new `PSObject` is constructed using an object, then the members of that object are made available to the script developer and CLR developer via the `PSObject`. These members are `BaseObject` members.
- **Adapted members:** When the object being wrapped is a meta-object, one that contains data in a generic fashion, its properties actually describe the contained data. It is the contained data that is interesting, not the description of the contained data. ETS solves this problem by introducing the notion of *adapters*, which modify the underlying .NET object to have the expected default semantics. A `PSObject` adapter is a way to surface a specific view of a `BaseObject`. For example, the ADO `DataRow` object has a `Table` property that has a `Column` property. If the object being passed down the pipeline is an ADO `DataRow` object, then the script developer probably wants to get directly at the contents of that data, not the description of the data. ETS enables a developer to directly access that data just like any other member. ETS automatically adapts a number of .NET meta-objects. Members that are exposed through an adapter are called adapted members of the object.
- **Extended members:** In addition to the base members and adapted members, `PSObject` allows an object to be extended with additional information. This additional information can be a new property or method that provides additional functionality in the scripting environment. For example, all the core cmdlets (e.g., `get-content`, `set-content`) take a `path` parameter; these can be made to work against any object by adding a `path` member to different object types so that they state their information in a common way, thereby enabling the cmdlets to work against those object types. Additionally, when a `PSObject` has no `BaseObject`, it is being used by the script developer to store information (essentially, it is used as a dynamically typed object), and all its members are "extended." All extended members may be defined on an instance (becoming instance members) or based on a `TypeName`.

Types of Members

Windows PowerShell's type system is so powerful that you can create a new property on an object dynamically, specify an alias to an already existing property, and create a new property by supplying a script block for getter/setter access. All these new properties are accessible in the same way as CLR members through `PSObject`'s properties/members. The enumerator shown in Figure 3-6 is available to specify the different member types.

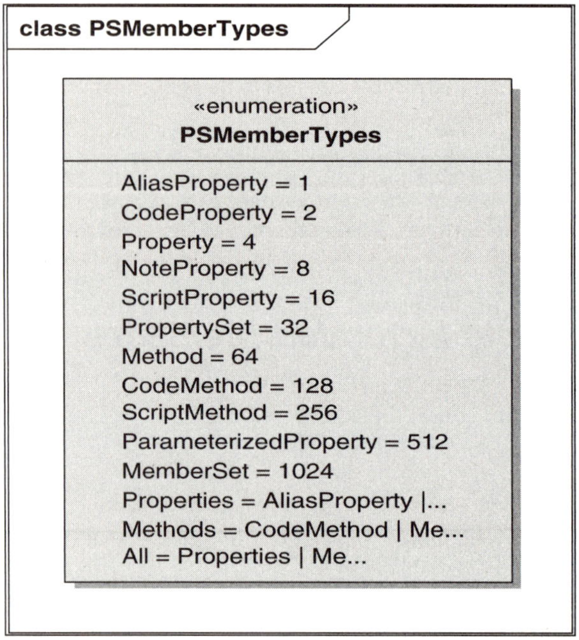

Figure 3-6: Specifying different member types with an enumerator

Figure 3-7 illustrates the different member types of a `PSObject` in more detail.

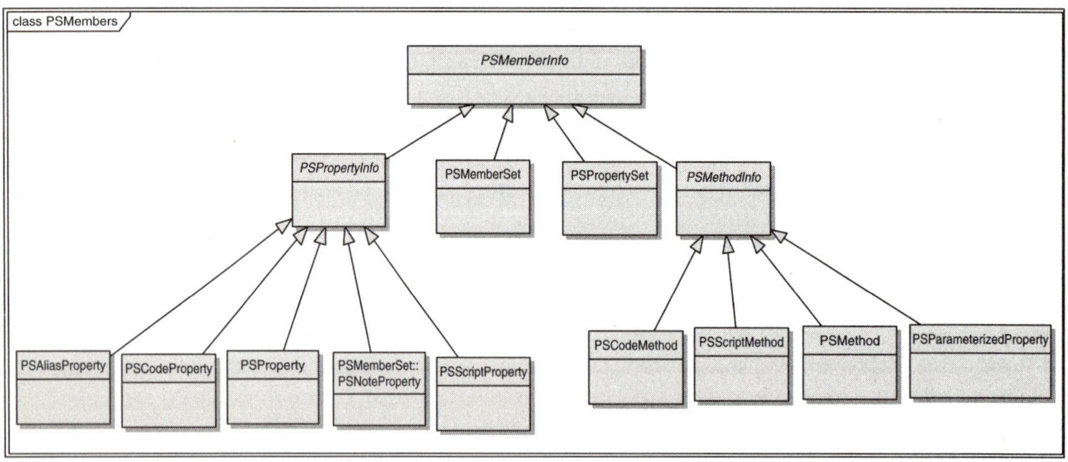

Figure 3-7: Member types of a `PSObject`

Properties

Properties are member types that can be treated as a property: Essentially, they can appear on the left-hand side of an expression if they have implemented a `set` operation, they take no arguments, and the `get` returns a value. `PSMemberTypes.Properties` includes the `Property`, `NoteProperty`, `AliasProperty`, `ScriptProperty`, and `CodeProperty` member types.

All properties derive from `PSPropertyInfo`, which is summarized in Figure 3-8.

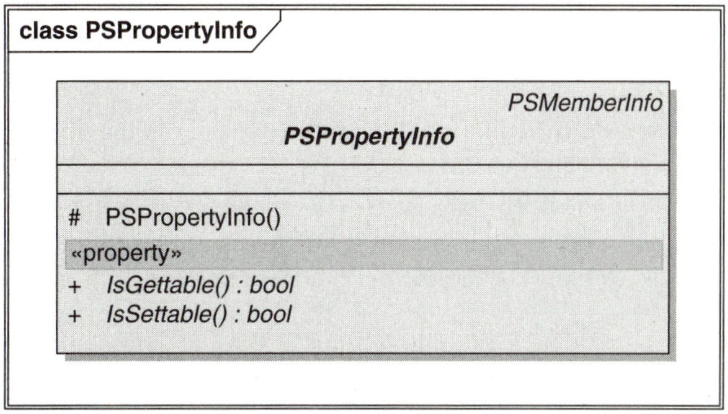

Figure 3-8: Property types of a `PSObject`

- `IsSettable` indicates whether this member has an accessible `set` operation (i.e., can be used on the LHS).
- `IsGettable` indicates whether this member has an accessible `get` operation (i.e., can be used on the RHS).

The following sections describe `PSMembers` that derive from `PSPropertyInfo`.

PSProperty

A `PSProperty` is one that is defined on the `BaseObject` or is made available through an adapter. It refers to both CLR fields as well as CLR properties. It may be either a `BaseObject` member or an adapted member. Figure 3-9 shows its definition, described here as follows:

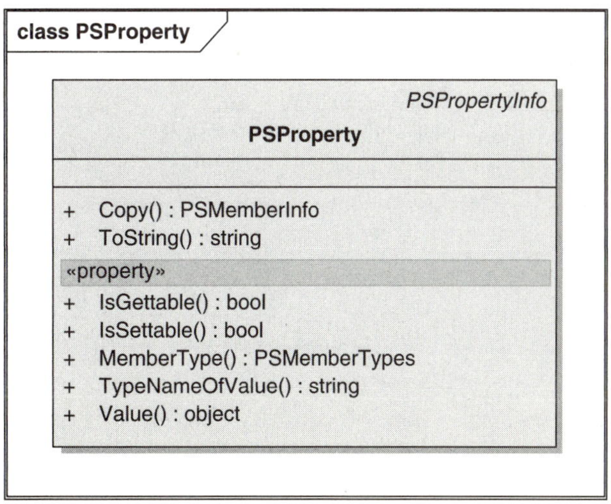

Figure 3-9: `PSProperty`

- `Constructor` does not exist on `PSProperty` because it exists solely on the `BaseObject`.
- `IsSettable` is determined by inspecting the underlying `BaseObject` or adapted view and determining whether a `set` operation is available.
- `IsGettable` is determined by inspecting the underlying `BaseObject` or adapted view and determining whether a `get` operation is available.
- `Value` retrieves or sets the value on that property or field. If the `get` or `set` is called and the operation is not available, then an `ExtendedTypeSystemException` (`GetValueException` or `SetValueException`) is thrown.
- `TypeNameOfValue` is the `TypeName` of the object that will be returned from a `get` operation or the `TypeName` needed as input for the `set` operation. In this case, the `TypeName` is the CLR full name.

PSNoteProperty

A `PSNoteProperty` is a name-value pairing in a `PSObject`. An `ExtendedMember`, it is used to contain an object in a parent `PSObject`. The `NoteProperty` retains the reference to the object to which it was set. It provides the same functionality in script as a field does in the CLR.

The definition of a `NoteProperty` is shown in Figure 3-10.

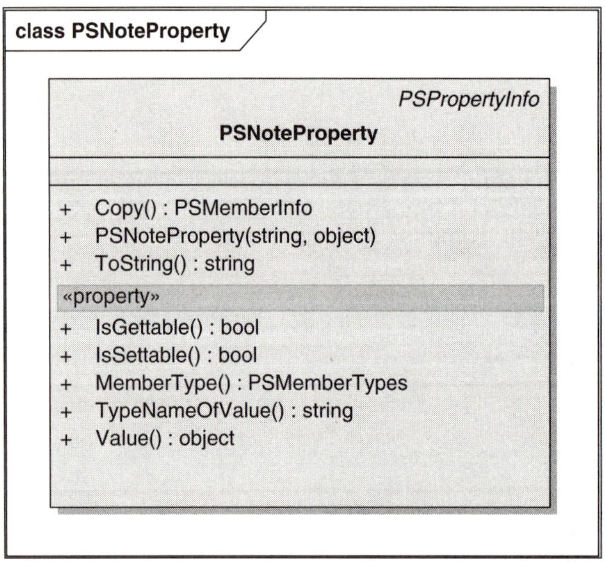

Figure 3-10: **`NoteProperty`**

- `Constructor` takes the name of the member to create and the value that will be stored in `Value`. Any object may be used for `Value`.
- `IsSettable` is `True`. `NoteProperty` does not have a `readonly` capability at this time.
- `IsGettable` is `True`. `NoteProperty` has no notion of `private` or `write-only` at this time.

- `Value` will retrieve or set the value of this Note.
- `TypeNameOfValue` is the `TypeName` of the object that will be returned from a `get` operation.

The following example adds a `NoteProperty` called `Title`, with an initial value of a string `Professional Windows PowerShell` to the variable `psobj`, which is a `PSObject`. It then sets the `Title` to the string `Professional Windows PowerShell Programming`:

```
PS C:\> $psobj = new-object system.management.automation.psobject
PS C:\> add-member -InputObject $psobj  -MemberType NoteProperty  -Name Title -
Value "Professional Windows PowerShell"
PS C:\> $psObj
Title
-----
Professional Windows PowerShell

PS C:\> $psobj.Title = "Professional Windows PowerShell Programming"
PS C:\> $psobj
Title
-----
Professional Windows PowerShell Programming

PS C:\>
```

PSScriptProperty

A `PSScriptProperty` is a "getter" or "setter" defined in script. An extended member, it provides similar functionality in a script to the property in the CLR.

The definition of a `ScriptProperty` is shown in Figure 3-11.

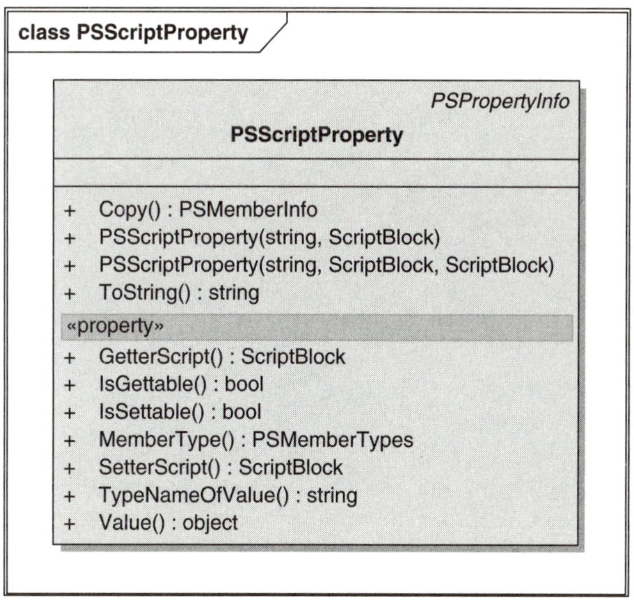

Figure 3-11: `ScriptProperty`

- Constructor takes the name of the member to create and the script blocks for get and/or set. At least one script block must be present. It stores these script blocks in the respective members GetterScript and SetterScript.
- IsSettable is True if SetterScript is not Null; otherwise, it is False.
- IsGettable is True if GetterScript is not Null; otherwise, it is False.
- Value will call the appropriate script block to perform the action. A get invokes the GetterScript and returns the value provided. A set invokes the SetterScript, passing it the object provided to it as $this.args.

> *If a* ScriptProperty is not associated with a PSObject, then $this evaluates+ *to* Null.

- TypeNameOfValue is the TypeName of the object that will be returned from a get operation. For PSScriptProperty this always returns System.Object.

The following example adds a ScriptProperty Cost, which dynamically calculates the sum of DevEffort and TestEffort:

```
PS C:\> $psobj = new-object system.management.automation.psobject
PS C:\> add-member -inputobject $psobj -membertype noteproperty -Name DevEffort
  -Value 5
PS C:\> add-member -inputobject $psobj -membertype noteproperty -Name TestEffort
  -Value 5 PS C:\> add-member -inputobject $psobj -membertype scriptproperty -Name
  Cost -Value {$this.TestEffort + $this.DevEffort}

PS C:\> $psobj
DevEffort                            TestEffort                              Cost
---------                            ----------                              ----
                                              5                                 5
10
```

The following example makes TestEffort always twice the value of DevEffort:

```
PS C:\> $psobj = new-object system.management.automation.psobject
PS C:\> add-member -inputobject $psobj -membertype noteproperty -name TestEffort 0
PS C:\> add-member -inputobject $psobj -membertype noteproperty -name _DevEffort 0
PS C:\> add-member -inputobject $psobj -membertype scriptproperty -name DevEffort -
value {$this._DevEffort} -secondvalue
 {
>> $this._devEffort = $args[0]; $this.TestEffort = 2*$this._devEffort}
>>
PS C:\> $psobj

TestEffort                    _DevEffort                                DevEffort
----------                     ----------                                ---------
                                        0                                        0
0


PS C:\> $psobj.DevEffort = 10
PS C:\> $psobj
```

```
TestEffort                    _DevEffort                    DevEffort
----------                    ----------                    ---------
                               20                            10
10


PS C:\>
```

PSCodeProperty

A `PSCodeProperty` is a "getter" or "setter" defined in a CLR language. An extended member, it provides similar functionality to a property in a CLR language; however, it may be added to a `PSObject` dynamically (based on the `TypeName` lookup or on an `Instance`).

In order for a `PSCodeProperty` to become available, a code developer must write the property in some CLR language, compile it, and ship the resultant assembly. The assembly must be available in the runspace where the code property is desired.

The definition of a `PSCodeProperty` is shown in Figure 3-12.

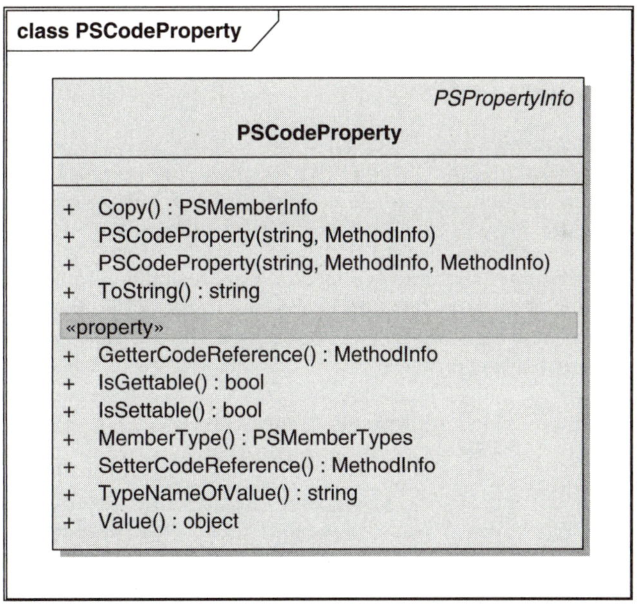

Figure 3-12: **`PSCodeProperty`**

- `Constructor` takes the name of the member to create and the `MethodInfo` for `get` and/or `set`. At least one `MethodInfo` must be present. It stores these in the respective members `GetterCodeReference` and `SetterCodeReference`.
- `IsSettable` is `True` if `SetterCodeReference` is not `Null`; otherwise, it is `False`.
- `IsGettable` is `True` if `GetterCodeReference` is not `Null`; otherwise, it is `False`.

- `Value` will call the appropriate method to perform the action. As shown earlier, a `get` invokes the `GetterCodeReference`, passing its containing `PSObject` instance, and returns the value returned from the invocation. A `set` invokes the `SetterCodeReference`, passing its containing `PSObject` instance as the first argument, and the object to use for the `set` value as the second argument.
- `TypeNameOfValue` is the `TypeName` of the object that will be returned from a `get` operation. In this case, the `TypeName` is the CLR full name.

The `PSCodeProperty` implementation must be thread-safe.

The following example shows the code necessary to create a `CodeProperty` that gets and sets the `TotalCost` given a `PSObject` that contains the `DevCost` and `TestCost`:

```
public class CodePropertyTotalCost
{
    public static int TotalCostGet(PSObject instance)
    {
        return (
            (int) instance.Properties["DevCost"].Value +
            (int) instance.Properties["TestCost"].Value
        );
    }

    public static void TotalCostSet(PSObject instance, int value)
    {
        int devvalue = value/2;

        instance.Properties["DevCost"].Value = devvalue;
        instance.Properties["TestCost"].Value = value - devvalue;
    }
}
```

Note that the methods that implement a `PSCodeProperty` are static. The `instance` data comes from the `PSObject` that is passed to the first parameter. In the case of the setter, the value to use is passed to the second parameter. When both a `get` and a `set` are defined, the second parameter to the `set` must be of the same type as the return of the `get`.

Assuming that the assembly which implements `CodePropertyTotalCost` is available and loaded in this runspace:

```
PS> $psobj = new-object system.management.automation.psobject
PS> add-member -inputobject $psobj -membertype noteproperty -name DevCost 3
Ps> add-member -inputobject $psobj -membertype noteproperty -name Testcost 3
PS> $x=[mynamespace.CodePropertyTotalCost].GetMethod("TotalCostGet")
PS> $y=[mynamespace.CodePropertyTotalCost].GetMethod("TotalCostSet")
PS> add-member -inputobject $psobj -membertype CodeProperty TotalCost $x $y
PS> $psobj.TotalCost
6
PS> $psobj.TotalCost=9
PS> $psobj.DevCost
4
PS> $psobj.TestCost
5
PS>
```

Notice that a `CodeProperty` is accessed identically to any other `Property` member and does not take any arguments.

PSAliasProperty

A `PSAliasProperty` references another property of a `PSObject`. It is an extended member, and its basic purpose is to perform a "rename" of the reference property. It may also convert that property to a different type upon its retrieval.

The definition of an `AliasProperty` is shown in Figure 3-13.

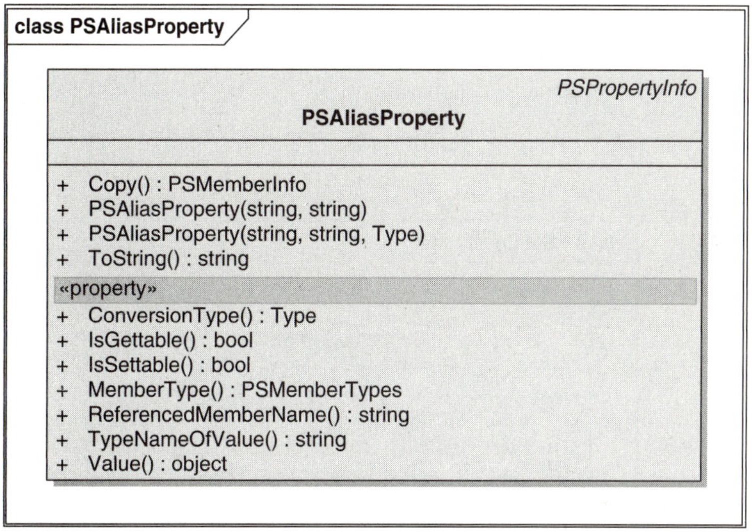

Figure 3-13: `AliasProperty`

- `Constructor` takes the name of the member to create and the name of the property to alias (the referenced `MemberName`). The referenced member may be of any `PSMemberType`.
  The overloaded constructor may also take a type to which the value of the referenced member will be converted (following the ETS conversion algorithm outlined later in this chapter).
- `IsSettable` is dynamically determined by examining the `IsSettable` of the referenced member.
- `IsGettable` is dynamically determined by examining the `IsGettable` of the referenced member.
- `Value` is gotten or set by dereferencing the value of the referenced member — conceptually, `referencedMember.Value`.
- `TypeNameOfValue` is the `TypeName` of the object that will be returned from a `get` operation.

The following example adds an `AliasProperty` called `path`, which renames the property `FullName` on the base `FileInfo` object:

```
PS C:\> $fileobj = get-childitem bootsect.bak
PS C:\> add-member -inputobject $fileobj -membertype aliasproperty -name path -
value fullname
```

```
PS C:\> $fileobj.path
C:\bootsect.bak
PS C:\> $fileobj.FullName
C:\bootsect.bak
PS C:\>
```

Methods

Methods are member types that can take arguments, may return some value, normally do significant work, and cannot appear on the left-hand side of an expression. Specifically, `PSMemberTypes.Methods` include `Method`, `ScriptMethod`, and `CodeMethod` member types.

Methods are accessed from script using the same syntax as other members with the addition of parentheses at the end of the member name.

All methods derive from `PSMethodInfo`, which is summarized in Figure 3-14.

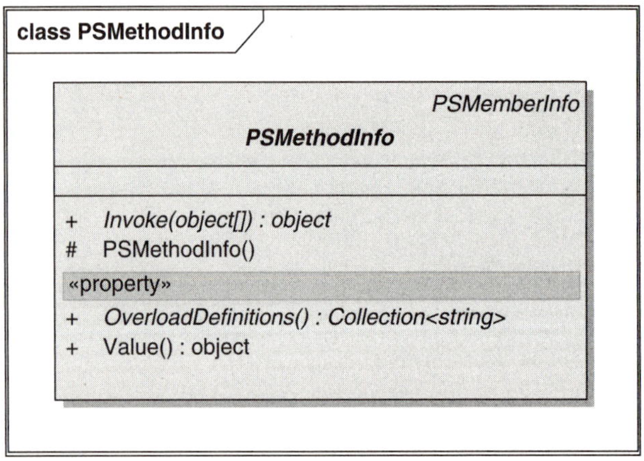

Figure 3-14: Methods derived from `PSMethodInfo`

- `Invoke` is the basic mechanism used to call (invoke) the specified method. It is passed in the arguments with which to call the method as an array of objects. Note that these arguments are the "value" only, no name.
- The order and type of the arguments must correspond to the expected parameters of the particular method being called. Type distance algorithms are used to match the arguments so that the correct overload is called (see the section "Distance Algorithm" later in this chapter).
- Type conversion is used after type distance is determined to convert the arguments passed to `invoke` to the type of parameters needed by the method being called.
- Optional parameters and "params" parameters are considered in the distance algorithm and in the invocation of the method.

- `Value` returns "this" instance of the derived method type (this approach still enables us to derive from `PSMemberInfo`). Note that this is "sealed," and therefore the derived method types do not have to deal with this. Any attempt to set the value throws `NotSupportedException`.
- `OverloadDefinitions` is a collection of strings that state which overloads are available. These contain the complete signature for those methods.

The following sections describe `PSMembers` that derive from `PSMethodInfo`.

PSMethod

A `PSMethod` is one that is defined on the `BaseObject` or is made available through an adapter.

The definition of a `PSMethod` is shown in Figure 3-15.

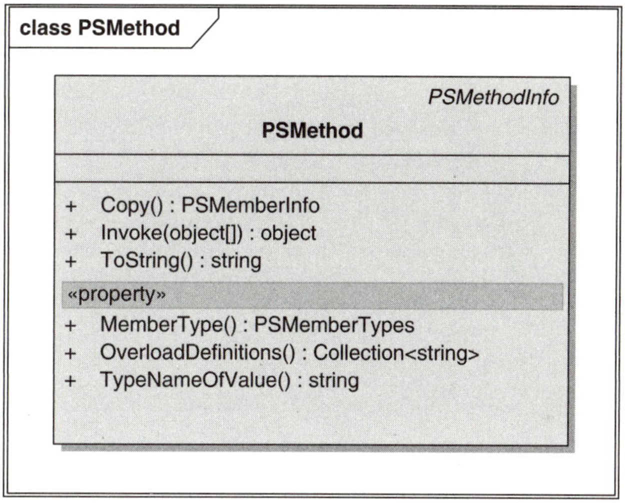

Figure 3-15: **`PSMethod`**

- `Invoke` calls the underlying CLR method on the adapter or `BaseObject`. If there is more than one definition of this method, then the `PSMethodInfo` base class uses the distance algorithm to determine which one to call.
- `OverloadDefinitions` gets the overloads from the CLR methods of this type using reflection.
- `TypeNameOfValue` returns `typeof(PSMethod).FullName`.

The following example uses the CLR method `split` to split a string on semicolons:

```
PS>
PS> $a="abc;xyz;kmh"
PS> $a.split(";")
abc
xyz
```

```
kmh
PS>
```

PSScriptMethod

A `PSScriptMethod` is an extended member method defined in the PowerShell language. It provides similar functionality to a method on the `BaseObject`, but it may be added to a `PSObject` dynamically (based on the `TypeName` lookup or on an `Instance`).

The definition of a `PSScriptMethod` is shown in Figure 3-16.

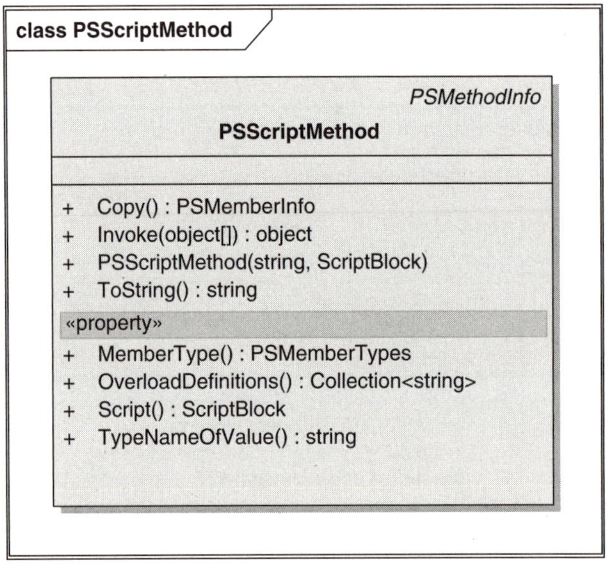

Figure 3-16: **`PSScriptMethod`**

- `Script` returns the `ScriptBlock` that defines this `ScriptMethod`.
- `Invoke` calls the underlying script block specified in the script.
- `OverloadDefinitions` will always be a collection of 1, as `ScriptMethods` do not support overloads yet.
- `TypeNameOfValue` returns `typeof(PSScriptMethod).FullName`.

```
PS C:\> $psobj = new-object system.management.automation.psobject
PS C:\> add-member -inputobject $psobj -membertype noteproperty -name DevCost -Value 2
PS C:\> add-member -inputobject $psobj -membertype noteproperty -name TestCost -Value 4
PS C:\> add-member -inputobject $psobj -membertype scriptmethod -name RealCost -Value {
>> param([int] $x)
>> return $x * ($this.TestCost + $this.DevCost)
>> }
>>
PS C:\> $psobj.RealCost(3)
18
PS C:\>
```

PSCodeMethod

A `PSCodeMethod` is an extended member method defined in a CLR language. It provides similar functionality to a method on the `BaseObject`, but it may be added to a `PSObject` dynamically (based on the `TypeName` lookup or on an `Instance`).

In order for a `PSCodeMethod` to become available, a code developer must write the method in some CLR language, compile it, and ship the resultant assembly. The assembly must be available in the runspace where the code method is desired.

The definition of a `PSCodeMethod` is shown in Figure 3-17.

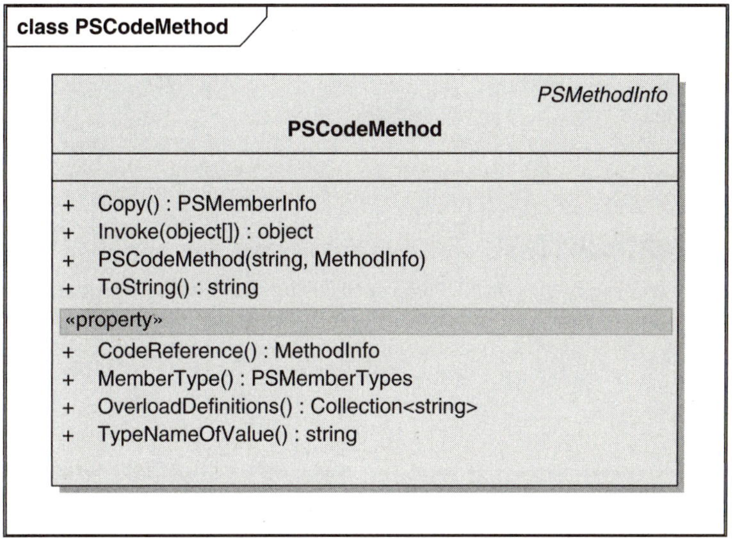

Figure 3-17: **`PSCodeMethod`**

- `Invoke` calls the underlying CLR method specified in the `CodeReference`.
- `OverloadDefinitions` gets the overloads from the CLR methods of this type using reflection.
- `TypeNameOfValue` returns `typeof(PSCodeMethod).FullName`.

The following example shows the code necessary to create a `CodeMethod` that computes the `RealCost` given a `multiplier` and a `PSObject` that contains a `TotalCost` property:

```
public class CodeMethodScheduleCost
{
    public static int RealCost(PSObject instance, int multiplier)
    {
      return (int)instance.Properties["TotalCost"].Value * multiplier;
    }
}
```

Note that methods which implement a `PSCodeMethod` are static. The instance data comes from the `PSObject`, which is passed to the first parameter. The number and type of the remaining parameters are up to the individual method. The `CodeMethod` implementation must be thread-safe.

There is currently no mechanism to create overloads (therefore, the `Overloads` collection is always of length 1).

Assuming that the assembly which implements `RealCost` is available on this runspace:

```
PS C:\> $psobj = new-object system.management.automation.psobject
PS C:\> add-member -inputobject $psobj -membertype noteproperty -name DevCost -
Value 2
PS C:\> add-member -inputobject $psobj -membertype noteproperty -name TestCost -
Value 4
PS C:\> add-member -inputobject $psobj -membertype scriptproperty -name TotalCost -
Value {$this.TestCost + $this.DevCost}
PS C:\> $x=[mynamespace.CodeMethodScheduleCost].GetMethod("RealCost")
PS C:\>add-member -inputobject $psobj -membertype CodeMethod -name RealCost -Value $x
PS C:\> $a.TotalCost
6
PS C:\> $a.RealCost(3);
18
PS C:\>
```

PSParameterizedProperty

A `PSParameterizedProperty` is how ETS exposes COM parameterized properties to the developer and engine. It combines parts of both a property and a method. It derives from `PSMethodInfo` because usage has shown this to be most effective (because anything taking arguments requires an "invoke"-style member instead of just a simple get/set interface). The definition of a `PSParameterizedProperty` is shown in Figure 3-18.

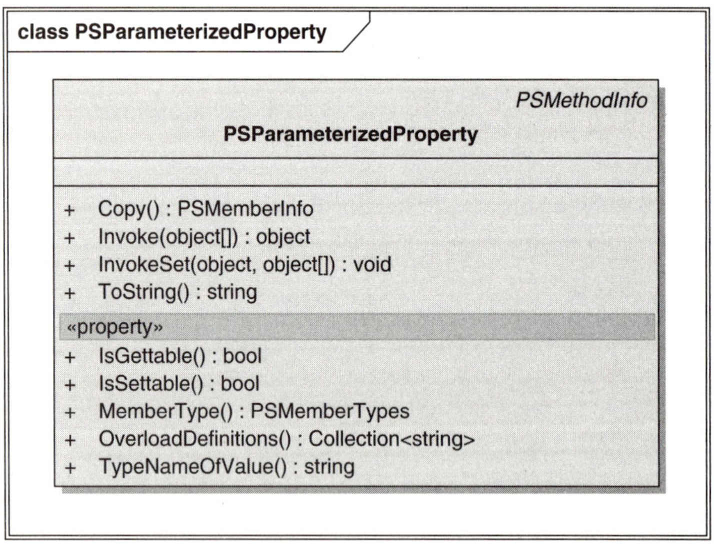

Figure 3-18: Definition of a `PSParameterizedProperty`

- `Constructor` is not public because a user may not create one of these. It is only exposed if an adapter provides it.
- `Invoke` calls the underlying COM parameterized property "getter" with the arguments passed in.
- `OverloadDefinitions` gets the overloads from the COM properties of this type using `IDispatch` and `TypeLibraries`.
- `InvokeSet` calls the underlying COM parameterized property "setter" with the arguments passed in and the `valueToSet` as the value to assign to that property.
- `IsSettable` is dynamically determined by examining the `IsSettable` of the referenced member.
- `IsGettable` is dynamically determined by examining the `IsGettable` of the referenced member.
- `TypeNameOfValue` returns `typeof(PSParameterizedProperty).FullName`.

Sets

`PSObject` is, at its most basic level, a named and dynamically typed collection of members. It is very useful to be able to partition these sets of members into different subsets so that the subset may be referenced together. There are two types of member subsets:

- `PropertySet` — A name to specify a number of properties
- `MemberSet` — A collection of any extended member types. These are defined more fully in the following subsections.

Taken together these sets offer powerful capabilities. For example, PowerShell defines a well-known `MemberSet` `PSStandardMembers` to define how parts of the PowerShell system will interact with a particular `PSObject`. One specific case is the `PropertySet` `DefaultDisplayPropertySet`, which is used by formatting and output to determine at runtime which properties to display for a given `PSObject`.

PSPropertySet

A `PSPropertySet` acts as an alias that points to *n* other properties. It is used to refer to a set of properties that have a common purpose or use. These properties may then be referred to as a "set" by single name.

You can normally use a `PropertySet` whenever a list of properties is requested.

The definition of a `PSPropertySet` is shown in Figure 3-19.

- `Constructor` takes the name of the member to create and an `IEnumerable<string>` that states the names of the properties to reference when `Value` is retrieved. The members referred to by `referencedPropertyNames` must be of type `PSMemberTypes.Properties` or `PSMemberTypes.PropertySet`.
- `Value` returns the `PSPropertySet` itself. An attempt to `set` value throws `NotSupportedException`.
- `TypeNameOfValue` is the fully qualified type name of `PSPropertySet` (i.e., `System.Management.Automation.PSPropertySet`).

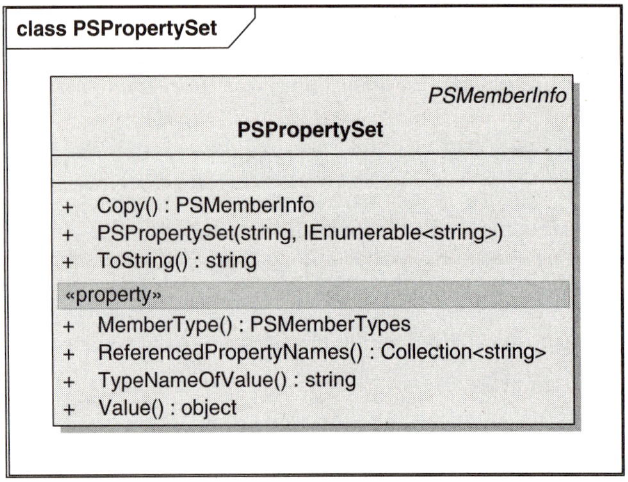

Figure 3-19: Definition of a PSPropertySet

For example, you could create a `PropertySet` that states the times of interest for a particular file:

```
PS C:\> $fileobj = get-childitem bootsect.bak
PS C:\>  $properties = new-object
system.collections.objectmodel.collection''1[System.String]
PS C:\> $properties.Add("CreationTime")
PS C:\> $properties.Add("LastAccessTime")
PS C:\> $properties.Add("LastWriteTime")
PS C:\> add-member -inputobject $fileobj -membertype propertyset -name Times
-value $properties
PS C:\> $fileobj | select-object Times

CreationTime                  LastAccessTime                LastWriteTime
------------                  --------------                -------------
10/19/2007 3:25:52 PM         10/19/2007 3:25:52 PM         10/19/2007 3:25:52 PM


PS C:\>
```

PSMemberSet

A `PSMemberSet` contains other extended members of any type. Importantly, the `this` pointer inside the `PSMemberSet` refers to the containing `PSObject`. Therefore, `ScriptProperties`, `ScriptMethods`, `AliasProperties`, `PropertySet`, and so forth may all reference the members in the `PSObject` (see Figure 3-20).

- `Constructor` takes the name of the `MemberSet` to create. An additional constructor takes the name of the `MemberSet` to create and an `IEnumerable<PSMemberInfo>` that specifies the members to add to that `MemberSet`.
- `Members` gets the collection of members contained in this `MemberSet`.
- `Methods` gets the collection of methods (`PSMemberTypes.Methods`) contained in this `MemberSet`.

- `Properties` gets the collection of properties (`PSMemberTypes.Properties`) contained in this `MemberSet`.
- `InheritMembers` tells this `MemberSet` to walk the `TypeNames` during a lookup of members. This means that any members of a parent type that are in a `MemberSet` of the same name will be available through this `MemberSet`. The default is `True`.
- `Value` returns the `PSMemberSet` itself. An attempt to `set` value throws `NotSupported`.
- `TypeNameOfValue` is the fully qualified type name of `PSMemberSet` (i.e., `System.Management.Automation.PSMemberSet`).

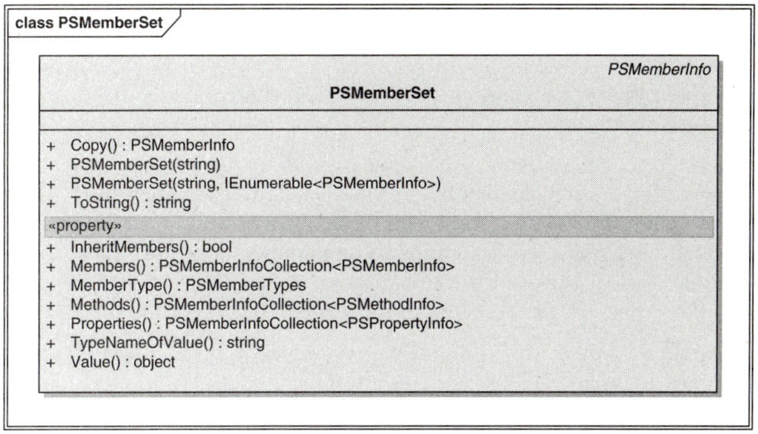

Figure 3-20: Members in the `PSObject`

For example, a `PSObject` with a `FileInfo` `BaseObject` contains members of `Mode` (a `ScriptProperty`), `LastWriteTime` (a `PSProperty`), `Length` (a `PSProperty`), and `Name` (a `PSProperty`). In the well-known `MemberSet` `PSStandardMembers`, a `PropertySet` member could be added that referred to those members.

`MemberSets` allow different parties to create `ExtendedMembers` in a less conflicting way; only the `MemberSet` name conflicts, its contained members do not.

ETS itself uses this functionality and defines a few well-known `MemberSets`, as described in the section "Standard MemberSets."

TypeNames

`TypeNames` is the list of `TypeNames` that this `PSObject` represents (it is a `Collection<String>`). Upon instantiation, `TypeNames` is set to the derivation hierarchy of the `BaseObject`. If there is no `BaseObject`, then `TypeNames` is empty.

A single `TypeName` is represented by a string, enabling the script developer to define new types dynamically. Therefore, `TypeNames` allows for dynamic derivation; that is, it allows a developer to state from which `TypeName` a `PSObject` should derive.

TypeNames are ordered such that the least index takes greatest precedence (e.g., members defined in TypeNames[0] will take precedence over members defined in TypeNames[1]). In other words, TypeNames lists the types from most specific to least specific. See the following section, "Lookup Algorithm," to learn how this is done.

Lookup Algorithm

A *lookup algorithm* is used any time a developer references a member — for example, accessing the member of a variable like $a.x (inside a script). For a code developer, this lookup algorithm is initiated while accessing the members, properties, methods, or index properties of PSObject.

Conceptually, the basic algorithm is designed to look up the members in the following order:

1. **Extended instance members:** These are the members added to an object using the add-member cmdlet.
2. **Extended type members:** This is done by walking up TypeNames against the TypeData file(s). Essentially, for each element in TypeNames (starting with Length-1), it walks the list of TypeConfigurationEntry (starting with 0) looking for the definition of an extended member for that type. When found, it adds those members (or returns the member if looking for a single member) and starts the lookup for the next TypeName. In this way, 0th TypeName and 0th TypeConfigurationEntry should win (i.e., override others later in the list).
3. **Adapted members:** This is done by querying the type adapter for properties and methods of the particular name(s) desired. This interface is not public at this time.

Notice that we do not actually lookup against the BaseMembers. This is because adapters hide the BaseObject in the default lookup. When the BaseObject is a .NET class, an internal default DotNet adapter is used. Therefore, an adapter is always available for any given object. As noted earlier, explicit access to BaseMembers is available through a hidden PSBase property in script. For a programmer, access to the original CLR object is available through the property ImmediateBaseObject (of the PSObject).

Naming collisions are not possible between extended instance members and extended type members — it is an error to add an extended instance member that would collide with an extended type member.

Naming collisions are currently possible between extended members and adapted members. In such a case, extended members override adapted members. Proper care needs to be taken while adding extended members through type files, through the add-member cmdlet, or by adding directly to a PSObject.

Distance Algorithm

Distance algorithms are used to determine which method to call when more than one method is possible (for example, when overloads are present). This is done by determining the distance between every argument and its corresponding parameter for each overload. The distance between an argument and a parameter is determined by a table with a heuristic approximation of the risk involved in the type conversion between the two types. The types that are understood (have an entry in this table) are as follows: char, int16, int32, int64, UInt16, UInt32, UInt64, float, double, decimal, bool, string, char[], regex, XmlDocument, object [].

A script developer may modify the results of the distance algorithm by "cast"ing the arguments to match the parameters of a certain overload.

This table is currently hard-coded, so it doesn't take into account the additional converters or constructors that might be specified by a developer.

PSObject Intrinsic Members and MemberSets

To facilitate developer access and control, `PSObject` supports five intrinsic members: `PSExtended`, `PSAdapted`, `PSBase`, `PSObject`, and `PSTypeNames`.

In order to allow developers to override the lookup algorithm and directly access each type of member, `PSObject` intrinsically supports three `MemberSets`:

- `PSExtended`: This `MemberSet` allows access to all extended members, and only extended members. No adapted members are present. For example, `$a.PSExtended.x` will get the `ExtendedMember x`. It will not make any access to the adapter if there is no `ExtendedMember` by that name (in this case, `x`).
- `PSAdapted`: This `MemberSet` allows access to all members made available through the adapter indicated by the `BaseObject`.
- `PSBase`: This `MemberSet` allows direct access to all public members on the `BaseObject`. No access is made to an `ExtendedMember` or an `AdaptedMember`.

`PSObject` allows script developers to directly access it (the meta-object) as needed. It does this by providing a `MemberSet` named `PSObject`. Therefore, `$a.PSObject.Members` references the `Members` property available on `PSObject` itself, returning a `PSMemberInfoCollection`.

As noted, the `TypeNames` list is *the* mechanism the system uses to determine the "type" of a `PSObject`. As shown in the section "Lookup Algorithm," the `TypeNames` list enables the developer to dynamically define derivation. `PSObject` supplies an intrinsic `NoteProperty` named `PSTypeNames` that references this list. Therefore, `$a.PSTypeNames` shows the `TypeNames` list for `$a`.

Errors and Exceptions

Errors can occur in the ETS at two points: during initialization (loading) of type data (see "Initialization Errors"), and when accessing a member of a `PSObject` or using one of the utility classes such as `LanguagePrimitivies`. (See the following section, "Runtime Errors.")

ETS does not swallow any exceptions.

Runtime Errors

With one exception noted below, all the exceptions thrown from the ETS during runtime are, or derive from, `ExtendedTypeSystemException`, which derives from `RuntimeException`. Therefore, they may be trapped by advanced script developers using the `Trap` statement in the PowerShell language.

All exceptions that occur when getting the value of a `PSMember` are of the type `GetValueException`. When the ETS itself recognizes the error, a `GetValueException` is thrown. When the underlying `get`, such as a `CodeProperty`, throws an exception, a `GetValueInvocationException` is thrown with the getter's exception as the inner exception.

All exceptions that occur during a set of the value of a `PSMemberTypes.Property` are of the type `SetValueException`. When the ETS itself recognizes the error, a `SetValueException` is thrown. If the underlying get, such as a `CodeProperty`, throws an exception, then a `SetValueInvocationException` is thrown with the getter's exception as the inner exception.

All exceptions that occur during the invocation of a `PSMemberTypes.Method` are of type `MethodException`. When the ETS itself recognizes the error, a `MethodException` is thrown. When the underlying `CodeMethod` throws an exception, a `MethodInvocationException` is thrown with the `CodeMethod`'s exception as the inner exception.

When an invalid cast is attempted, a `PSInvalidCastException` is thrown. Because this derives from `InvalidCastException`, it cannot be directly trapped from script. This means that the entity attempting the cast would need to wrap `PSInvalidCastException` in a `PSRuntimeException` in order for this to be trappable by script developers.

If an attempt is made to set a value of `PSPropertySet`, `PSMemberSet`, `PSMethodInfo`, or a member of a `ReadOnlyPSMemberInfoCollection`, a `NotSupportedException` is thrown.

All other exceptions are `ExtendedTypeSystemException` instead of more specific derived exceptions.

Initialization Errors

Errors in loading a `typexml` file should work like other PowerShell errors. If processing can continue, then it is a nonfatal error and it would call `WriteDebug` (because there's no `Error` pipe at this time). If a terminating error is found such that the rest of the file cannot continue, then the rest of the file is not processed (but does not throw a terminating exception). Note that there are no terminating errors at this time.

Information includes the following:

- Filename
- Line number
- Type in which the error occurred
- Member in which the error occurred
- Specific cause of the error

For example, adding a duplicate member `count` to the `System.Object` array would provide the following error:

```
DEBUG: Error loading Types.PSxml:
c:\temp\monad\types.PSxml(8) : Error in type "System.Object[]":
Member "Count" is already present.
```

Type Conversion

Type converters are used any time an attempt is made to convert an object of one type to another type (such as `string` to `int`). For example, the `ParameterBinding` algorithm performs type conversion when trying to bind incoming objects to a particular parameter and during casts in the PowerShell scripting language.

Attempts to convert one object to another type are separated into two different buckets:

- **Standard PowerShell Language conversions:** These are checked first and cannot be overridden.
- **Custom conversions**

Both are discussed in detail in the following sections.

Standard PS Language Conversion

Standard PS Language conversions follow the order shown in the following table when converting a value from one type to another type (note that `valueToConvert` is used to represent the object to convert).

From Type	To Type	Returns
null	String	String.Empty
	Char	'\0'
	Numeric	0 of the resultType
	Boolean	False
	Non-value-types	Null
	Nullable<T>	Null
DerivedClass	BaseClass	Original object
Anything	void	AutomationNull.Value
Anything	String	Calls the ToString mechanism (see the section "ToString Mechanism")
Anything	Boolean	LanguagePrimitives.IsTrue(valueToConvert)
Anything	PSObject	PSObject.AsPSObject(valueToConvert)
Anything	XMLDocument	Converts valueToConvert to String, and then calls the XMLDocument constructor
Anything	Nullable<T>	Converts to Nullable<T>(valueToConvert is first converted to type T. If conversion succeeds, then the converted value is used to convert to Nullable<T>.)
Array	Array	Tries to convert each array element

(continued)

From Type	To Type	Returns
Singleton	Array	array[0] = valueToConvert converted to the element type of the array
IDictionary	Hashtable	Hashtable(valueToConvert)
String	Char[]	valueToConvert.ToCharArray()
String	RegEx	RegEx(valueToConvert)
String	Type	Uses the valueToConvert to search in the internal representation of RunSpaceConfiguration.Assemblies
String	Numeric	If valueToConvert is "", then it returns 0 of the resultType. Otherwise, the culture "culture invariant" is used to produce a numeric value.
Integer	System.Enum	Converts the integer to the enumeration if the integer is defined in that enumeration. If the integer is not defined in that enumeration, then it throws an PSInvalidCastException.

Custom Converters

If none of the preceding Standard PowerShell Language conversions apply, then custom converters are checked.

If one of the following custom conversion operations throws an exception (i.e., the converter is found but it fails the conversion), then no further attempt to convert the object will be made and the original exception is wrapped in a `PSInvalidCastException`, which will then be thrown.

Custom converters are executed in the following order:

TypeConverter

This is a CLR defined type that can be assigned to a particular type using the `TypeConverterAttribute` or the `<TypeConverter>` tag in `TypeData` (see the "Type Configuration" section). If the `valueToConvert` has a `TypeConverter` that can convert to `resultType`, then it is called. If the `resultType` has a `TypeConverter` that can convert from `valueToConvert`, then it is called.

The CLR `TypeConverter` does not allow a single type converter to work for n different classes.

Parse

If the `valueToConvert` is a string and the `resultType` has a `Parse` method, then it is called.

`Parse` is a well-known method name in the CLR world.

- **Constructors:** If the `resultType` has a constructor that takes a single parameter of type `valueToConvert.GetType()`, then this is called.

- **Implicit cast operator:** If `valueToConvert` has an implicit cast operator that converts to `resultType`, then it is called. If `resultType` has an implicit cast operator that converts from `valueToConvert`, then it is called.
- **Explicit cast operator:** If `valueToConvert` has an explicit cast operator that converts to `resultType`, then it is called. If `resultType` has an explicit cast operator that converts from `valueToConvert`, then it is called.
- IConvertible: System.Convert.ChangeType is then called.

PSTypeConverter

A `PSTypeConverter` can be assigned to a particular type using the `TypeConverterAttribute` or the `<TypeConverter>` tag in the `TypeData` file (see the "Type Configuration" section for more details). If the `valueToConvert` has a `PSTypeConverter` that can convert to `resultType`, then this `PSTypeConverter` is called. If the `resultType` has a `PSTypeConverter` that can convert from `valueToConvert`, then it is called.

`PSTypeConverter` allows a single type converter to work for *n* different classes. For example, an `enum` type converter can convert a string to any `enum` (there doesn't need to be a separate type to convert each `enum`).

The `PSTypeConverter` class is defined as follows and shown in Figure 3-21.

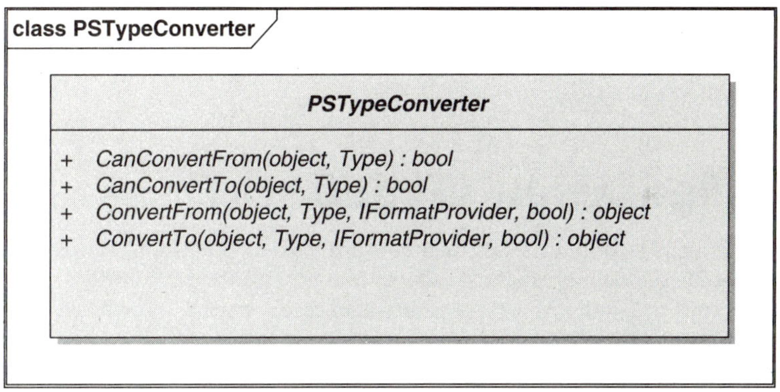

Figure 3-21: **`PSTypeConverter`** class

In order to use `PSTypeConverter`, attribute the class with `TypeConverterAttribute`, passing it your type converter derived from `PSTypeConverter`.

Specific Implementations of PSTypeConverter

Windows PowerShell ships with a custom `PSTypeConverter` called `ConvertThroughString`, which specifies that a particular destination type will always use `valueToConvert.ToString()` before being converted using the standard string conversions to the destination type:

```
public class ConvertThroughString : PSTypeConverter
{
    public override bool CanConvertFrom(object sourceValue, Type destinationType);
```

```
        public override object ConvertFrom(object sourceValue, Type destination-
Type, IFormatProvider formatProvider, bool ignoreCase); // for string conversions

    public override bool CanConvertTo(object sourceValue, Type destinationType);

      public override object ConvertTo(object sourceValue, Type destinationType, IFor-
matProvider formatProvider, bool ignoreCase);
}
```

ToString Mechanism

`PSObject` implements a version of `ToString` that is designed to allow customization of `ToString` and provide the most useful implementation of it. It does this by following the logic shown here:

- If there is a `PSCodeMethod` named `ToString`, then it is called and its value returned.
- If the `BaseObject` is `IEnumerable`, then the `Output-Field-Separator` (`$OFS`) separated list of the `ToString` of each element is returned — the `ToString` of the element might clearly be overridden using the other mechanisms. If the enumeration throws an exception, then the `BaseObject.ToString` is attempted.
- If the `BaseObject` is `PSNullBaseObject`, then the members of type `PSMemberTypes.Properties` are returned in hash table syntax.
- Otherwise, the `BaseObject.ToString` is called and its value returned. If `BaseObject.ToString` throws an exception, then this original exception is wrapped in an `ExtendedTypeSystemException`, which is then thrown.

Type Configuration (TypeData)

In the preceding examples, only instance members are used to keep them simple. However, all extended members may also be defined against a `TypeName` in a type configuration XML specification. Because XML is case sensitive, the nodes of `TypeData` are also case sensitive. However, the contents of those nodes are not case sensitive.

The following example defines the schema of a type configuration file. For the sake of brevity, I used the following logic to define the schema:

- Indentation represents containment. For example, the element `<Types>` contains the `<Type> element.`
- Symbols in square brackets (e.g., `[0..X]`) represent cardinality.
- `[0..Many]` indicates that a particular element can occur 0 to many times.

```
<Types> [1]
   <Type> [0..Many]
           <Name> [1]
           <Members> [0..1]
                  <NoteProperty> [0..Many]
                  <AliasProperty> [0..Many]
                  <ScriptProperty> [0..Many]
```

```
                  <CodeProperty> [0..Many]
                  <ScriptMethod> [0..Many]
                  <CodeMethod> [0..Many]
                  <PropertySet> [0..Many]
                  <MemberSet> [0..Many]
           <TypeConverter> [0..1]
                  <TypeName> [1]

<NoteProperty>
    <Value> [1]
    <TypeName> [0..1]

<AliasProperty>
    <ReferencedMemberName> [1]
        <TypeName> [0..1]

<ScriptProperty>
    <Name>
    <GetScriptBlock> [0..1]
    <SetScriptBlock> [0..1]

<CodeProperty>
    <Name> [1]
    <GetCodeReference> [0..1]
          <TypeName> [1]
          <MethodName> [1]
        <SetCodeReference> [0..1]
          <TypeName> [1]
          <MethodName> [1]


<ScriptMethod>
    <Name> [1]
     <Script> [1]

<CodeMethod>
    <Name> [1]
    <CodeReference> [1]
           <TypeName> [1]
           <MethodName> [1]

<PropertySet>
    <Name> [1]
    <ReferencedProperties>
           <Name> [1..Many]

<MemberSet>
    <Name> [1]
    <InheritMembers> [0..1]
    <Members> [0..1]
           <NoteProperty> [0..Many]
           <AliasProperty> [0..Many]
           <ScriptProperty> [0..Many]
           <CodeProperty> [0..Many]
```

```
            <ScriptMethod> [0..Many]
            <CodeMethod> [0..Many]
            <PropertySet> [0..Many]
            <MemberSet> [0..Many]
```

As per the preceding rules, there can be only one `<Types>` element in a type configuration file. However, there can be many `<Type>` elements inside a `<Types>` element.

If `<InheritMembers>` element is present, then it must have an `innerText`. That `innerText` must be either `True` or `False` (case-insensitive). By default, `MemberSets` inherit members (refer to the "PSMemberSet" section for more details).

If there is a definition conflict between different type configuration entries (or files), then the first one processed without errors wins.

If a schema check fails (e.g., a child element is of the wrong cardinality), then that entry is not processed. For example, if a `<Type>` element has two `<Name>` child elements, then that `<Type>` entry fails to be loaded into Windows PowerShell's type table.

Well-Known Members

In order for the PowerShell system itself to understand how to best operate against a particular `PSObject`, a set of *well-known members* is provided. For example, there is a particular member that defines what properties to display by default, or what properties to use for sorting. These members should be associated with each `PSObject` (either by adding `InstanceMembers` or `TypeMembers`) that want to participate in these activities.

Script Access

Scripts are able to access all extended members, adapted members, and base members, as well as the `PSObject` itself (the meta-object that contains all those). By default, script access has been optimized using the lookup algorithm described earlier. However, using the special `MemberSets` described above, script developers have complete access to all the different capabilities and abstractions of a `PSObject`. This approach enables both simple day-to-day usage as well as the creation of powerful scripts.

Summary

The Extended Type System (ETS) is one of the core elements of the Windows PowerShell Engine and it forms the basis of all object access and manipulation in Windows PowerShell. This chapter took a close look at the ETS, including the following topics:

- The `PSObject` and its various members
- Construction of the `PSObject`
- Different member types of the `PSObject`
- Details about each of the extended members that can be created and added to the `PSObject`

4

Developing Cmdlets

Developing cmdlets is one of the most common and powerful ways to extend PowerShell functionality. This chapter explains different aspects of authoring PowerShell cmdlets.

In a traditional shell such as a Unix shell or DOS's `cmd.exe`, each command is a standalone executable. Developing traditional command executables involves the following tasks:

- Parsing command lines, which normally includes command name, command parameter, and command arguments
- Processing command input, which normally is in text format
- Performing command logic, which can involve transforming command input into a different format for easier processing
- Generating command output, which typically is text writing to a console or outputting to a file
- Reporting errors in case command invocation is not successful

Unlike traditional commands, PowerShell cmdlets are .NET classes hosted in a PowerShell runtime environment. As a result, chores such as command-line parsing, input and output processing, and error reporting can be greatly simplified. This chapter illustrates how.

Getting Started

Developing a PowerShell cmdlet starts with the creation of a cmdlet class. The code in the following example implements the cmdlet `touch-file`, which updates the timestamp of a file to the current time. Please pay particular attention to the `Cmdlet` and `Parameter` attributes when reading through the code:

```
 [Cmdlet("Touch", "File")]
public class TouchFileCommand : PSCmdlet
```

```
{
    private string path = null;

    [Parameter]
    public string Path
    {
        get
        {
            return path;
        }
        set
        {
            path = value;
        }
    }

    protected override void ProcessRecord()
    {
        if (File.Exists(path))
        {
            File.SetLastWriteTime(path, DateTime.Now);
        }
    }
}
```

The cmdlet `touch-file` is implemented in the class `TouchFileCommand`, which derives from the `PSCmdlet` class. Cmdlet attributes of the class `TouchFileCommand` define the verb and noun that make up the cmdlet's name.

Within the `TouchFileCommand` class, the `Path` property is marked as a command parameter through the `Parameter` attribute. Logic for this command is implemented in the `ProcessRecord()` method, which simply calls the appropriate .NET API by setting `LastWriteTime` for the file.

To execute this command in PowerShell, specify the `-path` parameter and parameter arguments to the `touch-file` command, as shown here:

```
PS C:\user\gxie> dir


    Directory: Microsoft.PowerShell.Core\FileSystem::C:\user\gxie


Mode                LastWriteTime     Length Name
----                -------------     ------ ----
-a---          6/9/2007   4:47 PM        420 readme.txt


PS C:\user\gxie> touch-file -path c:\user\gxie\readme.txt
```

```
PS C:\user\gxie> dir


    Directory: Microsoft.PowerShell.Core\FileSystem::C:\user\gxie


Mode                LastWriteTime     Length Name
----                -------------     ------ ----
-a---         6/10/2007  10:44 AM        420 readme.txt
```

You can see that the timestamp for `c:\user\gxie\readme.txt` is updated to the current time.

Next, let's move on to look at how the PowerShell runtime environment interacts with the `TouchFileCommand` class when the `touch-file` cmdlet is invoked.

Command-Line Parsing

When PowerShell receives a command, it parses the command into a list of command elements, which includes the following:

- **Command name:** The first token of the command line
- **Command parameters:** Command elements starting with a hyphen (-)
- **Command arguments:** Command elements that are not command name or command parameters

For example, the full command `touch-file -path c:\user\gxie\readme.txt` will be parsed into a command element list including one command name (`touch-file`), one command parameter (`-path`), and one command argument (`c:\user\gxie\readme.txt`).

Command-line parsing is done by the PowerShell runtime environment without involving specific cmdlets. This simplifies the task for cmdlet development and at the same time delivers consistent command-line syntax across all cmdlets.

In PowerShell, a command argument may or may not be associated with a command parameter. This association, however, is not determined until the metadata for the specific command is consulted to determine whether a parameter is expecting an argument or not.

For example, at command-line parsing time, PowerShell doesn't know that the command argument `c:\user\gxie\readme.txt` is associated with the command parameter `-path`. This association is made later, at parameter binding time.

Command Discovery

Before a command can be invoked, PowerShell needs to determine whether the command is an alias, a function, a cmdlet, a script file, or even a native executable invocation. This step is called *command discovery*.

Command discovery of cmdlets is done through a cmdlet table, which is constructed when snap-ins are loaded into a PowerShell session. For example, when the snap-in assembly containing `TouchFileCommand` is loaded into a PowerShell session, the PowerShell Snapin Loader will find types in the snap-in assembly that meet the following criteria:

- Derive (directly or indirectly) from `PSCmdlet` class
- Include a `Cmdlet` attribute, which supplies a verb and a noun
- Provide a default public constructor so that an instance of the class can be instantiated

For each type that is discovered in this fashion, PowerShell constructs the necessary cmdlet metadata, and then adds the cmdlet metadata into the cmdlet table.

When a command is being invoked, PowerShell's command discovery consults the cmdlet table to determine whether the command matches any cmdlets within the table. If a match is found, then the related cmdlet metadata is retrieved for parameter binding and command invocation, as explained in the following sections.

Command metadata is constructed through reflection on the cmdlet type. It includes information such as the following:

- Name of the cmdlet (including verb and noun)
- The type that implements the cmdlet
- Parameters for the cmdlet

Parameter Binding

At this step, PowerShell binds command parameters and command arguments from the command into the cmdlet instance to be invoked.

Parameter binding is done based on cmdlet metadata retrieved during the command discovery. First, based on the type that implements the cmdlet, PowerShell will create an instance from it. Then, the parameter information in the cmdlet metadata is consulted to determine the list of allowed parameters, and whether a parameter expects an argument or not.

For the `touch-file` command example, based on cmdlet metadata, PowerShell found that `path` is a valid parameter that takes a string as its argument. With this information, the command argument `c:\user\gxie\readme.txt` will be associated with the command parameter `-path`.

To bind a parameter value into a cmdlet instance, setters of the corresponding property are called. For example, to bind `c:\user\gxie\readme.txt` to the parameter `-path`, the property `Path` of the `TouchFileCommand` instance is set to the string value `"c:\user\gxie\readme.txt"`.

After the parameter binding is completed, the cmdlet instance will have the parameter property values filled in. Then the cmdlet instance is ready to be invoked for command execution.

The complexity of parameter binding goes well beyond what is described here. In the section "Using Parameters," you will learn more details about the different kinds of parameters and how they are bound.

Command Invocation

Command invocation is done by calling appropriate methods for the cmdlet instance created during parameter binding. These methods include `BeginProcessing()`, `ProcessRecord()`, and `EndProcessing()`. All three methods, described in the following list, are virtual methods defined in the `PSCmdlet` base class and can be overridden in cmdlet implementation classes.

- `BeginProcessing()` provides the cmdlet with a chance to perform one-time-only start-up operations. This method is called only once, before all calls to `ProcessRecord()` and `EndProcessing()`.
- `ProcessRecord()` is a method most cmdlets override to do the bulk of their work. If a cmdlet is the first command in a pipeline, then this method is called once. Conversely, if a cmdlet is not the first command in pipeline, then this method is called for each pipeline input object.
- `EndProcessing()` is a method that cmdlets can derive to perform closing operations. This method is called after all `ProcessRecord()` calls are completed.

Optionally, you can override these three methods in child cmdlet classes. It is common for a cmdlet class to derive only one or two of these three methods.

Using Parameters

Command-line syntax of a cmdlet is shaped by parameters declared in the cmdlet class. To provide a rich and intuitive command-line user experience, PowerShell allows different aspects of a parameter to be defined, including the following:

- **Mandatory or optional:** A parameter can be mandatory or optional.
- **Positional or named:** A parameter can be identified by its position on the command line, or by an explicit name. For example, if you use the copy-item command, you usually specify the source and destination parameters without giving the parameter names.
- **Parameter validation:** Some validation rules can be attached to a parameter so that the parameter value will be validated before it is bound.
- **Parameter transformation:** Some transformation rules can be attached to a parameter so that a parameter value from a different type is transformed to the correct type expected by the parameter before it is bound.
- **Parameter Sets:** Parameters can be grouped into different parameter sets so that parameters from different sets can be mutually exclusive on the command line.

Mandatory Parameters

You can define mandatory parameters by setting the `Mandatory` property of the `parameter` attribute, as shown in the following example:

```
[Cmdlet("Touch", "File")]
public class TouchFileCommand : PSCmdlet
```

```
{
    private string path = null;

    [Parameter(Mandatory=true)]

    public string Path
    {
        get
        {
            return path;
        }
        set
        {
            path = value;
        }
    }

    protected override void ProcessRecord()
    {
        if (File.Exists(path))
        {
            File.SetLastWriteTime(path, DateTime.Now);
        }
    }
}
```

If a parameter is mandatory, then it needs to be bound (either from the command line or through pipeline input, which is discussed later) before the command logic can be invoked. If a mandatory parameter is not specified, then the user is prompted to provide a value, as shown in the following example:

```
PS C:\user\gxie> touch-file

cmdlet touch-file at command pipeline position 1

Supply values for the following parameters:
Path:
```

Positional Parameters

To use the `touch-file` cmdlet, users have to type the `-path` command parameter at the command line. Otherwise, a parameter binding failure will be reported, as shown here:

```
PS C:\user\gxie> touch-file c:\user\gxie\readme.txt

Touch-File : A parameter cannot be found that matches parameter name 'c:\user\
gxie\readme.txt'.
At line:1 char:11
+ touch-file <<<<  c:\user\gxie\readme.txt
```

This seems a little clumsy, however. To resolve this, positional parameters are supported in PowerShell to associate a command argument with a parameter based on its position. That way, the parameter name doesn't have to be explicitly mentioned in the command line.

To define a parameter to be positional, you can add a position value for the parameter, as shown in the following example:

```
[Cmdlet("Touch", "File")]
public class TouchFileCommand : PSCmdlet
{
    private string path = null;

    [Parameter(Mandatory=true, Position=1)]

    public string Path
    {
        get
        {
            return path;
        }
        set
        {
            path = value;
        }
    }

    protected override void ProcessRecord()
    {
        if (File.Exists(path))
        {
            File.SetLastWriteTime(path, DateTime.Now);
        }
    }
}
```

Now if you run the command without the `-path` command parameter, it will work, as shown in this example:

```
PS C:\user\gxie> touch-file c:\user\gxie\readme.txt

PS C:\user\gxie>
```

Parameter Binding for Positional Parameters

Now it's time to look at how positional parameters are bound. PowerShell uses the following process for binding positional parameters:

- First-named parameters (parameters whose names are explicitly typed out on the command line) are bound first.
- PowerShell puts unbound command arguments from the command line into a list called an *unbound argument list,* based on the position of arguments in the command line.
- PowerShell puts unbound positional parameters into a list called an *unbound positional parameter list,* based on the position value of the parameter declared in the cmdlet.
- The unbound argument list is matched against the unbound positional parameter list for binding command arguments to positional parameters. If there are more unbound arguments than positional parameters, then a parameter binding error is reported.

For example, assume a scenario in which a cmdlet `test-parameter` takes five parameters: `paramA`, `paramB`, `paramC`, `paramD`, and `paramE`, with `paramA`, `paramB`, and `paramC` declared to have positions 1, 2, and 3, respectively. Also assume that all five parameters expect an argument value. Now we can examine how these parameters will be bound for the command example shown here:

```
PS C:\user\gxie> test-parameter -paramD arg1 arg2 -paramB arg3 arg4
```

First, there are two named parameters in the command: `-paramD` and `-paramB`. They are bound first. As a result, `arg1` will be bound to `paramD`, and `arg3` will be bound to `paramB`. In addition, `arg2` and `arg4` are not bound, so we put them into an unbound argument list:

- Unbound argument list: `arg2`, `arg4`

Three parameters are unbound: `paramA`, `paramC`, and `paramE`. Because `paramE` is not positional, we put `paramA` and `paramC` into an unbound positional parameter list, which is ordered based on position value declared:

- Unbound positional parameter list: `paramA` (position = 1), `paramC` (position = 3)

Now we match the unbound argument list with the unbound positional parameter list. As a result, `arg2` is bound to `paramA` and `arg4` is bound to `paramC`.

Remaining-Argument Parameter

The remaining-argument parameter is a special positional parameter that takes the list of the remaining arguments after the named parameter binding and the positional parameter binding.

The following example illustrates how a remaining-argument parameter can be defined:

```
[Cmdlet("Test", "RemainingArgumentParameter")]
public class Test RemainingArgumentParameter Command : PSCmdlet
{
    private object[] arguments = null;

    [Parameter(ValueFromRemainingArguments=true)]
    public object[] Arguments

    {
        get
        {
            return arguments;
        }
        set
        {
            arguments=value;
        }
    }

    ...
}
```

Because in most cases there can be more than one remaining argument, normally the remaining-argument parameter is defined to be an array.

For example, let's assume that the `test-parameter` cmdlet mentioned earlier is expanded to take a sixth parameter, `paramF`, which takes its value from remaining arguments. Then, for the command

```
PS C:\user\gxie> test-parameter -paramD arg1 arg2 -paramB arg3 arg4 arg5 arg6
```

arguments `arg1`, `arg3`, `arg2`, and `arg4` will be bound to `paramD`, `paramB`, `paramA`, and `paramC`, as mentioned before. The remaining arguments are `arg5` and `arg6`, which are packed in an array and bound to the remaining-argument parameter, `paramF`.

Parameter Sets

Frequently, a cmdlet needs to have the capability to handle parameters that appear in different combinations. For the `touch-file` cmdlet described earlier, for example, it would be nice if the cmdlet could directly take a `FileInfo` object and directly operate on it.

To support this capability, PowerShell supports *parameter sets*, which organize parameters into mutually exclusive groups. At runtime, PowerShell will pick one parameter set depending on the parameters specified on the command line.

The following example is an enhanced version of the `touch-file` cmdlet, illustrating how parameter sets can be defined and used:

```
[Cmdlet("Touch", "File")]
public class TouchFileCommand : PSCmdlet
{
    private string path = null;

    [Parameter(ParameterSetName = "PathSet", Mandatory=true, Position=1)]

    public string Path
    {
        get
        {
            return path;
        }
        set
        {
            path = value;
        }
    }

    private FileInfo fileInfo = null;

    [Parameter(ParameterSetName = "FileInfoSet", Mandatory = true, Position = 1)]

    public FileInfo FileInfo
    {
        get
        {
            return fileInfo;
        }
        set
```

```
            {
                fileInfo = value;
            }
        }

        protected override void ProcessRecord()
        {
            if (fileInfo != null)
            {
                fileInfo.LastWriteTime = DateTime.Now;
            }

            if (File.Exists(path))
            {
                File.SetLastWriteTime(path, DateTime.Now);
            }
        }
    }
```

In the preceding example, you can see that a new parameter, `FileInfo`, is added to the cmdlet. In addition, because we want users to be able to specify either a `Path` or a `FileInfo` parameter from the command line, but not both, we put these two parameters into two different parameter sets, `PathSet` and `FileInfoSet`, respectively.

Now the `touch-file` cmdlet can be executed with either a `Path` or a `FileInfo` parameter but not both:

```
PS C:\user\gxie> touch-file -path c:\user\gxie\readme.txt

PS C:\user\gxie> $a = get-item c:\user\gxie\readme.txt

PS C:\user\gxie> touch-file -fileinfo $a
PS C:\user\gxie> touch-file -path c:\user\gxie\readme.txt -fileinfo $a

Touch-File : Parameter set cannot be resolved using the specified named parameters.
At line:1 char:11
+ touch-file <<<<  -path c:\user\gxie\readme.txt -fileinfo $a
```

Default Parameter Sets

If you run the `touch-file` command with no arguments, you will get a parameter set resolution failure, as shown here:

```
PS C:\user\gxie> touch-file

Touch-File : Parameter set cannot be resolved using the specified named parameters.
At line:1 char:11
+ touch-file
```

In this case, both `PathSet` and `FileInfoSet` are valid candidate parameter sets, but the PowerShell parameter binder is not able to decide which one to use. In this case, it makes sense for the parameter binder to use a more common parameter set for parameter binding. The default parameter set is designed for this purpose.

The following code illustrates how a default parameter set can be defined for a cmdlet:

```
[Cmdlet("Touch", "File", DefaultParameterSetName = "PathSet")]

public class TouchFileCommand : PSCmdlet
{
    ...
}
```

With this change, now you can execute the `touch-file` cmdlet again, with no arguments:

```
PS C:\user\gxie> touch-file


cmdlet touch-file at command pipeline position 1
Supply values for the following parameters:
Path:
```

The preceding example shows that the parameter binder has decided to use the default parameter set in this ambiguous situation.

Parameters That Belong to Multiple Parameter Sets

It is possible to define parameters that belong to several different parameter sets. One common scenario is for a parameter to belong to all parameter sets for the cmdlet. The parameter `Date` in the `touch-file` cmdlet is an example of this:

```
[Cmdlet("Touch", "File", DefaultParameterSetName = "PathSet")]
public class TouchFileCommand : PSCmdlet

{
    private string path = null;

    [Parameter(ParameterSetName = "PathSet", Mandatory=true, Position=1)]

    public string Path
    {
        ...
    }

    private FileInfo fileInfo = null;

    [Parameter(ParameterSetName = "FileInfoSet", Mandatory = true, Position = 1)]

    public FileInfo FileInfo
```

```
        {
            ...
        }

        DateTime date = DateTime.Now;

        [Parameter]
        public DateTime Date
        {
            get
            {
                return date;
            }
            set
            {
                date = value;
            }
        }

        protected override void ProcessRecord()
        {
            if (fileInfo != null)
            {

                fileInfo.LastWriteTime = date;

            }

            if (File.Exists(path))
            {

                File.SetLastWriteTime(path, date);

            }
        }
    }
```

`Date` is an optional parameter that enables users to specify a different date for the file's timestamp. If this parameter is not specified, then the file timestamp will be updated to the current time as before. It is obvious that this parameter applies to both cases: when the file information is specified through `Path` and when it is specified through `FileInfo`. Therefore, the `Date` parameter needs to be present on both parameter sets. The preceding code does exactly that by not setting `ParameterSetName` for the `Date` parameter, which means that this parameter applies to all parameter sets.

Now you can experiment with this enhanced version of the `touch-file` cmdlet. First, you can see that this parameter applies to both parameter sets: `PathSet` and `FileInfoSet`:

```
PS C:\user\gxie> touch-file -path c:\user\gxie\readme.txt -date 1/1/2000

PS C:\user\gxie> dir


    Directory: Microsoft.PowerShell.Core\FileSystem::C:\user\gxie
```

```
Mode                LastWriteTime     Length Name
----                -------------     ------ ----
-a---          1/1/2000  12:00 AM        420 readme.txt
PS C:\user\gxie> $a = get-item c:\user\gxie\readme.txt
```

```
PS C:\user\gxie> touch-file -fileinfo $a -date 2/1/2000
```

```
PS C:\user\gxie> dir


    Directory: Microsoft.PowerShell.Core\FileSystem::C:\user\gxie


Mode                LastWriteTime     Length Name
----                -------------     ------ ----
-a---          2/1/2000  12:00 AM        420 readme.txt
```

Next, note that the `Date` parameter is optional. Because of its absence, the file's timestamp will be updated to the current time:

```
PS C:\user\gxie> touch-file -path c:\user\gxie\readme.txt
PS C:\user\gxie> dir


    Directory: Microsoft.PowerShell.Core\FileSystem::C:\user\gxie


Mode                LastWriteTime     Length Name
----                -------------     ------ ----
-a---         6/10/2007   2:14 PM        420 readme.txt
```

Finally, if the `Date` parameter is the only parameter specified on the command line, parameter binding will default to the parameter set `PathSet`, which has the same effect as not specifying the `Date` parameter on the command line:

```
PS C:\user\gxie> touch-file -date 1/1/2000

cmdlet touch-file at command pipeline position 1
Supply values for the following parameters:
Path:
PS C:\user\gxie> touch-file

cmdlet touch-file at command pipeline position 1
Supply values for the following parameters:
Path:
```

Parameter Binding Related to Parameter Sets

PowerShell goes through the following phases to determine which parameter set to use during parameter binding:

- Named parameter binding
- Positional parameter binding
- Pipeline parameter binding

This section discusses parameter set logic related to the first two phases. Pipeline parameter binding and related parameter set decisions are discussed in the section "Processing Pipeline Input."

Named Parameter Binding

During this process, candidate parameter sets are narrowed down based on the parameter set to which the named parameter belongs. If ultimately there is no valid candidate parameter set, a parameter set resolution failure is reported.

The following example illustrates this process. Assume that the cmdlet `Test-ParameterSet1` has the following parameters:

- `ParamA` belongs to parameter set `SetX` and `SetY`
- `ParamB` belongs to parameter set `SetX`
- `ParamC` belongs to parameter set `SetY`

Assume the following command:

```
PS C:\user\gxie> Test-ParameterSet1 -ParamA arg1 -ParamB arg2 -ParamC arg3
Test-ParameterSet1 : Parameter set cannot be resolved using the specified named param-
eters.
At line:1 char:18
+ Test-ParameterSet1 <<<<  -ParamA arg1 -ParamB arg2 -ParamC arg3
```

Parameter resolution fails because binding `ParamA` results in the candidate parameter set to be `SetX` and `SetY`. Binding `ParamB` will further limit the candidate parameter set to be `SetX` only. Finally, when `ParamC` is bound, the parameter binder will find that it doesn't belong to any candidate parameter set, thereby resulting in the reported failure.

Positional Parameter Binding

Positional parameter binding is done after named parameter binding is completed. At the beginning of positional parameter binding, named parameter binding has already limited valid parameter sets to be one or more candidates. If there is only one valid parameter set, then parameters from that parameter set are used for positional parameter binding.

If there is more than one candidate parameter set, then the list of unbound positional parameters is built for each candidate parameter set. Then the first unbound positional parameters from the candidate parameter set will be matched against the first unbound argument, and the most suitable first unbound positional parameter will be chosen for binding (logic for deciding which one is most suitable is described in the next paragraph).

Next, parameter set information for the chosen positional parameter is used to narrow down the number of candidate parameter sets. Then the second unbound positional parameters from candidate parameter sets are considered for binding (to second unbound arguments) and candidate parameter sets are further narrowed down. This process continues until unbound positional parameters are exhausted. If conflicts regarding parameter sets occur during this process, a parameter set resolution error is reported.

The parameter binder decides on the most suitable unbound positional parameter based on the type of unbound argument that is being bound with. Following is the sequence of logic used:

- From the set of unbound positional parameters from different parameter sets, find the ones that have exactly the same value type as the type of unbound argument:
  - If only one parameter is found, then that parameter is chosen.
  - If more than one parameter is found but one of them is from the default parameter set, then the parameter from the default parameter set is chosen.
  - Otherwise, a random parameter is chosen from the list.
- If no unbound positional parameters are found to have exactly the same value type as the type of the unbound argument, find the ones that have value types that can be converted from the type of the unbound argument:
  - If only one parameter is found, then that parameter is chosen.
  - If more than one parameter is found but one of them is from the default parameter set, then the parameter from the default parameter set is chosen.
  - Otherwise, a random parameter is chosen from the list.

To illustrate this process, let's look at an example. Assume that cmdlet `Test-ParameterSet2` has the following parameter sets:

- **Parameter set SetX:** This includes the following positional parameters (in order): `ParamA` (of type `string`), `ParamB` (of type `int`)
- **Parameter set SetY:** This includes the following positional parameters (in order): `ParamA` (of type `string`), `ParamC` (of type `int`)
- **Parameter set SetZ:** This includes the following positional parameters (in order): `ParamD` (of type `object`), `ParamE` (of type `int`)

In addition, assume that parameter set `SetX` is the default parameter set. Now consider the following command:

```
PS C:\user\gxie> Test-ParameterSet2 "string" 12
```

The first argument of this command is a string. The second argument of this command is an integer.

Before position parameter binding, all three parameter sets are valid candidates. You bind the first unbound positional parameter, which can be either `ParamA` (from `SetX` and `SetY`) or `ParamD` (from `SetZ`). Because `ParamA`'s value type `string` exactly matches the type of the first unbound argument, it is chosen. As a result, now the valid parameter sets are narrowed down to `SetX` and `SetY` only.

Now you bind the second unbound positional parameter, which can be either `ParamB` (from `SetX`) or `ParamC` (from `SetY`). Because both parameters take a value type of `integer`, the one from the default parameter set is chosen. As a result, `ParamB` will be bound, and the candidate parameter sets is narrowed down to `SetX` only.

Please note that even after positional parameter binding it is possible for more than one parameter set to be valid. In this case, the parameter binder will report a parameter resolution failure unless this command takes pipeline input. If the command does take pipeline input (for example, if the command is the second command in the pipeline), then the parameter binder will have another shot at resolving the parameter set while binding pipeline inputs. This is discussed in the section "Processing Pipeline Input."

Parameter Validation

Parameter validation enables validation logic to be added to verify the parameter value before it is bound to a parameter. Parameter validation is specified through validation attributes defined on parameter properties.

The following example uses the `ValidateNotNullOrEmpty` attribute in the `Touch-File` cmdlet:

```
[Cmdlet("Touch", "File")]
public class TouchFileCommand : PSCmdlet
{
    private string path = null;

     [Parameter(ParameterSetName = "PathSet", Mandatory=true, Position=1)]

     [ValidateNotNullOrEmpty]

    public string Path
    {
        ...
    }

    private FileInfo fileInfo = null;

    [Parameter(ParameterSetName = "FileInfoSet", Mandatory = true, Position = 1)]
    public FileInfo FileInfo
    {
        ...
    }

    DateTime date = DateTime.Now;

    [Parameter]
    public DateTime Date
    {
        ...
    }

    protected override void ProcessRecord()
    {
        ...
    }
}
```

Now, if you build and run the new `touch-file` cmdlet with an empty path as shown here:

```
PS C:\user\gxie> touch-file -path ""
Touch-File : The argument cannot be null or empty.
```

```
At line:1 char:17
+ touch-file -path <<<<  ""
```

an error is reported that the `path` parameter cannot be null or empty.

PowerShell provides a list of parameter validation attributes out-of-the-box, including the following:

- `ValidateNotNull`: Validates that the parameter value is not null
- `ValidateRange`: Validates that the integer parameter value is in a specified range
- `ValidateCount`: Validates that the list parameter value has a number range of items
- `ValidateLength`: Validates that the string parameter value has a range of string length
- `ValidateSet`: Validates that the parameter value falls into a set specified
- `AllowNull`: Allows the parameter value to be null
- `AllowEmptyString`: Allows the string parameter value to be an empty string
- `AllowEmptyCollection`: Allows the list parameter value to take an empty collection

Custom Parameter Validation Attributes

Cmdlet developers can develop their own custom validation attributes. This can be done by deriving from the `ValidateArgumentsAttribute` class (directly or indirectly) and filling in logic for `ValidateElement`.

Following is an example that validates that a parameter value is an even number:

```
[AttributeUsage(AttributeTargets.Field | AttributeTargets.Property)]
public class ValidateEvenNumberAttribute : ValidateArgumentsAttribute
{
    protected override void ValidateElement(object element)
    {
        if (element == null || !(element is int))
        {
            throw new ArgumentException("Invalid parameter value");
        }

        int i = (int) element;

        if(i % 2 != 0)
        {
            throw new ArgumentException("Not an even number.");
        }
    }
}
```

The `Get-EvenNumber` cmdlet illustrates how to use this validation attribute:

```
[Cmdlet("Get", "EvenNumber")]
public class GetEvenNumberCommand : PSCmdlet
{
    int number = 0;
```

```
        [Parameter(Mandatory=true)]
        [ValidateEvenNumber]
        public int Number
        {
            get
            {
                return number;
            }
            set
            {
                number = value;
            }
        }

        protected override void ProcessRecord()
        {
        }
    }
```

Now try running the `Get-EvenNumber` cmdlet with an odd argument value for the `Number` parameter:

```
PS C:\user\gxie> get-evennumber -number 13
Get-EvenNumber : Cannot validate argument on parameter 'Number'. Not an even num
Ber.
At line:1 char:23
+ get-evennumber -number <<<<  13
```

As you can see, an error is reported because even number validation failed.

Parameter Transformation

In cmdlet development, parameters can be defined as any .NET types, from simple types such as `string`, `int` to complicated types such as `System.Process`. One common task, however, is to design the cmdlet so that parameter values can be easily typed in from the command line.

For example, assume that you want to develop a cmdlet `Unite-Rectangle`, which calculates the union of two rectangles:

```
Using System.Drawing;

[Cmdlet("Unite", "Rectangle")]

public class UniteRectangleCommand : PSCmdlet
{
    Rectangle rectangle1 = new Rectangle(0,0,0,0);

    [Parameter(Mandatory = true, Position = 1)]
    public Rectangle Rectangle1
```

```
        {
            get
            {
                return rectangle1;
            }
            set
            {
                rectangle1 = value;
            }
        }

        Rectangle rectangle2 = new Rectangle(0, 0, 0, 0);

        [Parameter(Mandatory = true, Position = 2)]
        public Rectangle Rectangle2
        {
            get
            {
                return rectangle2;
            }
            set
            {
                rectangle2 = value;
            }
        }

        protected override void ProcessRecord()
        {
            WriteObject(Rectangle.Union(rectangle1, rectangle2));
        }
    }
```

You can see that both parameters `Rectangle1` and `Rectangle2` have the type `System.Drawing.Rectangle`. To specify rectangle values for these command parameters, you would have to create rectangle objects first (using the `new-object` cmdlet) and then pass them to the new cmdlet, as shown in the following example:

```
PS C:\user\gxie> $r1 = new-object system.drawing.rectangle 1,2,1,1
PS C:\user\gxie> $r2 = new-object system.drawing.rectangle 3,4,1,1
PS C:\user\gxie> Unite-Rectangle $r1 $r2

Location : {X=1,Y=2}
Size     : {Width=3, Height=3}
X        : 1
Y        : 2
Width    : 3
Height   : 3
Left     : 1
```

```
Top       : 2
Right     : 4
Bottom    : 5
IsEmpty   : False
```

The first command creates a rectangle object with the left-bottom corner set to (1,2). The second command creates a rectangle object with the left-bottom corner set to (3,4). Both rectangles have a width and height of 1. After the rectangles are united, the smallest rectangle that can cover them both has a left-bottom corner of (1,2), with a width and a height of 3. The math works correctly, but having to create two rectangles beforehand is not desirable.

It would be nice to allow users to type a list, a string, or a hash table from the command line, which you would automatically convert into rectangles. To achieve this, *parameter transformation* comes in handy. Basically, a custom parameter transformation attribute can be defined with logic to convert parameter values from one format (for example, *list*) to another format (for example, *rectangle*). Then the attribute can be associated with a parameter so that this kind of transformation is done automatically during parameter binding.

The following code illustrates a custom `ListToRectangleConverterAttribute` class for converting a list into a rectangle:

```
Using System.Collection;

[AttributeUsage(AttributeTargets.Field | AttributeTargets.Property)]

public class ListToRectangleConverterAttribute : ArgumentTransformationAttribute
{
    public override object Transform(EngineIntrinsics ei, object inputData)
    {
        object input = inputData;

        if (input is PSObject)
            input = ((PSObject)input).BaseObject;

        if (input is IList)
        {
            IList list = input as IList;

            if (list.Count == 4)
            {
                return new Rectangle((int)list[0], (int)list[1],
                        (int)list[2], (int)list[3]);
            }
        }

        return inputData;
    }
}
```

In the preceding example, you can see that this class is derived from the `ArgumentTransformation-Attribute` class. The bulk of the work for this class is overriding the `Tranform` method to transform parameter values from one format to another. Inside the `Tranform` method, transformation is done selectively. More explicitly, you create a new `rectangle` object only if `inputData` is a list of four integers. Otherwise, `inputData` will be passed through as it is. This implementation is chosen so that you don't mistakenly convert `inputData` if it is already a `Rectangle`. In addition, passing through `inputData` allows another parameter transformation attribute down the chain to also process the data.

Now, use this attribute in the `Unite-Rectangle` cmdlet:

```
[Cmdlet("Unite", "Rectangle")]
public class UniteRectangleCommand : PSCmdlet
{
    Rectangle rectangle1 = new Rectangle(0,0,0,0);

     [Parameter(Mandatory = true, Position = 1)]

     [ListToRectangleConverter]

    public Rectangle Rectangle1
    {
        ...
    }

    Rectangle rectangle2 = new Rectangle(0, 0, 0, 0);

     [Parameter(Mandatory = true, Position = 2)]

     [ListToRectangleConverter]

    public Rectangle Rectangle2
    {
        ...
    }

    protected override void ProcessRecord()
    {
        WriteObject(Rectangle.Union(rectangle1, rectangle2));
    }
}
```

Now you can run the new `Unite-Rectangle` cmdlet by simply passing in two lists:

```
PS C:\user\gxie> Unite-Rectangle (1,2,1,1) (3,4,1,1)


Location : {X=1,Y=2}
Size     : {Width=3, Height=3}
X        : 1
Y        : 2
Width    : 3
Height   : 3
Left     : 1
Top      : 2
Right    : 4
Bottom   : 5
IsEmpty  : False
```

In addition, you can verify that directly passing a `Rectangle` object into either parameter will continue to work:

```
PS C:\user\gxie> $r2 = new-object system.drawing.rectangle 3,4,1,1
PS C:\user\gxie> Unite-Rectangle (1,2,1,1) $r2


Location : {X=1,Y=2}
Size     : {Width=3, Height=3}
X        : 1
Y        : 2
Width    : 3
Height   : 3
Left     : 1
Top      : 2
Right    : 4
Bottom   : 5
IsEmpty  : False
```

In summary, this section described how to declare a parameter to be mandatory and positional, how to use parameter sets, and how to validate and transform parameter values. In next section, you will learn how to make a parameter take pipeline input values.

Processing Pipeline Input

One of most popular PowerShell features is pipelining objects from one command to another command. For a cmdlet to be used in a pipeline, it needs to be able to handle pipeline input and generate pipeline output. In this section, you will learn techniques to handle pipeline input in a cmdlet.

PowerShell cmdlets can bind pipeline input to a parameter and access the parameter in the ProcessRecord() method of the cmdlet. The following example extends the `touch-file` cmdlet:

```
[Cmdlet("Touch", "File", DefaultParameterSetName = "Path")]
public class TouchFileCommand : PSCmdlet
{
    ...

     [Parameter(ParameterSetName = "FileInfo", Mandatory = true, Position = 1,
         ValueFromPipeline = true)]
    public FileInfo FileInfo
    {
        get
        {
            return fileInfo;
        }
        set
        {
            fileInfo = value;
        }
    }
    ...
```

```
        protected override void ProcessRecord()
        {
            if (fileInfo != null)
            {
                fileInfo.LastWriteTime = date;
            }

            if (File.Exists(path))
            {
                File.SetLastWriteTime(path, date);
            }
        }
    }
```

Comparing the preceding code with the example from the "Parameter Validation" section, the only change here is setting the `ValueFromPipeline` parameter to `true` for the `FileInfo` parameter. This informs the PowerShell engine that the parameter `FileInfo` will bind to pipeline input in case it is not specified from the command line.

Use the following to run this cmdlet:

```
PS C:\user\gxie> get-childitem *.txt | Touch-File -date 7/1/2007
PS C:\user\gxie> get-childitem *.txt


    Directory: Microsoft.PowerShell.Core\FileSystem::C:\user\gxie

Mode                LastWriteTime     Length Name
----                -------------     ------ ----
-a---          7/1/2007  12:00 AM        420 readme.txt
-a---          7/1/2007  12:00 AM        420 readme2.txt
```

In the first command of the preceding example, for each output object from `get-childitem*.txt`, the PowerShell engine will bind the `Touch-File` cmdlet's `FileInfo` parameter and call its `ProcessRecord()` method to update the timestamp of the file.

Cmdlets parameter can also bind to a property of a pipeline input object. Following is an example that binds the `path` parameter to a property of the pipeline input object:

```
    [Cmdlet("Touch", "File", DefaultParameterSetName = "Path")]
    public class TouchFileCommand : PSCmdlet
    {
        private string path = null;

         [Parameter(ParameterSetName = "Path", Mandatory=true, Position=1,
            ValueFromPipelineByPropertyName = true)]
        [Alias("FullName")]
        [ValidateNotNullOrEmpty]
```

```
        public string Path
        {
            get
            {
                return path;
            }
            set
            {
                path = value;
            }
        }

        private FileInfo fileInfo = null;

        [Parameter(ParameterSetName = "FileInfo", Mandatory = true, Position = 1)]
        public FileInfo FileInfo
        {
            get
            {
                return fileInfo;
            }
            set
            {
                fileInfo = value;
            }
        }

        DateTime date = DateTime.Now;

        [Parameter]
        public DateTime Date
        {
            get
            {
                return date;
            }
            set
            {
                date = value;
            }
        }

        protected override void ProcessRecord()
        {
            if (fileInfo != null)
            {
                fileInfo.LastWriteTime = date;
            }

            if (File.Exists(path))
            {
                File.SetLastWriteTime(path, date);
            }
        }
    }
```

In this example, instead of letting the FileInfo parameter take its value from the pipeline, you set TakeValueFromPipelineByPropertyName to be true for the parameter path. Furthermore, you define the alias FullName for the parameter path. Now, if the pipeline input object has either a path property or a FullName property, then that property value will be bound to the path parameter.

Run the touch-file command much as you did before:

```
PS C:\user\gxie> get-childitem *.txt | Touch-File -date 7/1/2007
PS C:\user\gxie> get-childitem *.txt


    Directory: Microsoft.PowerShell.Core\FileSystem::C:\user\gxie

Mode                LastWriteTime     Length Name
----                -------------     ------ ----
-a---          7/1/2007  12:00 AM        420 readme.txt
-a---          7/1/2007  12:00 AM        420 readme2.txt
```

You can see that the timestamp of both .txt files are updated. In this case, output of get-childitem *.txt contains a property named FullName (as shown below), which is bound to the path parameter of the touch-file cmdlet:

```
PS C:\user\gxie> get-childitem *.txt | get-member -membertype property


   TypeName: System.IO.FileInfo

Name              MemberType Definition
----              ---------- ----------
Attributes        Property   System.IO.FileAttributes Attributes {get;set;}
CreationTime      Property   System.DateTime CreationTime {get;set;}
CreationTimeUtc   Property   System.DateTime CreationTimeUtc {get;set;}
Directory         Property   System.IO.DirectoryInfo Directory {get;}
DirectoryName     Property   System.String DirectoryName {get;}
Exists            Property   System.Boolean Exists {get;}
Extension         Property   System.String Extension {get;}
FullName          Property   System.String FullName {get;}
IsReadOnly        Property   System.Boolean IsReadOnly {get;set;}
LastAccessTime    Property   System.DateTime LastAccessTime {get;set;}
LastAccessTimeUtc Property   System.DateTime LastAccessTimeUtc {get;set;}
LastWriteTime     Property   System.DateTime LastWriteTime {get;set;}
LastWriteTimeUtc  Property   System.DateTime LastWriteTimeUtc {get;set;}
Length            Property   System.Int64 Length {get;}
Name              Property   System.String Name {get;}
```

Pipeline Parameter Binding

Cmdlet parameters can be bound either to command arguments from the command line or to input objects from the pipeline. Command-line parameter binding happens once for each cmdlet invocation. It is performed before the BeginProcessing() method of the cmdlet implementation class is called.

Conversely, pipeline parameter binding happens once for each pipeline input object. It is performed before each call to the `ProcessRecord()` method of the cmdlet class.

Similar to command-line parameter binding, pipeline parameter binding also needs to pick the parameter to bind from valid parameter sets. It uses the following process to decide which parameter to bind first:

1. **Prepare parameter lists:** Unbound pipeline parameters from valid parameter sets are organized into two lists: One list (let's call it `ValueFromPipeline`) is for pipeline parameters taking pipeline input (i.e., the `ValueFromPipeline` property of the parameter attribute is set to true); another list (let's call it `ValudFromPipelineByPropertyName`) is for pipeline parameters taking pipeline input by property name (i.e., `ValueFromPipelineByPropertyName` is set to true). Pipeline parameters from default parameter sets are put at the beginning of these two lists so that they are considered for binding first.
2. **Bind next parameter:** The pipeline parameter binder uses four steps to determine which parameter to bind:
    a. **Bind parameters from the `ValueFromPipeline` list with *no* type conversion**. In this step, if one parameter from the list has exactly the same type as pipeline input object, then it will be bound. Otherwise, parameter binding goes to the next step.
    b. **Bind parameters from the `ValueFromPipelineByPropertyName` list with *no* type conversion**. In this step, if one parameter from the list matches a property's name of the pipeline input object and the parameter type matches the property type, then this parameter will be bound. Otherwise, parameter binding goes to the next step.
    c. **Bind parameters from the `ValueFromPipeline` list with type conversion**. In this step, if the pipeline input object can be converted into a type of parameter in the list, that parameter will be bound. Otherwise, parameter binding goes to the next step.
    d. **Bind parameters from the `ValueFromPipelineByPropertyName` list with *no* type conversion**. In this step, if the name of one property of the pipeline input object matches a parameter in the list and the property type can be converted to the parameter type, this parameter will be bound.
3. **Narrow down valid parameter sets:** If there is a parameter bound in the preceding steps, then parameter sets for the parameter bound will be used for narrowing down valid parameter sets. Then the pipeline binder will recalculate the unbound pipeline parameter list and bind the next parameter. This process will continue until no parameter can be bound.

To illustrate the process of pipeline parameter binding, let's expand the `touch-file` cmdlet to specify that both `Path` and `FileInfo` take their value from the pipeline:

```
[Cmdlet("Touch", "File", DefaultParameterSetName = "Path")]
public class TouchFileCommand : PSCmdlet
{
    private string path = null;

     [Parameter(ParameterSetName = "Path", Mandatory=true, Position=1,

       ValueFromPipeline = true, ValueFromPipelineByPropertyName = true)]
    [Alias("FullName")]
```

```
[ValidateNotNullOrEmpty]
public string Path
{
    get
    {
        return path;
    }
    set
    {
        path = value;
    }
}

private FileInfo fileInfo = null;

 [Parameter(ParameterSetName = "FileInfo", Mandatory = true, Position = 1,

    ValueFromPipeline = true)]

public FileInfo FileInfo
{
    get
    {
        return fileInfo;
    }
    set
    {
        fileInfo = value;
    }
}

DateTime date = DateTime.Now;

[Parameter]
public DateTime Date
{
    get
    {
        return date;
    }
    set
    {
        date = value;
    }
}

protected override void ProcessRecord()
{
    if (fileInfo != null)
    {
        fileInfo.LastWriteTime = date;
    }
```

```
            if (File.Exists(path))
            {
                File.SetLastWriteTime(path, date);
            }
        }
    }
```

Please note that the parameter `Path` is defined to take the value from either the pipeline object or a property of the pipeline object. In the preparation stage of pipeline parameter binding, the two pipeline parameter lists can be constructed as follows:

- ValueFromPipeline List: Path, FileInfo
- ValueFromPipelineByPropertyName List: Path

Now consider the following commands:

```
PS C:\user\gxie> $a = 'c:\user\gxie\readme.txt'
PS C:\user\gxie> $b = get-childitem readme2.txt
PS C:\user\gxie> $c = add-member -InputObject 0 -MemberType NoteProperty -Name P
ath -Value 'c:\user\gxie\readme3.txt' -passThru

PS C:\user\gxie> $a,$b,$c | touch-file -date 7/1/2007

PS C:\user\gxie> get-childitem


    Directory: Microsoft.PowerShell.Core\FileSystem::C:\user\gxie


Mode                LastWriteTime     Length Name
----                -------------     ------ ----
-a---          7/1/2007  12:00 AM        420 readme.txt
-a---          7/1/2007  12:00 AM        420 readme2.txt
-a---          7/1/2007  12:00 AM        420 readme3.txt
```

The first pipeline object is `$a`, which is a string. Because the type of the `Path` parameter is a string, it will be bound to take the value of `$a` during the step of binding parameters from the `ValueFromPipeline` list with no type conversion. With this, the timestamp of file `c:\user\gxie\readme.txt` will be updated.

The second pipeline object is `$b`, which is of type `FileInfo`. This matches the type for parameter `FileInfo`, `FileInfo`, so this parameter will take the value of `$b` during the step of binding parameters from the `ValueFromPipeline` list with no type conversion. With this, the timestamp of file `c:\user\gxie\readme2.txt` will be updated.

The third pipeline object is `$c`, which is a wrapped integer with a property named `Path`. First, an attempt to bind parameters from the `ValueFromPipeline` list will fail because neither parameter `Path` nor `FileInfo` is of type integer. During the step of binding parameters from the `ValueFromPipelineByPropertyName` list (with no type conversion), the `Path` parameter will be bound to a value of `$c.Path` because of type match and name match. With this, the timestamp of file `c:\user\gxie\readme3.txt` will also be updated.

At this point, you know how to make a cmdlet handle command-line input and pipeline input through command parameters. In the following sections, we discuss how to show cmdlet execution results to users. This includes cmdlet output and cmdlet execution errors.

Generating Pipeline Output

PowerShell cmdlets can write objects to the output pipe by using the `WriteObject()` method. The following example extends the `Touch-File` cmdlet to write `FileInfo` objects to the output pipe:

```
[Cmdlet("Touch", "File", DefaultParameterSetName = "Path")]
public class TouchFileCommand : PSCmdlet
{
    private string path = null;

    [Parameter(ParameterSetName = "Path", Mandatory=true, Position=1,
        ValueFromPipeline = true, ValueFromPipelineByPropertyName = true)]
    [Alias("FullName")]
    [ValidateNotNullOrEmpty]
    public string Path
    {
        get
        {
            return path;
        }
        set
        {
            path = value;
        }
    }

    private FileInfo fileInfo = null;

    [Parameter(ParameterSetName = "FileInfo", Mandatory = true, Position = 1,
        ValueFromPipeline = true)]
    public FileInfo FileInfo
    {
        get
        {
            return fileInfo;
        }
        set
        {
            fileInfo = value;
        }
    }

    DateTime date = DateTime.Now;

    [Parameter]
    public DateTime Date
```

```
        {
            get
            {
                return date;
            }
            set
            {
                date = value;
            }
        }

        protected override void ProcessRecord()
        {
            if (fileInfo == null && File.Exists(path))
            {
                fileInfo = new FileInfo(path);
            }

            if (fileInfo != null)
            {
                fileInfo.LastWriteTime = date;

                WriteObject(fileInfo);

            }
        }
    }
```

With this change, downstream cmdlets can continue processing the object, as shown in the following command:

```
PS C:\user\gxie> Get-ChildItem | Touch-File | Format-Table FullName, LastWriteTime

    FullName                                LastWriteTime
    --------                                -------------
    c:\user\gxie\readme.txt                 7/7/2007 1:51:26 PM
    c:\user\gxie\readme2.txt                7/7/2007 1:51:26 PM
    c:\user\gxie\readme3.txt                7/7/2007 1:51:26 PM
```

Reporting Errors

Cmdlet execution can encounter exceptions from different sources, including the following:

- .NET common language runtime (or CLR) or PowerShell — for example, the out of memory exception from CLR or the pipeline stopped exception from PowerShell
- Cmdlet logic itself
- Components on which the cmdlet depends

Cmdlets normally don't need to be concerned about exceptions from the CLR or PowerShell. These kinds of exceptions can be better handled by PowerShell. For exceptions from the other two sources, it is the cmdlet's responsibility to wrap the exceptions into error records and to report them.

There are two kinds of errors in PowerShell:

- **Non-terminating errors:** This kind of error is usually specific to the current pipeline object on which the cmdlet is operating. As a result, the cmdlet can skip the current object and move on to process the next object from the pipeline.
- **Terminating errors:** This kind of error indicates an issue with the cmdlet that prevents it from handling any pipeline objects. For example, the `Start-Service` cmdlet depends on the service controller for starting a service. If the service controller is not running, the `Start-Service` cmdlet will not be able to start any service. As a result, the whole cmdlet needs to be stopped.

For normal shells, error handling focuses on reporting errors. PowerShell also allows analyzing and acting upon the errors. Usually, errors during PowerShell command execution are accumulated into an array. Then users can analyze the error, fix the problem, and resend the objects not processed through the pipeline. To support this capability, PowerShell provides the `ErrorRecord` and `ErrorDetail` classes.

ErrorRecord

`ErrorRecord` is a class for providing information about errors that occurred during cmdlet execution. It tracks the following information:

- **Exception:** This is the underlying exception that caused the error. It provides an error message, call stacks, and so on to help diagnose the error.
- **Error category and Error ID:** These provide categorization information to help search for and group errors.
- **Target object:** This is normally the current pipeline object. With this, you can determine which pipeline objects were not successfully processed and need to be processed again.
- **InvocationInfo:** This provides context about this error. It includes information such as the cmdlet, the pipeline, and which line of a script file was being executed when the error happened.

To create an `ErrorRecord` object, just fill in information about the exception, error category, error ID, and target object, as shown in the following example:

```
[Cmdlet("Touch", "File", DefaultParameterSetName = "Path")]
public class TouchFileCommand : PSCmdlet
{
    private string path = null;

    [Parameter(ParameterSetName = "Path", Mandatory = true, Position = 1,
        ValueFromPipeline = true, ValueFromPipelineByPropertyName = true)]
    [ValidateNotNullOrEmpty]
    [Alias("FullName")]
    public string Path
    {
        get
        {
            return path;
        }
        set
        {
            path = value;
        }
    }
```

```
private FileInfo fileInfo = null;

[Parameter(ParameterSetName = "FileInfo", Mandatory = true, Position = 1,
    ValueFromPipeline = true)]
public FileInfo FileInfo
{
    get
    {
        return fileInfo;
    }
    set
    {
        fileInfo = value;
    }
}

DateTime date = DateTime.Now;

[Parameter]
public DateTime Date
{
    get
    {
        return date;
    }
    set
    {
        date = value;
    }
}

protected override void ProcessRecord()
{
    FileInfo myFileInfo = fileInfo;

    if (myFileInfo == null && File.Exists(path))
    {
        myFileInfo = new FileInfo(path);
    }

    if (myFileInfo != null)
    {
        try
        {
            myFileInfo.LastWriteTime = date;
        }
        catch (UnauthorizedAccessException uae)
        {
```

```
            ErrorRecord errorRecord = new ErrorRecord(uae,
                "UnauthorizedFileAccess",
                ErrorCategory.PermissionDenied,
                myFileInfo.FullName);
```

```
                WriteError(errorRecord);
                return;
            }

            WriteObject(myFileInfo);
        }
    }
}
```

There is no need to provide `InvocationInfo` during `ErrorRecord` construction. Information about that will be filled in when the error record is reported.

Use the following to run this command:

```
PS C:\user\gxie> get-childitem readme.txt


    Directory: Microsoft.PowerShell.Core\FileSystem::C:\user\gxie


Mode                LastWriteTime     Length Name
----                -------------     ------ ----
-a---         7/8/2007   6:49 PM        420 readme.txt


PS C:\user\gxie> get-childitem readme.txt | touch-file

Touch-File : Access to the path 'C:\user\gxie\readme2.txt' is denied.
At line:1 char:17
+ dir | touch-file <<<<
```

This reported error message is constructed from the exception message and `InvocationInfo`. The optional `InvocationInfo` provides the line, character, and script block shown at the bottom of this example error message.

ErrorDetails

Frequently, cmdlet developers find that error messages from the exception of the error record are too general to help users understand and troubleshoot the issue. To resolve this, error details can be attached to error records, as shown in the following example:

```
[Cmdlet("Touch", "File", DefaultParameterSetName = "Path")]
public class TouchFileCommand : PSCmdlet
{
    ...

    protected override void ProcessRecord()
```

```
        {
            FileInfo myFileInfo = fileInfo;

            if (myFileInfo == null && File.Exists(path))
            {
                myFileInfo = new FileInfo(path);
            }

            if (myFileInfo != null)
            {
                try
                {
                    myFileInfo.LastWriteTime = date;
                }
                catch (UnauthorizedAccessException uae)
                {
                    ErrorRecord errorRecord = new ErrorRecord(uae,
                        "UnauthorizedFileAccess",
                        ErrorCategory.PermissionDenied,
                        myFileInfo.FullName);

                    string detailMessage = String.Format("Not able to touch file
                        '{0}'. Please check whether it is readonly.",
                        myFileInfo.FullName);

                    errorRecord.ErrorDetails = new ErrorDetails(detailMessage);

                    WriteError(errorRecord);
                    return;
                }

                WriteObject(myFileInfo);
            }
        }
    }
```

There are two ways to construct an `ErrorDetails` object. The simplest way is to directly construct the object using a message string. A more complicated way is to construct the object based on a resource string and some placeholder arguments. To support internationalization, using a resource string is recommended.

Now if you run the command again, you will see that the message from the `ErrorDetails` object is reported from the console:

```
PS C:\user\gxie> get-childitem readme.txt | touch-file
```

```
Touch-File : Not able to touch file 'C:\user\gxie\readme2.txt'. Please check
whether it is readonly.
At line:1 char:17
+ dir | touch-file <<<<
```

Non-terminating Errors and Terminating Errors

To report non-terminating errors, the `WriteError()` method can be used as shown in the preceding example. This will not stop the cmdlet from processing the next pipeline object, as shown in this example:

```
PS C:\user\gxie> get-childitem


    Directory: Microsoft.PowerShell.Core\FileSystem::C:\user\gxie


Mode                LastWriteTime     Length Name
----                -------------     ------ ----
-a---         7/14/2007   6:49 PM        420 readme.txt
-ar--          7/1/2007  12:00 AM        420 readme2.txt
-a---         7/14/2007   6:49 PM        420 readme3.txt


PS C:\user\gxie> get-childitem | touch-file


Mode                LastWriteTime     Length Name
----                -------------     ------ ----
-a---         7/14/2007   6:49 PM        420 readme.txt
Touch-File : Access to the path 'C:\user\gxie\readme2.txt' is denied.
At line:1 char:17
+ dir | touch-file <<<<
-a---         7/14/2007   6:49 PM        420 readme3.txt
```

Because `readme2.txt` is read-only, the `touch-file` operation on it failed. However, this didn't stop the cmdlet from processing the next file, `readme3.txt`.

If you change the preceding code to throw a terminating error using the `ThrowTerminatingError()` method, the command output will be different, as you can see with the following:

```
PS C:\user\gxie> get-childitem | touch-file

Mode                LastWriteTime     Length Name
----                -------------     ------ ----
-a---         7/14/2007   6:49 PM        420 readme.txt
Touch-File : Access to the path 'C:\user\gxie\readme2.txt' is denied.
At line:1 char:17
+ dir | touch-file <<<<
```

In the preceding example, you can see that `readme3.txt` is not processed after the terminating error.

At this point, you have learned the core steps for creating a PowerShell cmdlet, including declaring cmdlet parameters, handling pipeline input, generating output, and reporting errors.

The next few sections cover several more advanced topics, including the following:

- How to make high-impact cmdlets more user friendly by supporting `ShouldProcess`
- How to make cmdlets to work with PowerShell paths and namespaces
- How to create help content for cmdlets

Supporting ShouldProcess

Some cmdlet actions can be destructive. Therefore, users should be reminded about the possible consequences of an action before it is performed. You can declare a cmdlet to support the `ShouldProcess()` method for this, as shown in the following example:

```
[Cmdlet("Touch", "File", DefaultParameterSetName = "Path",
    SupportsShouldProcess = true, ConfirmImpact = ConfirmImpact.Medium)]
public class TouchFileCommand : PSCmdlet
{
    ...

    protected override void ProcessRecord()
    {
        FileInfo myFileInfo = fileInfo;

        if (myFileInfo == null && File.Exists(path))
        {
            myFileInfo = new FileInfo(path);
        }

        if (myFileInfo != null)
        {
            if (this.ShouldProcess(myFileInfo.FullName,
                                   "set last write time to be " + date.ToString()))
            {
                try
                {
                    myFileInfo.LastWriteTime = date;
                }
                catch (UnauthorizedAccessException uae)
                {
                    ErrorRecord errorRecord = new ErrorRecord(uae,
                        "UnauthorizedFileAccess",
                        ErrorCategory.PermissionDenied,
                        myFileInfo.FullName);

                    string detailMessage = String.Format(
                        "Not able to touch file '{0}'. Please check whether
                        it is readonly.", myFileInfo.FullName);
```

```
                    errorRecord.ErrorDetails = new ErrorDetails(detailMessage);

                    WriteError(errorRecord);
                    return;
                }

                WriteObject(myFileInfo);
            }
        }
    }
}
```

The following steps can be used to make a cmdlet support `ShouldProcess`:

1. Declare the cmdlet to support `ShouldProcess` by setting the `SupportsShouldProcess` property of the cmdlet attribute to `true`.
2. Optionally set a confirm impact level by using the `ConfirmImpact` property of the cmdlet attribute. If this property is not set, then it defaults to `Medium`. You will learn more about confirming impact level in the next section.
3. Add logic to the code so that the `ShouldProcess` method is called before any destructive action is performed.

Use the following to run the preceding cmdlet:

```
PS C:\user\gxie> get-childitem | touch-file -whatif
```

```
What if: Performing operation "set last write time to be 7/15/2007 5:25:55 PM" on Tar-
get "C:\user\gxie\readme.txt".
What if: Performing operation "set last write time to be 7/15/2007 5:25:55 PM" on Tar-
get "C:\user\gxie\readme2.txt".
What if: Performing operation "set last write time to be 7/15/2007 5:25:55 PM" on Tar-
get "C:\user\gxie\readme3.txt".
```

```
PS C:\user\gxie> get-childitem | touch-file -confirm
```

```
Confirm
Are you sure you want to perform this action?
Performing operation "set last write time to be 7/15/2007 5:46:24 PM" on Target
 "C:\user\gxie\readme.txt".
[Y] Yes  [A] Yes to All  [N] No  [L] No to All  [S] Suspend  [?] Help
(default is "Y"):a

Mode                LastWriteTime     Length Name
----                -------------     ------ ----
-a---          7/15/2007   5:46 PM       420 readme.txt
-a---          7/15/2007   5:46 PM       420 readme2.txt
-a---          7/15/2007   5:46 PM       420 readme3.txt
```

Here, you can see that if the cmdlet is invoked with the `-whatif` parameter, then it will not perform the action but just show information about what would have been performed if the `-whatif` parameter were not specified.

When the `touch-file` cmdlet is called with the `-confirm` parameter, it prompts the user for a confirmation before the action is performed.

Confirming Impact Level

Sometimes, we want the cmdlet to prompt for confirmation even when the `-confirm` parameter is not specified. One way to do this is to set the confirm impact level of the cmdlet to be high. For example, you can change the `ConfirmImpact` parameter level of the `touch-file` cmdlet as follows:

```
[Cmdlet("Touch", "File", DefaultParameterSetName = "Path",

    SupportsShouldProcess = true, ConfirmImpact = ConfirmImpact.High)]

public class TouchFileCommand : PSCmdlet
{
    ...
}
```

Now if you run the cmdlet without the `-confirm` parameter, it will also prompt:

```
PS C:\user\gxie> get-childitem | touch-file


Confirm
Are you sure you want to perform this action?
Performing operation "set last write time to be 7/15/2007 5:46:24 PM" on Target
 "C:\user\gxie\readme.txt".
[Y] Yes  [A] Yes to All  [N] No  [L] No to All  [S] Suspend  [?] Help
(default is "Y"):a

Mode                LastWriteTime     Length Name
----                -------------     ------ ----
-a---         7/15/2007   5:46 PM        420 readme.txt
-a---         7/15/2007   5:46 PM        420 readme2.txt
-a---         7/15/2007   5:46 PM        420 readme3.txt
```

How does PowerShell decide when to prompt for confirmation? It determines whether to prompt by comparing the following:

- **Confirm preference level:** This is set in the session variable `$ConfirmPreference`. (The value of this variable is `High` by default.)
- **Confirm impact level:** This is set in the cmdlet declaration. (By default, this level is `Medium`.)

If the confirm impact level of the cmdlet is equal to or higher than the confirm preference level, it will prompt. If a cmdlet is invoked with the `-confirm` parameter, PowerShell will temporarily set the confirm preference level to be `Low`. This will cause prompting for all cmdlets except the ones that declare the confirm impact level to be `None`.

Setting `$ConfirmPreference` to be `None` will suppress all prompting related to the `ShouldProcess`:

```
PS C:\user\gxie> $ConfirmPreference = 'None'
PS C:\user\gxie> get-childitem | touch-file


Mode                LastWriteTime     Length Name
----                -------------     ------ ----
-a---         7/15/2007   5:46 PM        420 readme.txt
-a---         7/15/2007   5:46 PM        420 readme2.txt
-a---         7/15/2007   5:46 PM        420 readme3.txt
```

How do you prompt for confirmation regardless of confirm preference levels and confirm impact levels? To do this, you can use `ShouldContinue()`.

ShouldContinue()

`ShouldContinue()` allows a cmdlet to prompt unconditionally for confirmation. To prompt during `ShouldContinue()` calls, PowerShell doesn't consult confirm preference levels from the environment or confirm impact levels for the cmdlet. Actually, a cmdlet doesn't even have to declare `SupportsShouldProcess` to use `ShouldContinue()`.

Usage of `ShouldContinue` is very similar to `ShouldProcess`. Extending the preceding `touch-file` cmdlet example, you can simply change the `ShouldProcess()` call to a `ShouldContinue()` call to make it work, although we will not go through the details here.

Working with the PowerShell Path

There is a fundamental problem with the `touch-file` cmdlet we have so far. If a file path doesn't exist, we will simply fail silently. Consider the following example:

```
PS C:\user\gxie> get-childitem

Mode                LastWriteTime     Length Name
----                -------------     ------ ----
-a---         7/15/2007   5:46 PM        420 readme.txt
-a---         7/15/2007   5:46 PM        420 readme2.txt
-a---         7/15/2007   5:46 PM        420 readme3.txt


PS C:\user\gxie> touch-file junk.txt

PS C:\user\gxie>
```

To fix this, you can change the `touch-file` cmdlet implementation to report an error record if the file doesn't exist, as shown here:

```
[Cmdlet("Touch", "File", DefaultParameterSetName = "Path",
    SupportsShouldProcess = true, ConfirmImpact=ConfirmImpact.Medium)]
public class TouchFileCommand : PSCmdlet
```

```
{
    ...

    protected override void ProcessRecord()
    {
        FileInfo myFileInfo = fileInfo;

        if (myFileInfo == null)
        {
            if (File.Exists(path))
            {
                myFileInfo = new FileInfo(path);
            }
            else
            {
                string fullPath = System.IO.Path.GetFullPath(path);
                string message = String.Format("File '{0}' is not found",
                                               fullPath);
                ArgumentException ae = new ArgumentException(message);

                ErrorRecord errorRecord = new ErrorRecord(ae,
                    "FileNotFound",
                    ErrorCategory.ObjectNotFound,
                    fullPath);

                WriteError(errorRecord);
                return;

            }
        }

        ...
    }
}
```

For clarity, you can print the full path for the file in the error message. Now run the command again with a non-existing file:

```
PS C:\user\gxie> touch-file junk.txt

Touch-File : File 'C:\Documents and Settings\gxie\My Documents\junk.txt' is not
 found
At line:1 char:11
+ touch-file <<<<  junk.txt
```

You can see that an error record is reported, but why is `junk.txt` resolving to `C:\Documents and Settings\gxie\My Documents\junk.txt` instead of `c:\user\gxie\junk.txt` ? Now try running the `touch-file` cmdlet on an existing file:

```
PS C:\user\gxie> touch-file readme.txt

Touch-File : File 'C:\Documents and Settings\gxie\My Documents\readme.txt' is not
```

```
 found
At line:1 char:11
+ touch-file <<<<  junk.txt
```

It still fails because file resolution is not based on the current PowerShell directory. Instead, it used the current working directory (which is `C:\Documents and Settings\gxie\My Documents\`) when PowerShell started.

To resolve this issue, file resolution needs to be based on the current PowerShell path. This can be done using the `GetResolvedProviderPathFromPSPath()` method for file path resolution, as shown in the following example code:

```
[Cmdlet("Touch", "File", DefaultParameterSetName = "Path", SupportsShouldProcess =
true, ConfirmImpact=ConfirmImpact.Medium)]
public class TouchFileCommand : PSCmdlet
{
    private string path = null;

    [Parameter(ParameterSetName = "Path", Mandatory = true, Position = 1,
        ValueFromPipeline = true, ValueFromPipelineByPropertyName = true)]
    [ValidateNotNullOrEmpty]
    [Alias("FullName")]
    public string Path
    {
        get
        {
            return path;
        }
        set
        {
            path = value;
        }
    }

    private FileInfo fileInfo = null;

    [Parameter(ParameterSetName = "FileInfo", Mandatory = true, Position = 1,
        ValueFromPipeline = true)]
    public FileInfo FileInfo
    {
        get
        {
            return fileInfo;
        }
        set
        {
            fileInfo = value;
        }
    }

    DateTime date = DateTime.Now;

    [Parameter]
```

```
public DateTime Date
{
    get
    {
        return date;
    }
    set
    {
        date = value;
    }
}

protected override void ProcessRecord()
{
    if (fileInfo != null)
    {
        TouchFile(fileInfo);
        return;
    }

    ProviderInfo provider = null;
    Collection<String> resolvedPaths = GetResolvedProviderPathFromPSPath(path,
                                           out provider);

    foreach (string resolvedPath in resolvedPaths)
    {
        if (File.Exists(resolvedPath))
        {
            FileInfo myFileInfo = new FileInfo(resolvedPath);
            TouchFile(myFileInfo);
        }
        else
        {
            string message = String.Format("File '{0}' is not found",
                                          resolvedPath);
            ArgumentException ae = new ArgumentException(message);

            ErrorRecord errorRecord = new ErrorRecord(ae,
                "FileNotFound",
                ErrorCategory.ObjectNotFound,
                resolvedPath);

            WriteError(errorRecord);
            return;
        }
    }
}

private void TouchFile(FileInfo myFileInfo)
{
    if (myFileInfo != null)
```

```
            {
                if (this.ShouldProcess(myFileInfo.FullName,
                                       "set last write time to be " + date.ToString()))
                {
                    try
                    {
                        myFileInfo.LastWriteTime = date;
                    }
                    catch (UnauthorizedAccessException uae)
                    {
                        ErrorRecord errorRecord = new ErrorRecord(uae,
                            "UnauthorizedFileAccess",
                            ErrorCategory.PermissionDenied,
                            myFileInfo.FullName);

                        string detailMessage = String.Format("Not able to touch file
                                        '{0}'. Please check whether it is readonly.",
                                        myFileInfo.FullName);

                        errorRecord.ErrorDetails = new ErrorDetails(detailMessage);

                        WriteError(errorRecord);
                        return;
                    }

                    WriteObject(myFileInfo);
                }
            }
        }
    }
```

The preceding code also moves the logic for updating the file's timestamp into its own private method. Now run the `touch-file` command directly passing in a `readme.txt`:

```
PS C:\user\gxie> touch-file readme.txt


Mode                LastWriteTime     Length Name
----                -------------     ------ ----
-a---           7/15/2007   7:41 PM        420 readme.txt
```

It works. Please also note that the `GetResolvedProviderPathFromPSPath()` method not only expands the PowerShell file path from a relative path into an absolute path, it also performs pattern matching on wildcards in the file path. (This is the reason why `GetResolvedProviderPathFromPSPath()` returns a list of file paths instead of one file path.) Try this out as follows:

```
PS C:\user\gxie> touch-file readme*.txt


Mode                LastWriteTime     Length Name
----                -------------     ------ ----
-a---           7/15/2007   7:41 PM        420 readme.txt
-a---           7/15/2007   7:41 PM        420 readme2.txt
-a---           7/15/2007   7:41 PM        420 readme3.txt
```

You can see that the `touch-file` cmdlet gets globbing behavior for free when you use `GetResolved-ProviderPathFromPSPath()` for file path resolution.

Documenting Cmdlet Help

The last, but important, step of cmdlet development is documenting the cmdlet so that users can be better informed about its usage through the `Get-Help` cmdlet. PowerShell provides a standard help format for all cmdlets so that cmdlet developers can focus on the content of help.

Your first step is to create a help file. The name of the help file should be the snap-in `dll` name followed by the `-help.xml` extension. For example, if your `Touch-File` cmdlet were compiled into the assembly `TouchFileSnapin.dll`, the help file should be `TouchFileSnapin.dll-help.xml`.

Now let's look at the contents of this file:

```
<?xml version="1.0" encoding="utf-8" ?>

<helpItems schema="maml">

<command:command xmlns:maml="http://schemas.microsoft.com/maml/2004/10"
xmlns:command="http://schemas.microsoft.com/maml/dev/command/2004/10"
xmlns:dev="http://schemas.microsoft.com/maml/dev/2004/10">

    <!-- Cmdlet detail section-->

    <command:details>
        <command:name>
            Touch-File
        </command:name>
        <maml:description>
            <maml:para>Update timestamp of a file</maml:para>
        </maml:description>
        <maml:copyright>
            <maml:para></maml:para>
        </maml:copyright>
        <command:verb>Touch</command:verb>
        <command:noun>File</command:noun>
        <dev:version></dev:version>
    </command:details>
    <maml:description>
        <maml:para>
            The Touch-File cmdlet updates timestamp of a file to current time or
            the time specified on command line.
        </maml:para>
    </maml:description>

    <!-- Cmdlet syntax section-->

    <command:syntax>
        <command:syntaxItem>
            <maml:name>Touch-File</maml:name>
            <command:parameter required="true" variableLength="true"
```

```
          globbing="true" pipelineInput="true (ByValue)" position="1">
            <maml:name>Path</maml:name>
        </command:parameter>
        <command:parameter required="false" variableLength="false"
         globbing="false" pipelineInput="false" position="named">
            <maml:name>Date</maml:name>
        </command:parameter>
    </command:syntaxItem>
    <command:syntaxItem>
        <maml:name>Touch-File</maml:name>
        <command:parameter required="true" variableLength="false"
         globbing="false" pipelineInput="true" position="1">
            <maml:name>FileInfo</maml:name>
        </command:parameter>
        <command:parameter required="false" variableLength="false"
         globbing="false" pipelineInput="false" position="named">
            <maml:name>Date</maml:name>
        </command:parameter>
    </command:syntaxItem>
</command:syntax>

<!-- Cmdlet parameter section  -->

<command:parameters>
    <command:parameter required="true" variableLength="true" globbing="true"
     pipelineInput="true (ByValue)" position="1">
        <maml:name>Path</maml:name>
        <maml:description>
            <maml:para>
                Path to the file whose timestamp will be updated.
            </maml:para>
        </maml:description>
        <command:parameterValue required="true" variableLength="true">
            String
        </command:parameterValue>
        <dev:type>
            <maml:name>String</maml:name>
            <maml:uri/>
        </dev:type>
        <dev:defaultValue></dev:defaultValue>
    </command:parameter>
    <command:parameter required="true" variableLength="false" globbing="false"
     pipelineInput="true" position="1">
        <maml:name>FileInfo</maml:name>
        <maml:description>
            <maml:para>
                FileInfo object for the file whose timestamp will be updated.
            </maml:para>
        </maml:description>
        <command:parameterValue required="false" variableLength="false">
            System.IO.FileInfo
        </command:parameterValue>
        <dev:type>
            <maml:name>System.IO.FileInfo</maml:name>
            <maml:uri/>
```

```
            </dev:type>
            <dev:defaultValue></dev:defaultValue>
        </command:parameter>
        <command:parameter required="false" variableLength="false" globbing="false"
         pipelineInput="false" position="named">
            <maml:name>Date</maml:name>
            <maml:description>
                <maml:para>
                    New timestamp for the file. If this parameter is not specified,
                    it will default to current time.
                </maml:para>
            </maml:description>
            <command:parameterValue required="false" variableLength="false">
                DateTime
            </command:parameterValue>
            <dev:type>
                <maml:name>System.DateTime</maml:name>
                <maml:uri/>
            </dev:type>
            <dev:defaultValue>System.DateTime.Now</dev:defaultValue>
        </command:parameter>
    </command:parameters>

    <!-- Input - Output section-->

    <command:inputTypes>
        <command:inputType>
            <dev:type>
                <maml:name>System.String</maml:name>
                <maml:uri/>
                <maml:description>
                    <maml:para>
                        <!-- description  -->
                        String input will be bound to -Path parameter of
                        Touch-File cmdlet.
                    </maml:para>
                </maml:description>
            </dev:type>
            <maml:description></maml:description>
        </command:inputType>
        <command:inputType>
            <dev:type>
                <maml:name>System.IO.FileInfo</maml:name>
                <maml:uri/>
                <maml:description>
                    <maml:para>
                        <!-- description  -->
                        FileInfo object input will be bound to -FileInfo parameter
                        of Touch-File cmdlet.
                    </maml:para>
                </maml:description>
            </dev:type>
            <maml:description></maml:description>
        </command:inputType>
    </command:inputTypes>
```

```
<command:returnValues>
    <command:returnValue>
        <dev:type>
            <maml:name>System.IO.FileInfo</maml:name>
            <maml:uri/>
            <maml:description>
                <maml:para>
                    <!-- description  -->
                    FileInfo object will be write the output pipe.
                </maml:para>
            </maml:description>
        </dev:type>
        <maml:description></maml:description>
    </command:returnValue>
</command:returnValues>
<command:terminatingErrors />
<command:nonTerminatingErrors />

<!-- Notes section  -->

<maml:alertSet>
    <maml:title></maml:title>
</maml:alertSet>
<!-- Example section  -->
<command:examples>
    <command:example>
        <maml:title>
            ------------------------- EXAMPLE 1 -------------------------
        </maml:title>
        <maml:introduction>
            <maml:para>C:\PS></maml:para>
        </maml:introduction>
          <dev:code>Touch-File readme.txt</dev:code>
          <dev:remarks>
            <maml:para>
                This command will update timestamp of readme.txt file
                to current time.
            </maml:para>
            <maml:para></maml:para>
            <maml:para></maml:para>
            <maml:para></maml:para>
          </dev:remarks>
        <command:commandLines>
            <command:commandLine>
                <command:commandText></command:commandText>
            </command:commandLine>
        </command:commandLines>
    </command:example>
    <command:example>
        <maml:title>
            ------------------------- EXAMPLE 2 -------------------------
        </maml:title>
        <maml:introduction>
            <maml:para>C:\PS></maml:para>
        </maml:introduction>
```

```
          <dev:code>Touch-File readme.txt -date 1/1/2007 </dev:code>
          <dev:remarks>
            <maml:para>
               This command will update timestamp of readme.txt file to
               January 1st of 2007.
            </maml:para>
            <maml:para></maml:para>
            <maml:para></maml:para>
            <maml:para></maml:para>
          </dev:remarks>
        <command:commandLines>
            <command:commandLine>
                <command:commandText></command:commandText>
            </command:commandLine>
        </command:commandLines>
    </command:example>
    <command:example>
        <maml:title>
            ------------------------- EXAMPLE 3 -------------------------
        </maml:title>
        <maml:introduction>
            <maml:para>C:\PS></maml:para>
        </maml:introduction>
          <dev:code>Touch-File *.txt -date 1/1/2007 </dev:code>
          <dev:remarks>
            <maml:para>
               This command will update timestamp of all *.txt file in current
               directory to January 1st of 2007.
            </maml:para>
            <maml:para></maml:para>
            <maml:para></maml:para>
            <maml:para></maml:para>
          </dev:remarks>
        <command:commandLines>
            <command:commandLine>
                <command:commandText></command:commandText>
            </command:commandLine>
        </command:commandLines>
    </command:example>
    <command:example>
        <maml:title>
            ------------------------- EXAMPLE 4 -------------------------
        </maml:title>
        <maml:introduction>
            <maml:para>C:\PS></maml:para>
        </maml:introduction>
          <dev:code>Get-ChildItem *.txt | Touch-File -date 1/1/2007 </dev:code>
          <dev:remarks>
            <maml:para>
               Similiar to example 3, this command will update timestamp of
               all *.txt file in current directory to January 1st of 2007.
           </maml:para>
            <maml:para></maml:para>
            <maml:para></maml:para>
          </dev:remarks>
```

```
            <command:commandLines>
                <command:commandLine>
                    <command:commandText></command:commandText>
                </command:commandLine>
            </command:commandLines>
        </command:example>
    </command:examples>

    <!-- Link section  -->

    <maml:relatedLinks>
        <maml:navigationLink>
            <maml:linkText>Get-ChildItem</maml:linkText>
            <maml:uri/>
        </maml:navigationLink>
    </maml:relatedLinks>
</command:command>

</helpItems>
```

You can see that the help file is an XML file following the MAML schema. The content of a cmdlet help file contains several sections:

- **Cmdlet detail:** This section contains the cmdlet's name and a general description of the cmdlet.
- **Cmdlet syntax:** This section describes usage syntaxes for the cmdlet. Each parameter set of the cmdlet will translate to a syntax item in this section.
- **Cmdlet parameter:** This section has detailed information about the cmdlet's parameters.
- **Input–Output:** This section describes what types of input are expected by the cmdlet and what type of output will be generated by cmdlet.
- **Notes:** This section is mainly for remarks and examples.
- **Links:** This section refers to related help topics.

You can deploy this file (`TouchFileSnapin.dll-help.xml`) to be in the same directory as `TouchFileSnapin.dll` (or, if this file is localized, put it under a language subdirectory). That way, it will automatically be picked up by PowerShell's help system.

Following is the output for running the `get-help Touch-File`:

```
PS C:\> get-help touch-file -full


NAME

    Touch-File


SYNOPSIS

    Update timestamp of a file
```

SYNTAX

```
Touch-File [-Path] [-Date] [<CommonParameters>]

Touch-File [-FileInfo] [-Date] [<CommonParameters>]
```

DETAILED DESCRIPTION

```
The Touch-File cmdlet updates timestamp of a file to current time or the ti
me specified on command line.
```

PARAMETERS

```
-Path <String>
    Path to the file whose timestamp will be updated.

    Required?                    true
    Position?                    1
    Default value
    Accept pipeline input?       true (ByValue)
    Accept wildcard characters?  true

-FileInfo [<System.IO.FileInfo>]
    FileInfo object for the file whose timestamp will be updated.

    Required?                    true
    Position?                    1
    Default value
    Accept pipeline input?       true
    Accept wildcard characters?  false

-Date [<DateTime>]
    New timestamp for the file. If this parameter is not specified, it will
     default to current time.

    Required?                    false
    Position?                    named
    Default value                System.DateTime.Now
    Accept pipeline input?       false
    Accept wildcard characters?  false

<CommonParameters>
    This cmdlet supports the common parameters: -Verbose, -Debug,
    -ErrorAction, -ErrorVariable, -OutBuffer and -OutVariable. For more
    information, type, "get-help about_commonparameters".
```

INPUT TYPE

```
System.String
```

```
System.IO.FileInfo
```

RETURN TYPE

```
System.IO.FileInfo
```

NOTES

```
-------------------------- EXAMPLE 1 --------------------------

C:\PS>Touch-File readme.txt


This command will update timestamp of readme.txt file to current time.




-------------------------- EXAMPLE 2 --------------------------

C:\PS>Touch-File readme.txt -date 1/1/2007


This command will update timestamp of readme.txt file to January 1st of
2007.




-------------------------- EXAMPLE 3 --------------------------

C:\PS>Touch-File *.txt -date 1/1/2007


This command will update timestamp of all *.txt file in current directory
to January 1st of 2007.




-------------------------- EXAMPLE 4 --------------------------

C:\PS>Get-ChildItem *.txt | Touch-File -date 1/1/2007


Similiar to example 3, this command will update timestamp of all *.txt file
in current directory to January 1st of 2007.
```

```
This is an example of binding -FileInfo parameter of Touch-File cmdlet to
pipeline object
```

RELATED LINKS

```
Get-ChildItem
```

As shown in the preceding example, different sections of help output roughly correspond to sections in the help file.

Best Practices for Cmdlet Development

The goal of cmdlet development is to release a useful cmdlet to users. In this section, we discuss some best practices for cmdlet development to make the cmdlet user's life easier.

Naming Conventions

The most visible part of a cmdlet is its name (which include a verb and a noun) and related syntax. Since cmdlet users can literally get thousands of cmdlets from different vendors, it is important to name cmdlet verbs, nouns, and parameters consistently. That enables the usage of cmdlets to become more intuitive.

Cmdlet Verb Name

The cmdlet verb, when chosen carefully, can provide a clear indication of what the cmdlet does. Conversely, if the verb is not chosen properly, it can be very confusing to cmdlet users. Because of this, the PowerShell team has compiled a list of recommended verbs, which are available in Appendix B of this book. Following are some general guidelines:

- Select verbs from the recommended list if possible.
- Avoid using synonyms of verbs in the recommended list.
- When developing a set of cmdlets related with one noun (for example, `get-service` and `set-service`), select verbs from related verbsets in the recommended list.

Cmdlet Noun Name

The cmdlet noun describes the data that the cmdlet is processing. As with the cmdlet verb, the cmdlet noun needs to be descriptive and avoid confusion with other domains. Following are some guidelines from the PowerShell team regarding the naming of nouns:

- Always use the singular version of a noun — for example, use `get-user` instead of `get-users`.
- Use Pascal case for nouns in the cmdlet declaration. Even though PowerShell is case insensitive, it will preserve the cmdlet name casing when presenting information about the cmdlet. Using Pascal case will help users to understand more sophisticated cmdlet names.
- Avoid using abbreviations in the cmdlet noun.

Cmdlet Parameter Name

As with the cmdlet noun, the cmdlet parameter name should be Pascal-cased. In addition, parameters should not use names already used by PowerShell for common parameters, including the following:

- Debug
- Verbose
- ErrorAction
- WhatIf
- Confirm
- OutVariable
- ErrorVariable
- OutBuffer

The cmdlet verb, noun, and parameter names should not use any of following special characters: # , ( ) { } [ ] & - / \ $; : “ ‘ < > | ? @ `

Interactions with the Host

The cmdlet should not directly read input from and write output to the console using the `System.Console` class for following reasons:

- The PowerShell cmdlet may execute in a console host environment. The PowerShell engine can be hosted in a graphical shell or in a service application. In either case, there is no console.
- Directly reading input from and writing output to the console may interfere with the PowerShell command-line host, which has its own specific sequence for reading input and writing output.

Instead, the cmdlet should depend on the following cmdlet user feedback APIs for interacting with end users:

- **ShouldProcess/ShouldContinue:** As mentioned earlier, this enables the end user to decide whether to perform an action.
- **WriteDebug:** This will write some debug information to the PowerShell host. By default, this information is not displayed unless the cmdlet is invoked with the `-debug` option or `$debugpreference` is set not to be `SilentlyContinue`.
- **WriteVerbose:** This will write some verbose information to the PowerShell host. By default, this information is not displayed unless the cmdlet is invoked with the `-verbose` option or `$verbosepreference` is set not to be `SilentlyContinue`.
- **WriteWarning:** This will write some warning information to the PowerShell host. By default, this information is displayed but it can be turned off by setting `$warningpreference` to `SilentlyContinue`.
- **WriteProgress:** This will write processing progress information to the PowerShell host. By default, this information is displayed but it can be turned off by setting `$progresspreference` to `SilentlyContinue`.
- **WriteError:** As described earlier, this will write error messages to the PowerShell host.

If these user feedback APIs are not sufficient, you can directly use host APIs, as shown in the following code snippet:

```
[Cmdlet("Test", "Host"]
public class TestHostCommand : PSCmdlet
{
    ...
    protected override void ProcessRecord()
    {
        if(this.Host != null)
        {
            this.Host.UI.WriteLine("message");
        }

        ...
    }
    ...
}
```

Nonetheless, it is highly recommended that you consider user feedback APIs first. For details about APIs, please see Chapter 6 and Chapter 7.

Summary

This chapter has described different aspects of writing a basic cmdlet, including defining cmdlet parameters, handling pipeline input, generating pipeline output, and reporting cmdlet execution errors. Also described in this chapter were more advanced topics, including supporting `shouldprocess`, working with the PowerShell path, and providing help content for cmdlets. At the end of the chapter, you learned about some best practices for cmdlet development.

A special group of cmdlets in PowerShell are used for navigating and manipulating data stores. Examples of these cmdlets include `get-location`, `get-childitem`, `remove-childitem`, and more. A goal of PowerShell is to use this common set of cmdlets to manage different kinds of data stores. Even better, you can make these cmdlets work with your own special data store. To achieve this, all you need to do is write a PowerShell provider with logic for accessing your data store. This is the topic of the next chapter.

5

Providers

Provider is a common term used in computer science to describe a service or interface for accessing some form of data. ADO.NET, for example, is a data provider model for accessing databases. It presents a consistent interface for accessing the rows and tables in the database. By implementing a data provider for a particular database or backend data store, applications can access the data in the same way, regardless of how the data is stored in the backend. This enables the business logic of an application to decouple itself from the details of which database it's accessing — at least, that's the theory.

In the case of PowerShell, providers present consistent interfaces via the *provider cmdlets* to custom data stores. There are several types of providers in PowerShell and developers must choose which one to use for controlling access to their data store.

Each provider interface or base class is an abstraction of the relationships of the data and the operations performed on that data. Different types of data storage present their own unique complexities and thus have different patterns of usage. This has led to several different interfaces and classes that you can derive from when implementing your provider. How you want your data to be accessed will dictate what interfaces you implement.

Like cmdlets, providers are compiled into a .NET assembly and included in your PowerShell session via snap-ins. Unlike cmdlets, however, once the `add-pssnapin` command is executed, any providers in that snap-in are initialized and added. See Chapter 2 for information about how to create a snap-in containing your provider.

This chapter explains how to write a provider and describes the multiple design decisions that affect which interfaces or features to implement. For overall information regarding how providers work, execute the command **get-help about_provider**.

This chapter is comprised of several sections that take a layer based approach to explaining how to develop a provider. The example providers are covered in the order of least complex to most complex. Each of the different provider types is demonstrated with a sample XML provider that ultimately enables you to navigate, copy, or remove nodes from an XML document you map as a PSDrive. We also use a stripped down filesystem provider to illustrate the property and content provider interfaces.

Note that the CD for this book contains several sample providers. Some of the methods from them are discussed throughout this chapter.

Why Implement a Provider?

The same cmdlets used to access the file system and Registry (`get-item`, `set-location`, `new-psdrive`, `get-property`) are used to access your provider's internal data. The differences lie in which provider class you derive from, which affects what cmdlets actually work with your provider. Data comes in all different flavors, but when you consider it at a higher level, a few fundamental questions group similar forms of data storage together, such as the following:

- ❑ Is your data store hierarchical or flat?
- ❑ Can you navigate through your data store like a file system?
- ❑ Do the items in your store have properties or content associated with them or is the location the only piece of critical information?

In addition to these, there are other questions to address, and the goal of this chapter is to help you answer them for your specific needs. Because users will already have an understanding of how the provider cmdlets work for the standard PowerShell providers, they will easily be able to begin using your provider at a much more efficient level. In addition, this enables you to take advantage of all the other great things PowerShell provides, such as streaming objects through the pipeline, consistent formatting and output, scripts, functions, and more.

One of PowerShell's great features is the capability it provides to call methods and properties on .NET objects directly. This may tempt you to simply expose the objects from your data store and have users call methods and properties on them directly. This could work, but you wouldn't be taking advantage of all the work the provider infrastructure does for you and how the provider cmdlets fit in with the rest of PowerShell.

Providers versus Cmdlets

Why not just write a bunch of cmdlets for accessing objects and/or data? You could do that, but it would end up being more work in the long run and it wouldn't provide a seamless user experience. By implementing a PowerShell provider, you don't have to worry about parsing parameters, which parameters to expose, or what cmdlets to create. It takes a fair amount of design and work to create a set of consistent, intuitive cmdlets, and that's exactly what the PowerShell team has done with the provider cmdlets.

Here's a fun exercise you can perform to determine whether the provider model is right for you. As you already know, cmdlets follow a verb-noun syntax. Write down the cmdlets you would need based on how you want to expose your objects. Most likely you'll have a `set-xyz` and a `get-xyz`. You might even have a `move-xyz` and a `remove-xyz`. Now type the command **get-command *-item**. If you see a lot of matches with the verbs, and the only difference is the noun part, then implementing a provider is the way to go. If you have some leftover cmdlets that are not covered, such as for accessing items like data rows or things like configuration settings, keep in mind that you also have `*-itemproperty` and `*-content` cmdlets as well, which provide even more ways of accessing a provider's data. In fact, the Windows PowerShell SDK includes an example of an Access database provider that may prove insightful if you have some database objects you want to interact with.

Some examples of good candidates for a provider include the following:

- XML documents (we build an XML provider from the ground up in this chapter)
- Any management or configuration application involving network topology or browsing
- Active Directory (which is our most popular request ☺)
- File system
- Registry
- DOM-style interfaces (e.g., Web pages and COM interfaces for Microsoft Office documents)
- Window/GUI control browser
- Browsing .NET assemblies

Basically, anything hierarchical in nature fits well.

Hierarchical data is not a requirement, though. Flat data schemes are just as useful when exposed through PowerShell providers. In fact, several of the built-in providers for PowerShell are flat name-value pair containers. This includes functions, aliases, and variables, so anything name-value pair-based could fit under the provider umbrella also. Maybe you want to create a hashtable on steroids; someday that hashtable might break the all-time home run record!

Essential Concepts

The following sections describe a couple of concepts that apply to all the provider types. They are used so often it makes sense to discuss them before proceeding.

Paths

Paths are used to locate the items in your provider. It is extremely important to understand the different types of paths that can exist for a provider, as this will make developing your provider much easier. The path specified by the user may indicate which provider to use or it may indicate a location for the current provider.

Thinking of paths as analogous to file system paths will help you understand them better at first. However, keep in mind that providers other than yours may have a different path syntax that needs to be handled. The PowerShell providers support both the backslash ("\") and the forward slash ("/") as path separators. Your provider code should handle both of these, and you will probably end up normalizing the incoming paths to a consistent syntax that makes sense for your provider.

For the XML provider sample, we use XPath queries, which only understand forward slashes. This requires us to tweak the user-specified paths to ensure that they are in the right format for the XML document APIs.

Drive-Qualified Paths

To enable the user to access data located at a physical drive, your Windows PowerShell provider must support a *drive-qualified path*. This path starts with the drive name followed by a colon (:). This pattern is the same as the pattern you're used to seeing for the filesystem.

For example:

- **mydrive:\abc\bar:** Accesses the item location at `\abc\bar` in the drive named "mydrive," which was created for a provider
- **C:\windows\system32:** An easy example of a filesystem path for the C: drive
- **HKLM:\Software\Microsoft:** Path to the Registry key `\Software\Microsoft` in the HKLM drive, which is created by the `Registry` provider

Provider-Qualified Paths

A *provider-qualified path* starts with the name of the provider and a double-colon ("::"). The part of the path after the double-colon is referred to as the *provider-internal path*. The provider-internal path after the double-colon is passed as-is to the cmdlet for your provider.

For example:

- **FileSystem::\\share\abc\bar:** A provider-qualified path for the PowerShell `FileSystem` provider. The path that is passed to the provider cmdlet is `\\share\abc\bar`. This is one form of using UNC paths.
- **Registry::HKEY_LOCAL_MACHINE\Software\Microsoft:** This is a provider-qualified path that points to the same item as `HKLM:\Software\Microsoft`.

Provider-Direct Paths

This path starts with `\\` or `//` and is passed directly to the provider for the current location. Therefore, the path is passed as-is to the current provider.

For example:

- **PS C:\dev\projects > get-item \\server\uploads:** Because we're in the `FileSystem` provider currently, the path is passed as-is to the callback for the provider cmdlet `get-item` (`\\server\uploads`). The `FileSystem` provider then treats it as a UNC path. What should be done with a path of this syntax is provider-specific. In the case of the `FileSystem` provider, the first alphanumeric token indicates the server, and everything after that is used to locate a shared folder on that machine.
- **HKLM:\Software > get-item \\server\uploads:** Because we're in the `Registry` provider, the supplied path doesn't refer to a valid item. Thus, no item is returned.

Provider-Internal Paths

This is the part of path indicated after the double-colon (`::`) in a provider-qualified path.

For example, `FileSystem::\\share\abc\bar` is a provider-qualified path for the PowerShell `FileSystem` provider. The provider-internal path from this is `\\share\abc\bar`. The provider-internal path is passed as-is to the provider API and the provider.

Path Expansion

The provider infrastructure expands the path when it contains one of the following:

.\ : Indicates the current location

..\ : Indicates the start of the parent path of the current location

~ \ : Starts at the Home directory for the current provider (`$HOME` is variable set for the `FileSystem` provider)

\ : Starts at the root of the current drive

As you can see, there are several different types of paths, and they should all be handled in the callbacks of your provider. The provider infrastructure will perform path expansion for you. It does its best to create a full path from the user-specified path before invoking your provider's callbacks.

Drives

Drives provide a way to logically or physically partition a provider's data store so that operations are performed against the correct data store. For the filesystem, this means logical or physical drives that may be hard disk partitions or possibly logical drives that simply map to another location in the filesystem. In the case of the `Registry` provider, drives map to the different Registry hives (`HKCU`, `HKLM`, and so on). For the example XML provider you will create, you map XML documents as drives.

Windows PowerShell applies the following rules for a Windows PowerShell drive:

- The name of a drive can be any alphanumeric sequence.
- A drive can be specified at any valid point on a path, called a *root*.
- A drive can be implemented for any stored data, not just the filesystem.
- Each drive keeps its own current working location, enabling the user to retain context when shifting between drives.

Error Handling

Instead of using exceptions for handling errors, provider developers must create `ErrorRecord` objects and pass them to one of the error-handling methods defined in the `CmdletProvider` base class. `ErrorRecord` objects contain the exception that is causing the error as well as some extra metadata used by the provider infrastructure for housekeeping. You are highly encouraged to create and pass `ErrorRecord instances` to the approved methods, rather than throw an exception that will exit the provider virtual callback method. Here's an example of what this code would look like:

```
ErrorRecord error = new ErrorRecord(new ItemNotFoundException(),
                    "ItemNotFound", ErrorCategory.ObjectNotFound, null);
ThrowTerminatingError(error);
```

It's important to understand the different ways to handle errors in your provider code. Very similar to error handling in cmdlets, there are two main APIs to use for handling errors:

- **ThrowTerminatingError(ErrorRecord):** This has the effect of stopping the current operation. Even if the user specified multiple items or paths, the operation would not finish.
- **WriteError(ErrorRecord):** This method writes the `ErrorRecord` instance to the error pipeline, which the user sees and can interact with, but it doesn't stop the action from continuing.

Capabilities

Capabilities are specific pieces of functionality that providers may or may not choose to support. The full list of capabilities can be discovered by examining the `ProviderCapabilities` enumerated type. When implementing your provider, you indicate what capabilities that provider supports via an attribute on the class declaration. Users must also implement their provider in a certain way to achieve that support. Otherwise, it would be misleading to have a provider declare support for a capability but not actually implement it.

`The ShouldProcess feature` is one of the most typical examples of a capability that prompts the user to determine whether to continue with an operation that modifies one or more items in the provider's data store. In addition, if the user specifies the `-confirm` parameter to the cmdlet, the `ShouldProcess()` method will prompt the user for confirmation. The following table (taken from MSDN) lists the values of the `ProviderCapabilities` enumerated type and what they indicate:

Credentials	The Windows PowerShell provider has the ability to use credentials passed to the provider from the command line. When this is implemented and the user supplies credentials on the command line, the `Credential` property is populated with those credentials. If this capability is not supported and the user attempts to pass credentials, the Windows PowerShell runtime throws a `ProviderInvocationException` exception (which wraps a `PSNotSupportedException` exception).
Exclude	The Windows PowerShell provider implements the ability to exclude items in the data store based on a wildcard string. The Windows PowerShell runtime performs this operation if the provider does not supply this capability; however, a provider that implements this capability will typically perform better if it is available. When implemented, this capability should have the same semantics as the `WildcardPattern` class.
ExpandWildcards	The Windows PowerShell provider implements the ability to handle wildcards within a provider internal path. The Windows PowerShell runtime performs this operation if the provider does not supply this capability; however, a provider that implements this capability will typically perform better if it is available. When implemented, this capability should have the same semantics as the `WildcardPattern` class.
Filter	The Windows PowerShell provider implements the ability to perform additional filtering based upon some provider-specific string.

Include	The Windows PowerShell provider has the ability to include items in the data store based on a wildcard string. The Windows PowerShell runtime performs this operation if the provider does not supply this capability; however, a provider that implements this capability will typically perform better if it is available. When implemented, this capability should have the same semantics as the `WildcardPattern` class.
None	The Windows PowerShell provider provides no capabilities other than capabilities based on derived base classes.
ShouldProcess	The Windows PowerShell provider calls `ShouldProcess()` before making any modifications to the data store. This includes calls made within all `New`, `Remove`, `Set`, `Clear`, `Rename`, `Copy`, `Move`, and `Invoke` interfaces. This allows the user to use the `-whatif` parameter.

Most of these correspond to parameters on the provider cmdlets. Consider the parameters for `get-item`:

```
Get-Item [-path] <string[]> [-include <string[]>] [-exclude <string[]>]
[-f ilter <string>] [-force] [-credential <PSCredential>] [<CommonParameters>]
```

You can see that the `-include`, `-exclude`, `-filter`, and `-credential` parameters have the same name as the capability enumeration. The `CmdletProvider` base class has a property for each of these that is set to the value of the parameter, if present. In your provider's callback for the cmdlet being executed, you can check the value and use it accordingly.

Hello World Provider

Here's an example of the simplest provider that can possibly be created. It doesn't do much, but technically it is a provider:

```
[CmdletProvider("HelloWorldProvider",ProviderCapabilities.None)]
public class HelloWorldProvider : CmdletProvider
{
}
```

The provider attribute indicates the friendly name of the provider as well as any specific ''capabilities'' the provider implements. In this case, because we're only implementing the most basic provider, we declare our provider as supporting no extra capabilities. The friendly name of the provider is used to refer to the provider and can be used as a parameter to the `get-psprovider` cmdlet to retrieve the `ProviderInfo` object that contains the information for this provider.

At this point, you could include this class in a snap-in assembly and add it to your session. That's it, four lines of code. Of course, this provider won't prove very useful, as it doesn't do anything. Providing functionality for your provider is achieved through overriding the virtual methods in the base class. Let's assume you compiled the preceding code into a snap-in assembly and added it to the current session. You can verify it is loaded by the using the following command, which returns information for the provider by name:

```
PS C:\Documents and Settings\Owner> Get-PSProvider HelloWorldProvider
Name                 Capabilities                   Drives
----                 ------------                   ------
HelloWorldProvider   None                           {}
```

Again, not very useful at all. To unload the provider, remove the snap-in containing it with `remove-pssnapin`. Remember that `remove-pssnapin` unloads the snap-in and the provider, but the assembly is still in use by the process. The only way to get the assembly unloaded from the process is by exiting `powershell.exe`.

Here's another not terribly useful provider, but it shows the first two callback methods:

```
[Provider("HelloWorldProvider",ProviderCapabilities.None)]
public class HelloWorldProvider : CmdletProvider
{
   protected override ProviderInfo Start(ProviderInfo providerInfo)
   {
      providerInfo.Description = "This is my first provider that doesn't do much!";
      return providerInfo;
   }
   protected override void Stop()
   {
       // perform any cleanup
   }
}
```

Each of the provider base classes has virtual methods that can be overridden to add custom functionality. The `CmdletProvider` has `Start()` and `Stop()` virtual methods, which are invoked when the provider is initialized and when it is being removed, respectively. These are done at snap-in add and removal time. The `ProviderInfo` object that is passed and returned by `Start()` is the same object returned by `get-psprovider`. By overriding the `Start()` method, the developer can create a custom `ProviderInfo` derived object with more information than just the properties on `ProviderInfo`. Let's look at the properties on the `ProviderInfo` object:

- **Name:** This is the friendly name of the provider. This name is also used in the case of fully qualified provider paths. `Get-psprovider <name>` will return the `ProviderInfo` or `ProviderInfo` derived instance for the providers that match the search criteria. The provider name can be used to retrieve help information for a provider, e.g., `Get-help <name> -category provider`. To get more information about the `FileSystem` provider, use the command `get-help filesystem-category provider`.
- **Capabilities:** Indicates the provider's specific capabilities
- **Drives:** The current drives that exist for each provider. Several drives are created at startup when the provider is initially created, but they can be changed via `new-psdrive` or `remove-psdrive`.
- **Description:** The description of what this provider does. This is set by the provider code inside a callback when the provider is first created and initialized.

- **PsSnapin:** The snap-in to which the provider belongs
- **Home:** This is an optional value that can be set to the home path for your provider. This might be used in cases where you want certain operations to always use home as the base path. For built-in providers, this is only set by the `FileSystem` provider and only makes sense for container and navigation providers that have a sense of hierarchy.

Built-in Providers

Before we start looking at writing our own provider, let's examine the providers that PowerShell has already implemented and provides you out of the box. It's a good idea to interact with these providers to get a feel for the provider cmdlets. Use your trusty `get-psprovider` command to retrieve the list of currently loaded providers. `Get-psprovider` returns one or more `ProviderInfo` objects depending on the search parameters given to the cmdlet:

```
PS C:\Documents and Settings\Owner> get-psprovider
Name                 Capabilities                                Drives
----                 ------------                                ------
Alias                ShouldProcess                               {Alias}
Environment          ShouldProcess                               {Env}
FileSystem           Filter, ShouldProcess                       {C, G, A, D...}
Function             ShouldProcess                               {Function}
Registry             ShouldProcess                               {HKLM, HKCU}
Variable             ShouldProcess                               {Variable}
Certificate          ShouldProcess                               {cert}
```

Output from `get-psprovider` displays the "built-in" providers of PowerShell. Any user-created providers loaded via a snap-in would appear in this list as well.

Alias Provider

The `Alias` provider derives from the `ContainerCmdletProvider` base class. For a full explanation of what cmdlets and operations the `ContainerCmdletProvider` supports, skip to the "Base Provider Types" section. Aliases can be created, removed, and modified via the `*-item` cmdlets. They can also be listed or retrieved via the `get-item` and `get-childitem` cmdlets. Even though the `*-item` cmdlets give you full access to alias management, there are also specific `*-alias` cmdlets that basically do the same thing that the `*-item` cmdlets do for the alias provider. The `alias` cmdlets were provided because they are more intuitive for people new to PowerShell and not familiar with providers.

The following example demonstrates different ways to retrieve all the currently defined aliases:

```
PSH> get-childitem alias:
PSH> get-alias
PSH> get-alias *
```

This next example shows two different ways to create a new alias, `foo`, that calls `get-command`:

```
PSH> new-alias foo get-command
PSH> new-item -path alias:foo -value get-command
```

Here, the `Alias` provider has a single drive called "`alias`," and all the aliases exist in the root level of that drive. Don't let the fact that the name of the provider and the drive are the same.

For more information about the `alias` provider, you can access its help information by typing the command **PS > help alias–Category provider**.

Environment Provider

The `Environment` provider derives from the `ContainerCmdletProvider` base class. See the "Base Provider Types" section to find out what cmdlets and operations this provider supports. Like the `Alias` provider, the `Environment` provider has ways to access environment variables other than just the `*-item` cmdlets.

The following example gets all the `Environment` variables by getting all the items in the `env:` drive:

```
PSH> get-childitem env:
PSH> $env:myenv=5
PSH> new-item -path env:myenv -value 5
```

For more information about the `Environment` provider, you can access its help information by typing the command **PS > help environment–Category provider**.

FileSystem Provider

The `FileSystem` provider derives from `NavigationCmdletProvider`. This base class, which derives from the `ContainerCmdletProvider` class, adds navigational capabilities through the `*-location` cmdlets, in addition to being able to access items by their path. The content of the files is exposed by the `IContentCmdletProvider` interface. The properties of the files, such as DateTime stamps or creation and access info, are exposed via the `IPropertyCmdletProvider` interface.

The default drives created for this provider are whatever drives you find in your Explorer window. This means that physical drives, logical drives, network drives, or mapped drives will be available in this provider. Drives that are created using the `new-psdrive` cmdlet in PowerShell only live for the duration and context of the process in which they were created. Therefore, drives are not shared across instances of PowerShell. The following example demonstrates the command that would create a new `PSDrive` for the PowerShell `FileSystem` provider and set its root to the specified path:

```
PS C:\Documents and Settings\Owner> new-psdrive -name mydocs -psprovider Filesystem -
root 'C:\Documents and Settings\Owner\My Documents'
```

For more information about the `FileSystem` provider, you can access its help information by typing the command **PS > help filesystem–Category provider**.

Function Provider

The `Function` provider derives from the `ContainerCmdletProvider` base class. Like the `Alias` and `Environment` providers, it has a one-level container of functions that exist in the root directory of the single drive created. In this case, that drive is "function:". Functions can be created by using the `new-item` cmdlet, as well as by declaring a function in a script or on the command line. By dot-sourcing a script that contains any functions, those functions are then available for access in the `Function` provider as if they were created using `new-item`. Here's an example of creating a function using `new-item` and then invoking that function to determine whether it is defined:

```
PS C:\Documents and Settings\Owner> new-item function:\dirtxt -val "get-childite
m *.txt"

CommandType     Name                                Definition
-----------     ----                                ----------
Function        dirtxt                              get-childitem *.txt

PS C:\Documents and Settings\Owner> dirtxt

    Directory: Microsoft.PowerShell.Core\FileSystem::C:\Documents and Settings\
    Owner

Mode                LastWriteTime     Length Name
----                -------------     ------ ----
-a---          9/4/2007  10:13 PM         10 blah.txt
-a---         8/28/2003   6:52 AM        921 reglog.txt
```

For more information about the `Function` provider, you can access its help information by typing the command **PS** > **help function–Category provider**.

Registry Provider

The `Registry` provider derives from the `NavigationCmdletProvider` base class. Because it derives from `NavigationCmdletProvider`, you can change locations within the different drives of the Registry. In the context of the `Registry` provider, drives map to Registry hives. By default, only two drives are created: `HKCU` and `HKLM`. One could just as easily map a new drive to one of the other hives. The following command would create a drive for the `HKEY_USERS` hive:

```
PSH> new-psdrive -name HKU -psprovider registry -root HKEY_USERS
```

One interesting thing to note about the `Registry` provider is the decision to implement the values for the Registry settings under the keys as properties, rather than using the name as part of the item's path.

The following set of commands show how to access the settings of Registry keys that are exposed as item properties in the `Registry` provider:

```
PS C:\Documents and Settings\Owner> dir
HKLM:\Software\Microsoft\PowerShell\1\PowerShellEngine
PS C:\Documents and Settings\Owner> get-itemproperty
HKLM:\Software\Microsoft\PowerShell\1\PowerShellEngine

PSPath                    : Microsoft.PowerShell.Core\Registry::HKEY_LOCAL_MACHINE\
Software\Microsoft\PowerShell\1\PowerShellEngine
PSParentPath              : Microsoft.PowerShell.Core\Registry::HKEY_LOCAL_MACHINE\
Software\Microsoft\PowerShell\1
PSChildName               : PowerShellEngine
PSDrive                   : HKLM
PSProvider                : Microsoft.PowerShell.Core\Registry
```

```
ApplicationBase          : C:\WINNT\system32\WindowsPowerShell\v1.0
ConsoleHostAssemblyName : Microsoft.PowerShell.ConsoleHost,Version=1.0.0.0,
Culture=neutral,PublicKeyToken=31bf3856ad364e35,ProcessorArchitecture=msil

ConsoleHostModuleName    : "C:\WINNT\system32\WindowsPowerShell\v1.0\
Microsoft.PowerShell.ConsoleHost.dll"
PowerShellVersion        : 1.0
RuntimeVersion           : v2.0.50727
```

Whether you expose the leaf nodes of your data store as items accessible via paths, as properties (`*-itemproperties`), or as content (`*-content`) is up to you and should ultimately be determined by what best fits your data store. This is just one of several design decisions that need to be kept in mind when determining how you want users to access your provider. The concepts of provider properties and content are explained more thoroughly in the section "Optional Provider Interfaces."

For more information about the `Registry` provider, you can access its help information by typing the command **PS > help registry–Category provider**.

Variable Provider

The `Variable` provider derives from the `ContainerCmdletProvider` base class. It has a single-level container of all the variables at the root of the single drive created for this provider, "variable:." The following example demonstrates retrieving a variable using `get-item`:

```
PS C:\Documents and Settings\Owner> $myvar="3"
PS C:\Documents and Settings\Owner> get-item variable:\myvar

Name                           Value
----                           -----
myvar                          3
```

For more information about the `variable` provider, you can access its help information by typing the command **PS > help variable–Category provider**.

Certificate Provider

The `Certificate` provider derives from the `NavigationCmdletProvider` base class. It allows you to access the various certificates on the machine. Things such as code-signing certificates can be viewed here and also retrieved for signing PowerShell scripts if security is a concern.

For more information about the `certificate` provider, access its help information by typing the command **PS > help certificate–Category provider**.

Base Provider Types

This section discusses the provider base classes from which your provider class will derive. These base classes are layered so that each successive class derives from the previous one, adding additional features. Simply choose what point of functionality you want to hook in at and derive from that class. There are also optional interfaces that can be implemented in isolation, such as `IPropertyCmdletProvider`. These interfaces are orthogonal to the base provider type that all providers ultimately derive from. In addition, a single provider may implement multiple "provider" interfaces.

We will cover each provider class and interface, and the cmdlets that are supported by them.

CmdletProvider

All provider classes ultimately derive from this base class. Most providers don't derive from this class directly, however, as it only has the `Start()` and `Stop()` callbacks. These enable developer code to be executed when the provider is initialized and terminated, respectively. These events occur at snap-in adding and removal time. More important, this class has several methods and properties for interacting with the provider infrastructure, host, and session state that will be used by providers implementing the other base classes. The actual methods and properties are examined later in this chapter.

DriveCmdletProvider

The `DriveCmdletProvider` class defines a provider that enables the creation and removal of drives. This class has methods the user can override to provide specific functionality when the drive cmdlets are executed and for initialization of any default drives.

The `DriveCmdletProvider` class derives from `CmdletProvider` and supports the following cmdlets:

- **new-psdrive:** This cmdlet creates a drive for a given provider. The following arguments are mandatory when creating a new `PsDrive`: `Name`, `PsProvider`, and `Root`. The values for these parameters are used to create a `PsDriveInfo` object, which is passed to a virtual method (`NewDrive()`), which the provider implementer overrides to provide custom functionality for this cmdlet. It is possible to return an instance of a custom drive object, but that object must derive from `PSDriveInfo`. In fact, this is a popular way for users to persist data such as connections or path information for the drives of a provider. A provider may also add dynamic parameters, which may or may not be mandatory. See the section "DriveCmdletProvider" for more information about dynamic parameters. The object written to the pipeline from this cmdlet is a `PsDriveInfo` object.
- **remove-psdrive:** This cmdlet removes the specified drive. This in turn causes the provider infrastructure to invoke a virtual callback method on the `DriveCmdletProvider` class, giving the implementer a chance to perform any cleanup for the removal of the drive. In the case of our `XMLProvider` examples, you use this to save any changes to the XML document back to the original file that was used to create the drive.

ItemCmdletProvider

By deriving from this base class, your provider supports operations for the `DriveCmdletProvider` as well as accessing items located by their paths. These paths point to items inside your data store. The path(s) supplied to the cmdlets supported by a provider of this type point to one or more items, and don't support navigation. Nor do they differentiate between a container and leaf node. The operations users can perform on these items include retrieving them, clearing them, or invoking them, which performs some provider-specific action.

Providers deriving from this class only support provider-qualified paths. That means the user must always specify the provider in the path. The provider infrastructure strips out the provider name and passes the provider internal path to the callbacks for each cmdlet.

How do you access an item for a given drive? Good question. Because a drive-qualified path doesn't work, the path must have a format like the following `Provider::drive:\path1\path2`. Then the string `drive:\path1\path2` will be passed to the callback method for your cmdlet. If your provider had no drives and was a single data store, then whatever was present after `Provider::` would be passed to your cmdlet callbacks.

Items that are written to the pipeline have properties added regardless of the type of object that provider outputs. The following properties are added as `NoteProperties` to the `PSObject` that wraps the object your provider emits via a call to `WriteItemObject()`:

- **PSPath:** The fully qualified provider path. It has the following syntax: `snapin\provider::drive:\path`.
- **PSProvider:** The provider to which this item belongs
- **PSIsContainer:** This indicates whether this item is a container or not; this is taken from the `isContainer` Boolean passed in the call to `WriteItemObject()` from inside your provider code.

Some of the `*-item` cmdlets don't write objects to the pipeline, but they can if the `-PassThru` parameter is supplied. `Set-item` is one such cmdlet, and several of the other `*-item` cmdlets in the other provider base types support this as well. Using `get-command` or `get-help` for a specific `*-item` cmdlet will indicate whether or not it supports the `-PassThru` parameter.

The `ItemCmdletProvider` class derives from `DriveCmdletProvider` and supports the following cmdlets:

- **get-item:** Retrieves the item at the specified location. The path supplied is specific to that provider, and the implementer is responsible for parsing the path to ultimately determine what item, if present, should be returned. This does not return "content" for that item if the provider also implements the `IContentCmdletProvider` interface. The `Get-content` cmdlet must be used in that case. The object at the specified path is written to the pipeline via a call to `WriteItemObject()`, which is defined in the `CmdletProvider` base class. `Get-item` may return one or more objects from a single path. For the sample XML provider, it's possible to have multiple XML nodes of the same name, in which case `get-item` may return multiple nodes. It is also possible for the user to specify multiple paths and/or a single path to be expanded into multiple paths if your provider supports wildcard expansion.
- **clear-item:** Deletes the contents or value of the item at the specified location but does not delete the item. An example of this for the `Variable` provider would be to clear the value of the variable if it existed but not remove it.
- **set-item:** Sets an item at the specified location with the indicated value. It is up to the provider to determine the semantics of setting an item that already exists versus one that doesn't. In most cases it probably won't matter, but your provider may need to make a distinction in some cases.
- **invoke-item:** Invokes the default action for an item at the specified location. For the Filesystem provider, this would mean invoking the application associated with the file's extension.

ContainerCmdletProvider

By deriving from this base class, your provider will support operations for the `ItemCmdletProvider` as well as the cmdlets for dealing with a multilayered data store. A container provider is similar to an N-tree and is the first provider that introduces a sense of hierarchy. There is no support for nested containers, though. Nested containers are only supported in navigation providers. The container provider does allow the user to interact hierarchically with the items in the data store.

The `ContainerCmdletProvider` class derives from `ItemCmdletProvider` and supports the following cmdlets:

- **Copy-item:** Copies items for a provider from one location to another. The item(s) that are copied are specific to the provider. The `-recurse` parameter indicates that all items underneath the specified item should be copied as well.
- **Get-childitem:** Gets the items and child items in one or more specified locations. The items returned may be containers or not. If the specified path points to a leaf node, this cmdlet performs similarly to `get-item`. However, if the path points to a container, all the items inside the first level of that container would be displayed. In the case of the filesystem, all the files and directories in a specified directory would be returned but not the files in the subdirectories. All files and directories could be returned if the `-recurse` parameter is specified.
- **New-item:** Creates one or more items for the provider at the specified location(s). An optional `-value` parameter is used to pass the data used to create the item(s) for your provider. For navigation providers, the `-type` parameter may be needed to indicate whether the new item is a container or a leaf node, but for a container provider only child items can be created.
- **Remove-item:** Deletes the item(s) at the specified location(s) for the provider. Unlike `clear-item`, this cmdlet does actually remove the item so that it no longer exists; thus, `get-item` would not return the recently removed item.
- **Rename-item:** Renames a single item at the specified location. This cmdlet doesn't need to differentiate between containers and non-containers because it is only renaming a single item. The renamed item is still in the same container, it just has a different name.
- **Set-location:** Sets the location context for the provider to the specified path if it exists and is a container for the provider. If a relative path is supplied, then the new location is the current location for the current drive plus the user-supplied relative path. This, of course, assumes the user is currently inside the provider for which the location is being changed. Otherwise, a drive-qualified or provider-qualified path must be supplied. This will change the context to the new provider, and for navigation providers sets the `CurrentLocation` property for the drive to which the user is moving.
- **Pop-location:** Changes the current location to the location most recently pushed onto the stack. You can pop the location from the default stack or from a stack that you create by using `push-Location`. `Pop-location` works across providers, so if the last path you put on the default stack was from the `Registry` provider (Registry key) and you were currently in the `FileSystem` provider, `pop-location` would switch your current provider context to the Registry and set your path accordingly.
- **Push-location:** The `push-location` cmdlet pushes the current location onto a default stack or onto a stack that you create. If you specify a path, `push-location` pushes the current location

onto the stack and then changes to the location specified by the path. You cannot push a location onto the stack unless it is the current location.

- **Get-location:** Returns the current location and writes it to the pipeline so it can be displayed, stored in a variable, or piped into another command.
- **resolve-path:** Interprets the wildcard characters in a path and displays the items and containers at the location specified by the path. This may result in one or more paths being returned.
- **test-path:** Indicates whether the specified location actually exists for this provider. Returns a Boolean with the value of `true` if it exists; otherwise, it returns `false`.

NavigationCmdletProvider

This base class supports all operations from the `ContainerCmdletProvider` as well as relative paths and nested containers. Using the filesystem as an example, nested containers would be directories and subdirectories that the container provider does not support. Relative paths allow you to use the current location as the starting point when passing paths to the provider cmdlets. Instead of having to type the full path of an item each time, you can simply type the relative path inside the current container you are in. Again, this is analogous to directories on the filesystem, but providers enable you to extend this concept to any data store, which in fact is what the `Registry` and `Certificate` providers do.

The `NavigationCmdletProvider` class derives from `ContainerCmdletProvider`. It supports the following cmdlets:

- **join-path:** Combines two paths into a single path, using a provider-specific delimiter between paths. The resulting path is written to the pipeline as a string. This cmdlet is useful when creating paths based on variables and strings, and eliminates the need for users to know the path delimiter for the provider. This example joins the specified paths, and passes that path to `set-location`, which changes the current location to the new value:

```
PS C:\> join-path winnt system32 | set-location
PS C:\winnt\system32>
```

- **move-item:** Moves one or more items from one location or container in the provider to another. The items being moved may be containers or child nodes. Specifying the `-recurse` parameter copies all sub-items and subcontainers as well.

Optional Provider Interfaces

In addition to deriving from one of the Windows PowerShell base classes, your Windows PowerShell provider can support other functionality by deriving from one or more of the following provider interfaces. This section defines those interfaces and the cmdlets supported by each. It does not describe the parameters for the interface-supported cmdlets. Cmdlet parameter information is available online using the `Get-Command` and `Get-Help` cmdlets.

IContentCmdletProvider

The `IContentCmdletProvider` interface defines a content provider that performs operations on the content of a data item. The definition of content varies for each provider and may not even exist for some providers. Support for content means the items in your data store need to support more complex operations than set, clear, and get. This interface returns reader and writer objects such as the stream classes in .NET. This makes it ideal for modifying stream-based data or sequential data structures such as lists, collections, or anything row-based. Key-based data structures such as hashtables are better suited for the `IPropertyCmdletProvider`. You may need to implement both if the items in your data store have properties and content that are separate from each other.

This interface is optional, but in order for it to make sense, your provider class must minimally derive from the `ItemCmdletProvider` base class. Otherwise, your provider won't have support for items and paths for which you are trying to modify the content.

By implementing this interface, your provider is declaring support for several cmdlets that return objects derived from other specific interfaces, such as `IContentRead` and `IContentWriter`. There is some extra overhead in using the content interfaces to modify the items in your data store. There are three interfaces to implement, and how you want users to modify the items in your data store is an important design consideration. It may be that the objects returned by the `*-item` cmdlets already have public APIs for doing all the modifications needed, but if the data is laid out sequentially, then support for the content cmdlets may make sense.

`IContentCmdletProvider` supports the following cmdlets:

- **get-content:** The `get-content` cmdlet gets the content of the item at the location specified by the path. It reads the content one "line" at a time and returns an object for each line. This cmdlet ends up calling `GetContentReader()` from the `IContentCmdletProvider` interface. The provider implementer is responsible for returning an `IContentReader` derived instance, which is used to retrieve the content of the item one object or line at a time. In the case of a file, this would return each line as a separate object.
- **set-content:** The `set-content` cmdlet sets the content of the item at the specified location. An array of objects is used as the value. The provider developer is responsible for creating an `IContentWriter` derived object, which iterates through the object array value and sets the content of the item with these objects. How the objects are converted and "streamed" to the item in the data store is very provider specific. In the case of a text file, this would be line by line, but your items may have a very specific binary structure that warrants data marshalling, or maybe you store objects directly.
- **add-content:** This cmdlet appends the specified content to the existing content of the item at the specified path. This uses the `IContentWriter` interface in the same manner as `set-content`. It performs a seek operation to the end of the item's content and then writes the supplied values.
- **clear-content:** This cmdlet clears the content of the item at the specified location but does not delete the item.

IPropertyCmdletProvider

The `IPropertyCmdletProvider` interface defines a property provider that enables access to the properties of one or more items in your provider. Think of this as a static hashtable. You can get, set, or clear the values of the properties but you can't modify the property names. The properties that you want to allow access for are the same for all the items in your data store and they will never change.

`IPropertyCmdletProvider` supports the following cmdlets:

- **clear-itemproperty:** Sets properties of the specified items to the "clear" value. This means the property still exists but it has no value. This is similar to `clear-item` or `clear-content` but for properties.
- **get-itemproperty:** Retrieves properties from one or more items at the specified locations. The property values are written to the pipeline.
- **set-itemproperty:** Sets the value of the property to the supplied value for the items at the specified locations. This cmdlet can take a single name and value to set the property of the items or it can take a `PSObject`, in which case it extracts all the properties from the object and uses those name-value pairs to set the properties of the item.

IDynamicPropertyCmdletProvider

The `IDynamicPropertyCmdletProvider` interface, derived from `IPropertyCmdletProvider`, defines a provider that supports dynamic or runtime properties for its items. This type of provider handles operations for which properties can be defined at runtime — for example, a `new-itemproperty` operation. Such operations are not possible on items that have statically defined properties.

The `IDynamicPropertyCmdletProvider` interface derives from the `IPropertyCmdletProvider` class. It supports the following cmdlets:

- **copy-itemproperty:** Copies a property from the specified item to another item
- **move-itemproperty:** Moves a property from the specified item to another item
- **new-itemproperty:** Creates a new property on the specified items and streams the resultant objects
- **remove-itemproperty:** Removes a property for the specified items
- **rename-itemproperty:** Renames a property of the specified items

ISecurityDescriptorCmdletProvider

The `ISecurityDescriptorCmdletProvider` interface adds security descriptor functionality to a provider. This interface allows the user to get and set security descriptor information for an item in the data store. This interface supports the following cmdlets:

- **get-acl:** Returns the security descriptor for the items at the specified locations. The security descriptor contains the ACL (Access Control List) for the resource that the items refer to, which is used to check permissions such as read/write.
- **set-acl:** Sets the security descriptor for the items at the specified locations, which will update the permissions for the resources to which the items refer.

CmdletProvider

The most basic provider derives from the `CmdletProvider` base class. The `CmdletProvider` class provides several methods and properties used by providers to implement their custom functionality. In addition to these, there are some virtual callback methods for when the provider is instantiated and removed from the session. The `DriveCmdletProvider` base class enables you to add and remove drives but it still doesn't create a useful provider by itself. Although it is possible to create providers from either of these classes, in most cases developers should derive from one of the following classes to implement their own PowerShell providers:

- **ItemCmdletProvider:** Serves as a base class for providers that expose an item as a PowerShell path. It only supports provider-qualified paths.
- **ContainerCmdletProvider:** Serves as a base class for PowerShell providers that perform operations such as rename, remove, and copy; and checks existence against items that are appropriate for containers.
- **NavigationCmdletProvider:** Serves as the base class for PowerShell providers that perform operations against items in a multilevel data store.

Here's another look at the basic `HelloWorld` provider:

```
[Provider("HelloWorldProvider",ProviderCapabilities.None)]
public class HelloWorldProvider : CmdletProvider
{
   protected override ProviderInfo Start(ProviderInfo providerInfo)
   {
      providerInfo.Description = "This is my first provider that doesn't do much!";
      return providerInfo;
   }
   protected override void Stop()
   {
       // perform any cleanup
   }
}
```

Let's discuss the two virtual callback methods in more detail:

```
protected override CmdletProvider.Start(ProviderInfo providerInfo) { ... }
```

This method is invoked when the provider is instantiated and added to the current PowerShell session. There are two ways for the provider to be added. When the snap-in containing the provider is added, the `Start()` method is called. The other way to add your provider to PowerShell is by creating a custom shell, specifying your provider and the assembly containing the provider. This causes the provider to be instantiated and added at startup of the custom shell. In the preceding code example, we don't do much other than set a custom description. This description can then be retrieved via `get-psprovider HelloWorldProvider` after the snap-in is loaded. Although it's not done here, it is common to create a custom `ProviderInfo` derived object to store or persist data for the provider. This allows the provider-specific data to be passed along via the `ProviderInfo` instance, which is available as a property on the `CmdletProvider` class, and also available via `get-psprovider` from the command line. In this respect, the custom `ProviderInfo` class enables the user to pass provider-specific data between the command line and the internal implementation of the provider.

Now consider the following method:

```
protected void CmdletProvider.Stop() { ... }
```

This method is invoked when the provider is being removed from the current PowerShell session. The provider is removed when the snap-in containing the provider is removed. This allows the provider to perform cleanup of any resources created during the lifetime of the provider.

There is a virtual method called `StartDynamicParameters()`, *which is supposed to allow runtime defined parameters during creation of the provider. At the time of writing, however, this callback doesn't actually get called back, so don't worry about it.*

Methods and Properties on CmdletProvider

The `CmdletProvider` base class also has several methods and properties that the developer will undoubtedly use to perform actions such as writing objects to the pipeline, error handling, and executing commands internally. The reader should refer to the Windows PowerShell SDK on MSDN to see the full list. This section describes some of the important methods of `CmdletProvider` that most providers will end up using, as shown here:

```
public void WriteItemObject(object item, string path, bool isContainer);
```

Developers can call this method when they want to write an item to the pipeline. This will happen when the user executes `get-item` for an item that actually exists. The `path` parameter is the value that is added to the object for the `PsPath` property, which is discussed in the `ItemCmdletProvider` previously. The `isContainer` Boolean indicates whether the item is a container. This value should always be `false`, except for the container and navigation providers that support containers. A single `get-item` or `get-childitem` call may result in multiple calls to this method. If so, it's up to the developer to determine the order in which the items are written to the pipeline, as that will affect the order in which the user sees them.

```
public void WriteError(ErrorRecord errorRecord);
public void ThrowTerminatingError(ErrorRecord errorRecord);
```

These methods are invoked by a provider when an error is encountered that the user should be notified about. They are discussed further in the "Error Handling" section later in this chapter. The most important thing to understand here is that `ThrowTerminatingError()` stops the current operation from continuing, whereas `WriteError()` does not. `ThrowTerminatingError()` ends up throwing an exception, so you don't have to worry about returning from your callback after calling it.

The following methods display some information text to the user:

```
public void WriteVerbose(string text);
public void WriteWarning(string text);
```

The text supplied to `WriteVerbose()` is only displayed if the user specifies the `-verbose` parameter of the provider cmdlet. `WriteWarning()` always displays its text in yellow. Sprinkling your provider code with `WriteVerbose()` statements makes it possible for the user to gain some extra insight more easily if an error has occurred. For example, sometimes the path specified as a parameter to the cmdlet will not be the same as the path in the callback method for that cmdlet.

The `ShouldProcess()` methods are used by providers that support the `ShouldProcess` capability:

```
public bool ShouldProcess(string target);
public bool ShouldProcess(string target, string action);
public bool ShouldProcess(string verboseDescription, string verboseWarning,
                    string caption);
public bool ShouldProcess(string verboseDescription, string verboseWarning,
               string caption, out ShouldProcessReason shouldProcessReason);
```

By declaring support for the ShouldProcess capability, the developer must call ShouldProcess() before executing any operations that would modify the data store or an item in that data store. Typical operations where this should be used are set-item, clear-item, and so on. If the user specifies the -confirm or -whatif cmdlet parameter, invocation of ShouldProcess() prompts the user to indicate what the operation is. Then, for -confirm, it waits for the user to respond to indicate whether it should continue with the operation. If the user does not specify -confirm or –whatif, then calls to ShouldProcess() do nothing. This feature is quite handy when creating complex pipelines of multiple commands and there is some doubt as to exactly what items will be modified or deleted in your provider. Because a single path may return multiple items, ShouldProcess() should be called for each item being modified. Users can choose yesToAll to stop the prompting if they desire.

Like ShouldProcess(), the following method prompts the user and waits for their input before continuing with the operation:

```
public bool ShouldContinue(string query, string caption);
public bool ShouldContinue(string query, string caption, ref bool yesToAll, ref
                           bool noToAll);
```

However, ShouldContinue() always prompts the user, whereas ShouldProcess() only prompts when -whatif or -confirm are specified at the command line. ShouldContinue() should be used in cases where there is some ambiguity about the operation or the item in question, thus requiring the user to verify the course of action.

Following is the ProviderInfo instance that is created for your provider:

```
protected internal ProviderInfo ProviderInfo { get; }
```

This is written to the pipeline via get-psprovider. It has some useful information, such as the current drives for this provider and its capabilities.

This next property contains a reference to the drive in which the current operation is being performed:

```
protected PSDriveInfo PSDriveInfo { get; }
```

This will come in handy when you need to determine which drive of your data store to look in for the item you're retrieving or modifying. This base class property is only set for the Container-CmdletProvider and NavigationCmdletProvider classes. If your provider is deriving from ItemCmdletProvider, you will have to parse the path yourself to determine the drive. You can use the base.ProviderInfo.Drives to retrieve the PSDrive based on name.

In the following example, SessionState refers to the context of the current PowerShell session:

```
public SessionState SessionState { get; }
```

Think of this as all the currently defined variables, aliases, functions, providers, and drives that exist in the powershell.exe process. Notice how all of these concepts have providers associated with them. That's because they are nothing more than data stores. Each runspace has its own session state, and powershell.exe currently only allows a single runspace. The SessionState object provides a way to access these data stores that would normally require cmdlets. Rather than having to execute get-variable in a separate pipeline, SessionState has a PSVariable property that returns a PSVariableIntrinsics, which allows the developer to add, remove, and get variables defined in the current PowerShell session. This enables your provider to easily create or set a number of variables when it is initialized, which it may use when accessing the data store. Note the use of the word "intrinsics" in the property or classname as this usually indicates an object you can use to execute commands via internal APIs, rather than at the command line or by creating and executing a pipeline.

The `CommandInvocationIntrinsics` object enables you to execute scripts or any arbitrary command line from within your provider in the current runspace:

```
public CommandInvocationIntrinsics InvokeCommand { get; }
```

`ProvideIntrinsics` enables you to execute provider cmdlets through an API for your provider:

```
public ProviderIntrinsics InvokeProvider { get; }
```

It has a property for each type of provider functionality (item, content, property, security). Therefore, rather than having to execute a `get-item` or `get-content` cmdlet from within your provider, you can use this class to perform those operations via internal APIs.

The following base class property enables the developer to access any dynamic parameters that may have been supplied for the current operation:

```
protected object DynamicParameters { get; }
```

This is only set when the user supplies a dynamic parameter that the provider cmdlet supports.

The following example indicates one or more items to exclude when performing an operation. For example, the user could exclude text files with "`*.txt`" when calling `get-item` for the filesystem:

```
public Collection<string> Exclude { get; }
```

A filter is a provider-specific path that can be used when retrieving items from the data store:

```
public string Filter { get; }
```

Rather than `-Exclude` or `-Include`, which are used after retrieval to thin out the list of items to return, the `-Filter` value is used at the time of accessing the data store so that the operation may return the exact set of items desired.

The following flag indicates that the operation should continue regardless of any warning scenarios:

```
public SwitchParameter Force { get; }
```

What may be considered a warning is provider specific, but typically this involves copying over or creating an item that already exists. Otherwise, your provider may want to prompt the user.

Use the following to indicate one or more items to include when performing an operation:

```
public Collection<string> Include { get; }
```

For example, the user could specify only text files with "`*.txt`" when calling `get-item` for the filesystem.

DriveCmdletProvider

The previous provider wasn't very useful. Providers present a consistent interface to a data store. Drives represent the partitioning of that data store or possibly the data stores themselves. In the case of our sample XML provider, a drive is mapped to an XML document. If you were writing an SQL or database provider, a drive would most likely be a connection to the database. The `NewDrive()` method takes a `PSDriveInfo` object and returns an instance of `PSDriveInfo`. The simplest thing to do here would be to return the instance passed to the method. In fact, this is what the default implementation does if the method is not overridden by the developer.

Sometimes, however, you may want to attach some extra information to your drive. This is accomplished by creating your own `PSDriveInfo` derived class and creating an instance of that class with the `PSDriveInfo` instance. In the case of our sample XML provider, we use the `-path` dynamic parameter to set the `DocumentPath` property of our `XmlDriveInfo` object. This is used to create our `XmlDocument`, which we would use for accessing the elements in the XML document.

The `NewDriveDynamicParameters()` callback enables you to add runtime parameters to the `new-psdrive` cmdlet that are specific to your provider. Let's say you wanted to add a `-path` parameter to the `new-psdrive` cmdlet for our sample XML provider. You would create a collection of `RuntimeDefinedParameter` objects and add a single parameter object with the name `-path`, and specify the type of the parameter. This indicates to the provider infrastructure that `new-psdrive` for that provider has extra dynamic parameters.

All of the properties of a parameter that can be defined using the normal mechanism of attributes for cmdlets can be specified at runtime as well. Note that it is possible to make a dynamic parameter mandatory. Because we made the `-path` parameter mandatory, the user must supply a value for it when invoking `new-psdrive` for our XML provider. The object instantiated by the provider implementer and returned by the `NewDriveDynamicParameters() callback` indicates that there is a dynamic parameter "-path" and that it is mandatory. The provider infrastructure uses the information from this object to populate the `DynamicParameters` property of the `CmdletProvider` class. This `DynamicParameters` property is available to your cmdlet callbacks and is how you extract values for them. `DynamicParameters` is always set to the dynamic parameters for the current cmdlet being executed.

For providers that implement the `DriveCmdletProvider` base class or higher, the `InitializeDefaultDrives()` virtual method is invoked to allow the provider to create any initial drives. Drives created in this method are generally the drives you want to be available to the user without them having to use `new-psdrive`. In the example of the `FileSystem` provider, this would be any drives already present in the operating system's filesystem. Create the `PSDriveInfo` derived objects and return a collection of them. In the following example, we have overridden the method but return null. This is basically the same as not overriding the function at all. Because our sample XML provider maps drives to XML files, we don't start out with any default drives.

If you are going to create drives in `InitializeDefaultDrives()`, use names that won't clash with already existing drives. Drive names are globally unique, and if you try to initialize a drive that already exists, the user will get an error when your provider is starting up (i.e., when the snap-in is being loaded). The provider will still load, but the user will have to manually create the drive or your provider might be left in an indeterminate state.

The `RemoveDrive()` callback method enables us to perform any cleanup for the specific drive being removed. This is called when the drive is being removed via `remove-psdrive` or the provider is shutting down from its snap-in being removed or the user exiting the shell. In the case of our XML provider, we use an `XmlDocument` instance to represent the XML file for our drive. If any changes were made to the document we would want to save them. This is done in `RemoveDrive()`. No dynamic parameters are available for `remove-drive`.

At this point, we're actually using input from the user to control what we map our drive to. The user must supply a `path` parameter to the XML document we use. What if the file doesn't exist or some other error occurs when trying to access it? This is the point at which we must discuss how error handling is managed in our provider. We will show a quick example of the most typical way to handle errors.

Errors should be handled by creating an instance of the `ErrorRecord` class and then calling either `WriteError()` or `ThrowTerminatingError()`. Which method you should use to pass your `ErrorRecord` instance to the user depends upon the priority and severity of the error. The main consideration is whether the error should stop the current operation from continuing. If the answer is yes, then call `ThrowTerminatingError()`, which stops the current operation and throws an exception, which the user can interact with to determine the next course of action. If the error shouldn't stop the current operation, use `WriteError()`. Also available is `WriteWarning()`, which should be used to indicate much less severe errors that the user may not need to actually worry about. The following is an `XmlDriveProvider.cs` sample XML provider:

```
public abstract class ItemCmdletProvider : DriveCmdletProvider
{
        protected ItemCmdletProvider();

        // clear-item cmdlet
        protected virtual void ClearItem(string path);
        protected virtual object ClearItemDynamicParameters(string path);

        // get-item cmdlet
        protected virtual void GetItem(string path);
        protected virtual object GetItemDynamicParameters(string path);

        // invoke-item
        protected virtual void InvokeDefaultAction(string path);
        protected virtual object InvokeDefaultActionDynamicParameters(string path);

        // Used to validate path before attempting other operations
        // or callbacks
        protected abstract bool IsValidPath(string path);

        // used by multiple cmdlets to verify item exists at a location
        protected virtual bool ItemExists(string path);
        protected virtual object ItemExistsDynamicParameters(string path);

        // set-item cmdlet
        protected virtual void SetItem(string path, object value);
        protected virtual object SetItemDynamicParameters(string path, object value);
}
```

Here's the class declaration for the `XmlDriveInfo` class that derives from `PSDriveInfo`. The constructor for our custom drive class must call the base constructor, which takes a `PSDriveInfo` reference. By using the `XmlDriveInfo` class, you can set any properties or values in addition to the methods and properties of `PSDriveInfo`.

```
public class XmlDriveInfo : PSDriveInfo
 {
     private string _path;
     private XmlDocument _xml;
     public string DocumentPath
     {
         get { return _path; }
     }
     public XmlDocument XmlDocument
     {
         get { return _xml; }
         internal set { _xml = value; }
     }
     public XmlDriveInfo(string path, PSDriveInfo drive)
         : base(drive)
     {
         _path = path;
         _xml = new XmlDocument();
         _xml.Load(_path);
     }
}
```

ItemCmdletProvider

The `ItemCmdletProvider` base class is where you can begin to see how useful providers are. By using paths, you can allow items to be retrieved, cleared, and tested for existence. This is also where you need to come up with a path syntax for the provider that you can use to identify items within the data store. Naturally hierarchical data structures will have paths similar to the `FileSystem` or `Registry` provider. However, in those cases, you'll probably want to derive from the `Container` or `Navigation` classes to provide even more useful access to your data store. Even if that's the case, this section describes how you would implement just the methods in the `ItemCmdletProvider` for now.

`ItemCmdletProvider` derives from `DriveCmdletProvider`, so the methods for that class should be overridden as well. Most of the method names are self-explanatory enough to indicate when they would be invoked and what their purpose is.

Here's the public API surface of the class to show what methods you can override:

```
public abstract class ItemCmdletProvider : DriveCmdletProvider
{
        protected ItemCmdletProvider();
        // clear-item cmdlet
        protected virtual void ClearItem(string path);
        protected virtual object ClearItemDynamicParameters(string path);
        // get-item cmdlet
        protected virtual void GetItem(string path);
```

```
        protected virtual object GetItemDynamicParameters(string path);
        // invoke-item
        protected virtual void InvokeDefaultAction(string path);
        protected virtual object InvokeDefaultActionDynamicParameters(string path);
        // Used to validate path before attempting other operations
        // or callbacks
        protected abstract bool IsValidPath(string path);
        // used by multiple cmdlets to verify item exists at a location
        protected virtual bool ItemExists(string path);
        protected virtual object ItemExistsDynamicParameters(string path);

        // set-item cmdlet
        protected virtual void SetItem(string path, object value);
        protected virtual object SetItemDynamicParameters(string path, object value);
    }
```

The callback methods here each correspond to a specific cmdlet. Not overriding the method that corresponds to the cmdlet with the same name (`get-item ->GetItem()`) means an error will be reported to the user indicating that your provider doesn't support that operation if they try to use that cmdlet. Of course, that may be desired behavior if your provider can't support that operation. Note that this is different from `DriveCmdletProvider`, where there is a reasonable default action for `new-psdrive` and `remove-psdrive` if the `NewDrive()` and `RemoveDrive()` methods are not overridden.

For example, suppose your `ItemCmdletProvider` didn't support `clear-item`, only `get-item` and `set-item`. By not overriding the `ClearItem()` method, the following error would occur when the user tried to call `clear-item` for your provider (sssume you've created a provider "`XmlItemProvider`" and it has a drive called "`foo`"):

```
PS C:\Documents and Settings\Owner> clear-item Xmlitemprovider::foo:\rootpath
Clear-Item : Provider execution stopped because the provider does not
support this operation.
At line:1 char:11
+ clear-item  <<<< Xmlitemprovider::blah:\Objs\Obj
```

In addition, there is a method that returns optional dynamic parameters for almost every cmdlet. Using `get-item` as an example, there is a `GetItemDynamicParameters()`callback method. The associated dynamic parameter methods can either be declared and return null or just not be overridden at all to indicate that there are no dynamic parameters for that particular cmdlet. Whether or not your cmdlets need dynamic parameters is provider specific. In the case of our sample XML provider, every cmdlet returns a `-namespace` dynamic parameter. This is due to an internal implementation detail specifying that using XPath query strings and the `XmlDocument.SelectNodes()` method require the namespaces to specify whether the document has any namespace other than the default (which is no namespace defined).

As a result, the sample XML providers automatically check all namespaces when looking up items by their path, but if a namespace is specified by the user via the `-namespace` dynamic parameter, then only that namespace is used when searching for the item located by the path. Again, this is one of those internal implementation details that vary according to the details of your provider/data store. This is also exactly the reason why dynamic parameters exist for all the provider cmdlets. Otherwise, it would make it difficult to create useful providers for some data stores.

Let's start by looking at the declaration of our provider that supports "items":

```
[CmdletProvider("XmlItemProvider", ProviderCapabilities.ShouldProcess)]
public class XmlItemProvider : ItemCmdletProvider
{
   ...
}
```

This is very similar to the class declaration for the drive provider. We derive from `ItemCmdletProvider`, which has the extra methods to override. However, if you look closely, we supply a different value for `ProviderCapabilties` to the `CmdletProviderAttribute`. For our `XmlItemProvider`, we declare support for `ShouldProcess`. This means that we will call `ShouldProcess()` before modifying any of the items in our XML document.

Now look at the methods we want to override:

```
protected abstract bool IsValidPath(string path);
```

First, we must look at `IsValidPath()` as it's the only abstract method. This method is used to determine whether a path is syntactically correct. The path doesn't have to actually exist; it should just verify that the syntax of the path is correct. The provider infrastructure calls this method before any other callbacks. This enables callbacks invoked after this one to go on the assumption that the syntax of the path is valid. This method doesn't correspond to a specific cmdlet and is in fact invoked for the majority of the provider cmdlers. It is used as an early detector to stop or continue the operation. If the path is invalid, then it can't possibly point to an item, so you may as well stop at that point.

The following method is invoked when the provider needs to verify the existence of an item at the specified path:

```
protected virtual bool ItemExists(string path);
```

The `Item` provider uses this callback as a frontline of defense before calling the `ClearItem()`, `InvokeDefaultAction()`, and `GetItem()` callbacks. This enables those methods to concentrate on performing the action on the item and not worry about whether the item exists or not. In fact, this method is called quite often by the other cmdlets for the container and navigation provider classes. It's important that this method support the different types of paths, as discussed earlier in the chapter.

The following is an example of what `ItemExists()` looks like for the `XmlItemProvider` included with the sample code:

```
protected override bool ItemExists(string path)
{
     base.WriteVerbose(string.Format(
                   "XmlItemProvider::ItemExists(Path = '{0}')",path));

     string npath = XmlProviderUtils.NormalizePath(path);
     string xpath = XmlProviderUtils.PathNoDrive(npath);

     XmlDriveInfo drive = XmlProviderUtils.GetDriveFromPath(path,base.ProviderInfo);
```

```
        if (drive == null)
        {
              return false;
        }

        XmlDocument xml = drive.XmlDocument;
        if (xml.SelectSingleNode(xpath,drive.NamespaceManager) == null)
             return false;
        else
             return true;
   }
```

Let's examine this method line by line:

```
WriteVerbose(string.Format(
    "XmlItemProvider::ItemExists(Path = '{0}')" , path));
```

This is a personal preference, but I'm a big fan of providing a way to display the methods as they are entered and the parameter values being passed (just like the old `printf()` days). By including this call to `WriteVerbose()`, you can see the information by specifying the `-verbose` parameter when any cmdlet that ends up calling `ItemExists()` is executed. That happens to be `get-item`, `clear-item`, and `invoke-item`.

Here's an example of what the output of `WriteVerbose()` looks like when the `-verbose` parameter is specified. Notice how the user-specified path "`XmlItemProvider::foo:\Objs\one`" is stripped of the provider, and the provider-internal path "`foo:\Objs\one`" is passed to the callback methods:

```
PS C:\Documents and Settings\Owner> get-item XmlItemProvider::foo:\Objs\one -ver
bose
VERBOSE: XmlItemProvider::ItemExists(Path = 'foo:\Objs\one')
VERBOSE: XmlItemProvider::GetItem(Path = 'foo:\Objs\one')

PSPath          : provider1snapin\XmlItemProvider::foo:\Objs\one
PSProvider      : provider1snapin\XmlItemProvider
PSIsContainer   : False
att1            : dude1
#text           : blah
```

```
string npath = XmlProviderUtils.NormalizePath(path);
```

Although Windows PowerShell providers support both forward '/' and backslash '\' as path separators, the XPath query syntax we use for retrieving items in our XML document only supports the forward slash. This is a common scenario whereby some tweaking is needed by the provider to create a valid path for searching its internal data store. Therefore, `XmlProviderUtils.NormalizePath()` simply converts all back slashes to forward slashes and returns the resulting string.

```
string xpath = XmlProviderUtils.PathNoDrive(npath);
```

The XPath query string doesn't know or care about provider names and drives, so we need to make sure it begins with the root node of the `XmlDocument`. However, provider paths may be fully qualified or drive qualified, which means we need to strip the prepended provider or drive info from the path. For example, "`XmlItemProvider::drive:\root\child1`" would become "`\root\child1`," which is a valid XPath query string. When we derive our provider from the container or navigation provider base class, the path values passed to ItemExists() may be fully qualified or drive qualified. We should handle all the cases even though for now our XmlItemProvider only supports provider-qualified paths.

```
XmlDriveInfo drive = XmlProviderUtils.GetDriveFromPath(path,base.ProviderInfo);
if (drive == null)
{ return false; }
```

It turns out that even though the specified path may include the drive in it (drive::\root\childnode), the provider infrastructure doesn't parse the path to determine the drive for providers that dervive directly from ItemCmdletProvider. The ContainerCmdletProvider and NavigationCmdletProvider classes have more logic in them that would parse the user-specified path and populate the PSDriveInfo property on the CmdletProvider base class. Keep in mind, however, that for the item provider, this doesn't happen, so you need to extract the drive and then search the current drives for the provider to get the current drive. That's what this utility method does; and if the drive doesn't exist, obviously the item doesn't exist, so you return false:

```
XmlDocument xml = drive.XmlDocument;
if (xml.SelectSingleNode(xpath,drive.NamespaceManager) == null)
   return false;
else
 return true;
```

Remember that we created our own XmlDriveInfo class, which inherited from PSDriveInfo, so we could store our own provider-specific data in it. This is where that becomes useful. Each drive is associated with a particular XmlDocument, and we use the SelectSingleNode() method on the XmlDocument to retrieve the items based on the path. This is a prime example of when the provider concepts are mapped to the internal details of your data store. In the case of our sample XML provider, we're simply passing the paths to the SelectSingleNode() method with some preprocessing that removes the drive and/or changes "\" to "/".

If SelectSingleNode() returns null, that means no nodes were found, which means the item doesn't exist. In ItemExists(), we use SelectSingleNode()because we only care that at least one item exists. In the other *-item cmdlet callback methods, we use SelectNodes() because a single path may return multiple items.

Now take a look at GetItem():

```
protected override void GetItem(string path)
{
      WriteVerbose(string.Format(
                  "XmlItemProvider:: GetItem (Path = '{0}')",path));

      string npath = XmlProviderUtils.NormalizePath(path);
      string xpath = XmlProviderUtils.PathNoDrive(npath);

     XmlDriveInfo drive = XmlProviderUtils.GetDriveFromPath(path,base.ProviderInfo);

      if (drive == null)
      {
            return;
      }

      XmlDocument xml = drive.XmlDocument;
```

```
        XmlNodeList nodes = xml.SelectNodes(xpath,drive.NamespaceManager);

        foreach(XmlNode node in nodes)
        {
              WriteItemObject(node, path, false);
        }
}
```

You've probably noticed that the first couple of lines are the same as they are in `ItemExists()`. A good developer would have put them in a separate method. Bad developer! Bad developer! Anyway, the thing to note here is what you actually do with the nodes that are retrieved by the specified path:

```
foreach(XmlNode node in nodes)
{
     WriteItemObject(node, path, false);
}
```

`WriteItemObject()` is how we pass the items back to the user. Each item should be written into the pipeline separately via a call to `WriteItemObject()`. We also pass the path and indicate whether the item is a container, which is always `false` in the case of the item provider. As mentioned previously, a handful of extra properties are tacked onto your items as they are written to the pipeline. Two of those properties (`PSPath` and `PSIsContainer`) are the values supplied in the call to `WriteItemObject()`.

The following method is invoked when the user executes the `invoke-item` cmdlet for your provider:

```
protected virtual void InvokeDefaultAction(string path);
```

If this operation doesn't apply to your provider, simply don't override the method; the infrastructure will indicate that your provider doesn't support it. An example of where this action does make sense is for the `FileSystem` provider. `Invoke-item` in that case will cause the application associated with the file's extension to launch with that file opened.

At this point, you're probably starting to see how you map the provider paths to our internal data store. Of course, it will vary greatly upon your data store and how you actually identify the items in it. For our sample XML provider, we use XPath queries as the glue between the provider paths and the XML document that is our data store. The last method worth looking at shows how you perform the `clear-item` for our sample XML provider. The `SetItem()` method isn't discussed here but it can be examined by looking at the `XmlItemProvider.cs` sample code file.

```
protected virtual void ClearItem(string path) { ...}
```

This is called when the user invokes `clear-item` for this provider. The path supplied here is exactly the same as specified at the command line. It is up to the provider to do any wildcard expansion or path manipulation. Note that if the user uses the `-literalPath` parameter instead of `-path`, then escape characters will not be interpreted. Remember that the escape character in PowerShell is the backtick. If multiple paths are supplied to `clear-item` (`-path` takes a `string[]`), then this method is called back for each path separately. This is true for all the callback methods for the `*-item` cmdlets that take a `string[]` as the path.

Once the item or items indicated by the path are retrieved, the developer must decide what the "clear" action means. Usually this means not deleting the item but emptying or removing the contents. This way, `get-item` still returns an object but it has no value.

Now let's look at the ClearItem() callback method. This method retrieves any XML nodes pointed to by the user-supplied path and "clears" them. In the case of our XML provider, clearing an item means removing any child nodes but leaving the node intact. Notice that we call ShouldProcess() before executing any action that would modify the internal data store:

```
protected override void ClearItem(string path)
{
     WriteVerbose(string.Format("XmlItemProvider::ClearItem(Path = '{0}')",path));

      string npath = XmlProviderUtils.NormalizePath(path);
      string xpath = XmlProviderUtils.PathNoDrive(npath);

     XmlNodeList nodes = GetXmlNodesFromPath(xpath);

     // throw terminating error if we can't find any items at path
     // This is unexpected since ItemExists() was already called and must have
     // returned true for ClearItem() to even be invoked.
     // ------------------------------------------------
     if (nodes == null || nodes.Count == 0)
     {
          ErrorRecord error = new ErrorRecord(new ItemNotFoundException(),
                   "ItemNotFound", ErrorCategory.ObjectNotFound, null);
          ThrowTerminatingError(error);
     }

     foreach (XmlNode node in nodes)
     {
          // ShouldProcess() enables use of -whatif & -confirm flags for clear-item
          // If path returns more than a single XMLNode, we call ShouldProcess()
          // for each node not one call to ShouldProcess for the entire operation
          // ------------------------------------------------------------
          if (base.ShouldProcess(node.Name))
          {
               node.RemoveAll();
          }
     }
}
```

Note the call to ShouldProcess() before we actually "clear" the XmlNode. How you "clear" items in each data store is provider specific.

That's it for the ItemProviderCmdlet class. We have our first cmdlets to access the items in our provider's data store, but the operations are limited. The next provider class enables even more functionality on top of this class.

ContainerCmdletProvider

The ContainerCmdletProvider class derives from ItemCmdletProvider and adds support for several more of the *-item cmdlets. It also introduces the concept of *location* via the set-location and get-location cmdlets. With the item provider type, each item was identified by a path but there is no relationship between the items — at least not through the cmdlets supported by ItemCmdlet-Provider. This changes with the ContainerCmdletProvider, which introduces the classical parent-child relationship. Like a binary tree in which each node may have child nodes, the items in the container provider may have child items as well. `Get-childitems` is a new cmdlet for this provider that highlights this fact. If the objects in your data store have any kind of hierarchical relationship, you should probably at least derive from `ContainerCmdletProvider`. Read the introduction to `NavigationCmdletProvider` to determine whether your provider should support navigation.

Like before, several callback methods are inherited, each corresponding to a specific cmdlet. In addition, each of those has a callback method for dynamic parameters, which you may or may not need to override. If you don't have any dynamic parameters, then simply don't override those methods.

Here's a list of new methods inherited from `ContainerCmdletProvider`:

```
public abstract class ContainerCmdletProvider : ItemCmdletProvider
{
        protected ContainerCmdletProvider();

        // copy-item
        protected virtual void CopyItem(string path, string copyPath, bool recurse);
        protected virtual object CopyItemDynamicParameters(string path,
string destination, bool recurse);

        // get-childitems
        protected virtual void GetChildItems(string path, bool recurse);
        protected virtual object GetChildItemsDynamicParameters(string path,
bool recurse);

        // These methods get called before the other callbacks
        protected virtual void GetChildNames(string path, ReturnContainers
returnContainers);
        protected virtual object GetChildNamesDynamicParameters(string path);
        protected virtual bool HasChildItems(string path);

        // new-item
        protected virtual void NewItem(string path, string itemTypeName,
object newItemValue);
        protected virtual object NewItemDynamicParameters(string path,
string itemTypeName, object newItemValue);

        // remove-item
        protected virtual void RemoveItem(string path, bool recurse);
        protected virtual object RemoveItemDynamicParameters(string path,
bool recurse);

        // rename-item
        protected virtual void RenameItem(string path, string newName);
        protected virtual object RenameItemDynamicParameters(string path,
string newName);
}
```

Each new cmdlet has its own callback method as well as an additional callback for dynamic parameters. Nothing new there. Let's look at some example code from our sample XML provider, included with the sample code as `XmlContainerProvider.cs`.

The class declaration is similar to the other providers except that we derive from a different base class:

```
[CmdletProvider("XmlContainerProvider", ProviderCapabilities.ShouldProcess)]
public class XmlContainerProvider : ContainerCmdletProvider
{
   ...
}
```

Let's examine some of the callback methods:

```
protected virtual void CopyItem(string path, string copyPath, bool recurse);
```

`Copy-item` is the first cmdlet that actually moves around items in the data store. Previously, we only changed the value of items in the data store. Now with the cmdlets supported by `ContainerCmdlet-Provider`, we will begin to move items around to different locations or paths. Let's look at the code from the sample XML provider:

```
protected override void CopyItem(string path, string copyPath, bool recurse)
{
    WriteVerbose(string.Format("XmlContainerProvider::CopyItem(Path =
'{0}', CopyPath = '{1}', recurse = '{2}')", path, copyPath, recurse));

    string xpath = XmlProviderUtils.NormalizePath(path);

    XmlNodeList nodes = GetXmlNodesFromPath(xpath);

    if (nodes == null || nodes.Count == 0)
    {
          ErrorRecord error = new ErrorRecord(new ItemNotFoundException(),
                    "ItemNotFound", ErrorCategory.ObjectNotFound, null);
          WriteError(error);
    }

    XmlNode destNode = GetSingleXmlNodeFromPath(copyPath);
    if (destNode == null )
    {
           ErrorRecord error = new ErrorRecord(new
ItemNotFoundException("Destination item not found"),
                "ItemNotFound", ErrorCategory.ObjectNotFound, copyPath);
            WriteError(error);
    }

    XmlDocument xmldoc = GetXmlDocumentFromCurrentDrive();

    foreach (XmlNode nd in nodes)
    {
         if (base.ShouldProcess(nd.Name))
         {
             destNode.AppendChild(nd.Clone());
         }
    }
}
```

If you're paying close attention, you can see that I'm making a couple of assumptions here. In fact, there are a few scenarios I'm not handling (I'm doing this on purpose, of course). Everything looks OK up until the point where I retrieve the `destNode` from the `copyPath`. The code assumes that there is already a node located at `copyPath` to copy the items to. In terms of the filesystem, I would be assuming that the `copyPath` is a directory and that it exists, but in fact there are several situations that can occur here that a provider should handle.

What we will discuss now are some of the boundary cases that may occur when the `copy-item` cmdlet is being executed for your provider. These boundary cases are due to the existence or non-existence of the `copyPath` and `destNode` parameters in the `CopyItem()` callback. These values are ultimately derived from the command-line parameters of similar names for `copy-item`.

How you handle the following scenarios depends mostly upon the details of your provider. There are probably some standard ways of dealing with these cases, and understanding how the built-in PowerShell providers handle them (i.e., filesystem) might give you some insight about how your provider should behave.

Let's assume you have the following XML document for the sake of this discussion:

```
<root>
    <one>blah</one>
    <two>blah2</two>
    <three>blah3</three>
</root>
```

Scenario 1

There's already an XML node at the place indicated by `copyPath`. In this case, you can simply copy the XML nodes retrieved from `path` to that node (this is the scenario I've handled):

```
copy -path drive:/root/one -destination drive:/root/two
```

This operation copies the "`one`" node and adds it as a child of the "`two`" node. This makes the XML document look like the following (notice how the `one` node was copied inside the `two` node; it didn't copy over it):

```
<root>
  <one>blah</one>
  <two>blah2<one>blah</one></two>
  <three>blah3</three>
</root>
```

Scenario 2

There's not a node at the `copyPath`, but the `copyPath` up until the last item name exists. Using initial XML doc again, the following operation would enact this scenario:

```
copy-item -path drive:/root/one -destination drive:/root/four
```

In this case, a new node should be placed under `root` with the name "`four`" and the inner text value of "`blah`" (`<four>blah</four>`).

This scenario is not handled by the above `CopyItem()` *code sample.*

Scenario 3

The `copyPath` doesn't exist but neither does a parent. Again, assuming the initial XML doc, the following command highlights this scenario:

```
copy-item -path drive:/root/one -destination drive:/foo/four
```

What should you do here? Should you write an error and fail to complete the operation? Should you create the necessary items from the root of the document to the end node? In this case, a typical behavior might be failure unless `-force` is specified. The presence of the `-force` indicates that the operation should be completed unless there is a catastrophic failure preventing it from happening. Otherwise, create or overwrite any items that need to be in order to finish.

Why the long example here? The reason is because I wanted to highlight the kinds of decisions that you, as a developer, will have to make when writing your provider. The details of your provider will in many cases dictate the behavior for some of the boundary cases when moving items around your data store. Another question that needs to be answered for container providers is whether your `copy-item` and `move-item` cmdlets support the `-recursive` flag. In most cases, a "move" action implicitly means moving all the items within the container recursively. And with the "copy" operation, usually you want to allow the user to control whether to copy just the first level of items or the whole heirarchy of items located recursively inside the container being copied. Again, this all depends on the internal details of your provider's data store and the relationships between the objects in it.

The notion of nested containers helps resolve some of these issues. All three of these scenarios have a well-understood behavior when it comes to the filesystem, which is a navigational provider that supports nested containers. That's another thing to keep in mind when deciding which provider base class to derive your provider from.

Now let's look at the implementation of `new-item`. Notice that we had to check the existence of the `-Force` parameter for the case where an item already exists at the path. Then, once we have everything we need, we call `ShouldProcess()` before actually creating the item. In this sample code we create an `ErrorRecord` and call `WriteError()` if the parent XML node doesn't exist. If the path were "drive:\root\a\b," the parent node would be located at "drive:\root\a." Without a valid parent node, we can't create a new XML node inside of it. One other option would be to create all nodes up to and including the child node ("b" in this case). And looking at the `FileSystem` provider, that's what `-Force` does. It will create nested directories if needed when the `-Force` parameter is supplied. For our sample XML provider I chose not to do that because it may create unwanted XML nodes in the XML document.

```
protected override void NewItem(string path, string itemTypeName, object
newItemValue)
        {
    WriteVerbose(string.Format("XmlNavigationProvider::RemoveItemNewItem(Path =
'{0}', itemtype = '{1}', newvalue = '{2}')",
                path, itemTypeName, newItemValue));

            // first check if item already exists at that path
            // -------------------------------------------------
           FFstring xpath = XmlProviderUtils.NormalizePath(path);

            // we need to get the parent of the new node so we can add to its children
```

```
            // we do this by chopping the last item from the path if there isn't
already an item
            // at the path. in which case we need to check force flag or error out
            // for example: new item path = drive:/root/one/two
            // the parent node would be at drive:/root/one
            // ------------------------------------------
            XmlNode parent = null;

            XmlNode destNode = GetSingleXmlNodeFromPath(xpath);

            if (destNode != null)
            {
                parent = destNode.ParentNode;
                if (base.Force)
                    destNode.ParentNode.RemoveChild(destNode);
                else
                {
                    // write error
                    ErrorRecord err = new ErrorRecord(new
ArgumentException("item already exists!"), "AlreadyExists",
                        ErrorCategory.InvalidArgument, path);
                    WriteError(err);
                    return;
                }
            }
            else
            {
                parent = GetParentNodeFromLeaf(xpath);
            }

            // Need to handle case where the parent node doesn't exist
            if (parent == null)
            {
                // write error
                ErrorRecord err = new ErrorRecord(new
ItemNotFoundException("ParentPath doesn't exist"), "ObjectNotFound",
                    ErrorCategory.ObjectNotFound, path);
                WriteError(err);
                return;
            }

            string endName = GetLastPathName(xpath);
            XmlDriveInfo drive = base.PSDriveInfo as XmlDriveInfo;
            XmlDocument xmldoc = drive.XmlDocument;

            XmlNode newNode = xmldoc.CreateNode(itemTypeName, endName,
parent.NamespaceURI);

            // lets call shouldprocess
            if (ShouldProcess(path))
            {
                parent.AppendChild(newNode);
            }
        }
```

NavigationCmdletProvider

This, the final provider class, derives from `ContainerCmdletProvider` and adds a few additional virtual methods to override. The most important concept added by the navigational provider is the nested containers and the ability to change locations among them. Just like directories in the filesystem, these containers can be used as the current location (and in fact the `PSDriveInfo` object has a `CurrentLocation` property that stores this value) for performing operations on the items in your data store. The ability to use relative paths from the current location saves a lot of typing and makes discovery of your provider much easier.

```
public abstract class NavigationCmdletProvider : ContainerCmdletProvider
{
     protected NavigationCmdletProvider();

     // used by the provider infrastructure as well as useful
     // for you callback methods when handling container vs non-container operations
     protected virtual string GetChildName(string path);
     protected virtual string GetParentPath(string path, string root);
     protected virtual bool IsItemContainer(string path);

     // join-path
     protected virtual string MakePath(string parent, string child);

     // move-item
     protected virtual void MoveItem(string path, string destination);
     protected virtual object MoveItemDynamicParameters(string path,
string destination);

     // used to create the handle realtive paths by the provider infrastructure
     protected virtual string NormalizeRelativePath(string path, string basePath);
}
```

One of the most important things to remember is the support for relative paths. This means your callbacks need to handle both relative and absolute paths. Luckily, you don't need to go back and rewrite all the methods we implemented earlier. This is because for navigational providers, the infrastructure inserts extra callbacks that developers can override to create the appropriate full path from a relative path. The next few methods help in achieving this.

The following methods are invoked by the provider infrastructure in various cases to construct the appropriate path and/or put together the path from the container plus child item specified. In addition, the `NavigationCmdletProvider` supplies a default implementation for these methods. These default implementations work for any path syntax that only uses the forward slash and the backslash ("/" and "\") as path separators. If your provider is doing anything with its paths that violates this, you'll most likely have to override one or more of them yourself.

The default implementations for these methods always normalize the path to use the backslash. Because the XPath query strings we use only support the forward slash, we need to renormalize the paths in our cmdlet callbacks. That's why you'll notice that the XML provider always calls `XmlProvider-Utils.NormalizePath()` first in every callback so that the path is in the right format for `XmlNode.SelectNodes()` and `XmlNode.SelectSingleNode()`.

The following method returns the last childname from the supplied path:

```
protected virtual string GetChildName(string path);
```

For example, if `path=\root\path1\path2`, then this method returns `path2`. This is one of the virtual methods that already has a default implementation. The default implementation works for paths that only use the "/" or "\" as path separators (i.e., the filesystem). Therefore, if the paths for your provider follow the same format as the filesystem, then you won't need to override this method.

This method returns the parent path for a given path:

```
protected virtual string GetParentPath(string path, string root);
```

This means everything to the left of the last path separator. Therefore, if `path = \root\path1\path2`, this method should return `\root\path1`. This method is used by the other callbacks when relative paths are supplied. It has a default implementation for "/" and "\" path separators.

Here is another method that has a default implementation for the "/" and "\" path separators:

```
protected virtual string NormalizeRelativePath(string path, string basePath);
```

This method actually converts paths beginning with ".\" or "..\" to the correct relative path. If you override this method, then be sure to check for those special path tokens.

This next callback is invoked when the user executes `join-path`:

```
protected virtual string MakePath(string parent, string child);
```

It is also the method that is called to create the full path that is passed to the actual cmdlet callback. The provider infrastructure invokes this method and `ItemExists()` for almost every provider cmdlet. As a result, special care should be taken to ensure that these two methods are reliable and handle all the possible path types. There is a default implementation of `MakePath()` that supports "/" and "\" as the path separators.

Because the XPath queries we've been using need to use the forward slash, as long as you make sure to normalize the path in all the other callback methods by replacing "\" with "/" you're fine. You can use the default implementation of `MakePath()` and the other methods and you're only one step from supporting navigation and relative paths.

You do need to override the `IsItemContainer()` callback:

```
protected virtual bool IsItemContainer(string path);
```

This is called by `set-location` to ensure that you're trying to move to an actual container.

The following sample code is from our XML sample provider. It determines whether an item is a container based on the `NodeType` property of the `XmlNode` reference. This method doesn't check whether or not the container has any items in it. Its sole purpose is to return a Boolean indicating whether it's a container or not:

```
protected override bool IsItemContainer(string path)
{
        // see if item exists at path and indicate if it is container
        // if its a container, we can set-location to it
        string xpath = XmlProviderUtils.NormalizePath(path);
```

```
        XmlNode  node  = GetSingleXmlNodeFromPath(xpath);

        if (node == null)
            return false;
        else
           return IsNodeContainer(node);
}

private bool IsNodeContainer(XmlNode xmlNode)
{
    // only certain types of XmlNodes can be containers
    if ((xmlNode.NodeType == XmlNodeType.Entity) ||
                (xmlNode.NodeType == XmlNodeType.Element) ||
                (xmlNode.NodeType == XmlNodeType.Document))
    {
        return true;
    }
    else
    {
         return false;
    }
}
```

Now let's look at the callback for the `move-item` cmdlet:

```
protected virtual void MoveItem(string path, string destination);
```

The other new callback in the `NavigationCmdletProvider` class is `MoveItem()`, which is called when the user executes the `move-item` cmdlet. Let's take a look at the implementation for that callback. If you think about what a move operation really does, it's the same as a copy and remove. Thus, we simply combined the code from those two callbacks previously defined in the `ContainerCmdletProvider`. Notice the call to `ShouldProcess()` before each potential change to the XML document.

```
protected override void MoveItem(string path, string destination)
{
      WriteVerbose(string.Format("XmlNavigationProvider::MoveItem(Path =
'{0}', destination = '{1}')", path, destination));

      string xpath = XmlProviderUtils.NormalizePath(path);

      XmlNodeList nodes = GetXmlNodesFromPath(xpath);

      XmlNode destNode = GetSingleXmlNodeFromPath(destination);

      XmlDocument xmldoc = GetXmlDocumentFromCurrentDrive();

      foreach (XmlNode nd in nodes)
      {
           if (base.ShouldProcess(nd.Name))
           {
                destNode.AppendChild(nd.Clone());
```

```
                    // remove node from old location
                    nd.ParentNode.RemoveChild(nd);
                }
            }
        }
```

IPropertyCmdletProvider

Implementing this interface declares support for the `get-itemproperty`, `set-itemproperty`, and `clear-itemproperty` cmdlets. Each of the cmdlet callback methods also has an associated dynamic parameter callback that must be overridden because it's an interface. To indicate that the cmdlet has no dynamic parameters, simply return `NULL`.

Let's look at the methods for the interface:

```
public interface IPropertyCmdletProvider
{
        // clear-itemproperty
        void ClearProperty(string path, Collection<string> propertyToClear);
        object ClearPropertyDynamicParameters(string path, Collection<string>
propertyToClear);

        // get-itemproperty
        void GetProperty(string path, Collection<string> providerSpecificPickList);
        object GetPropertyDynamicParameters(string path, Collection<string>
providerSpecificPickList);

        // set-itemproperty
        void SetProperty(string path, PSObject propertyValue);
        object SetPropertyDynamicParameters(string path, PSObject propertyValue);
}
```

For some sample code that illustrates how to use this interface, I decided to implement a minimalistic `FileSystem` provider. In fact, the `SampleFileSystemProvider` class only supports `get-item` and the property and content interfaces. The file and directory items in the `FileSystem` provider have a static set of properties; and, furthermore, we restrict access to certain ones. This may or may not be the case for your provider but it makes for an interesting example.

In designing the sample XML provider, I was considering treating XML attributes as properties. The attributes can be changed at runtime, however, which indicates the need for the `IDynamicProperty-CmdletProvider` *interface not the* `IPropertyCmdletProvider` *interface. The former allows runtime properties, whereas the latter doesn't. Thus, I chose to use the well-known* `FileSystem` *as an example.*

Let's take a closer at look the callback for `get-itemproperty`:

```
public void GetProperty(string path, Collection<string> providerSpecificPickList)
{
     WriteVerbose(string.Format("SampleFileSystemProvider::GetProperty(path =
'{0}')", path));

     // TODO: We should probably do more argument preprocessing here but
     // more importantly, we're not handling any exception that might occur as
```

```
        // a result of accessing the properties of the file. There may be a FILE I/O
        // or permissions problem. We should add a try-catch block that calls
        // ThrowTerminatingError() if any exceptions are thrown.
        // --------------------------
        FileSystemInfo fileinfo = null;

        // First check if we have a directory,
        // ---------------------------------
        DirectoryInfo dir = new DirectoryInfo(path);
        if (dir.Exists)
        {
            fileinfo = dir;
        }

        // now check for file
        // -----------------
        FileInfo file = new FileInfo(path);
        if (file.Exists)
        {
             fileinfo = file;
        }

        // item doesn't exist at path, call WriteError() and do nothing else
        if (fileinfo == null)
        {
             ErrorRecord error = new ErrorRecord(new ArgumentException(
            "Item not found"),"ObjectNotFound", ErrorCategory.ObjectNotFound, null);
               WriteError(error);
        }
        else
        {

               // create PSObject from the FileSystemInfo instance
               PSObject psobj = PSObject.AsPSObject(fileinfo);


               // create the PSObject to copy properties into and that we will return
               PSObject result = new PSObject();

               foreach (string name in providerSpecificPickList)
               {

                   // Copy all the properties from the original object into 'result'
                   PSPropertyInfo prop = psobj.Properties[name];
                   object value = null;
                   if (prop != null)
                   {
                       value = prop.Value;
                   }
                   else
                   {
                       WriteWarning(string.Format("Property name
'{0}' doesn't exist for item at path '{1}'",
                               name, path));
```

```
                }
                result.Properties.Add(new PSNoteProperty(name, value));
            }

            WritePropertyObject(result, path);
        }
    }
```

The first thing we do is try to retrieve the item specified by the path. The `ItemExists()` method is called before this but we still check for the case where no item is located at the path. Once we have an item, we create a `PSObject` from it. Using `PSObject` makes it much easier to check the public properties of the object. `PSObject` internally creates an internal hashtable for all the public properties via reflection and exposes them through its `Properties` collection.

Once we determine whether the property we're looking for exists or not, we add a new `PSNoteProperty` for each property to a blank `PSObject`. This `PSObject` is then written to the pipeline via `WritePropertyObject()`. As indicated in the comments, you treat a non-existent property as a warning and add a `NULL` value to the returned result for the property. How you handle this case will vary from provider to provider.

IDynamicPropertyCmdletProvider

This interface derives from `IPropertyCmdletProvider`, so your provider must implement the methods defined in both. As previously stated, the "dynamic" properties can be added and removed at runtime. Although an example is not provided here, the code is very similar to the `IPropertyCmdletProvider` methods. Any property values added, changed, or removed should be written to the pipeline via `WriteItemProperty()` as a `PSObject` so that users specifying the `-PassThru` parameter can see them.

Here's a sample of the new methods for this interface:

```
public interface IDynamicPropertyCmdletProvider : IPropertyCmdletProvider
{
        // copy-itemproperty
        void CopyProperty(string sourcePath, string sourceProperty,
string destinationPath, string destinationProperty);
        object CopyPropertyDynamicParameters(string sourcePath,
string sourceProperty, string destinationPath, string destinationProperty);

        // move-itemproperty
        void MoveProperty(string sourcePath, string sourceProperty,
string destinationPath, string destinationProperty);
        object MovePropertyDynamicParameters(string sourcePath,
string sourceProperty, string destinationPath, string destinationProperty);

        // new-property
        void NewProperty(string path, string propertyName,
string propertyTypeName, object value);
        object NewPropertyDynamicParameters(string path, string propertyName,
string propertyTypeName, object value);

        // remove-property
        void RemoveProperty(string path, string propertyName);
        object RemovePropertyDynamicParameters(string path, string propertyName);
```

```
        // rename-property
        void RenameProperty(string path, string sourceProperty,
string destinationProperty);
        object RenamePropertyDynamicParameters(string path,
string sourceProperty, string destinationProperty);
    }
```

IContentCmdletProvider

By implementing this interface, your provider is declaring support for the `get-content`, `set-content`, `add-content`, and `clear-content` cmdlets. These cmdlets use a row/stream-based interface to read or write data to the item in your data store. In addition to callback methods for each cmdlet, two interfaces must be implemented to actually do the reading and writing to the item. These new interfaces are `IContentReader` and `IContentWriter` and they are returned by the `GetContent()` and `SetContent()` methods, respectively.

Let's look first at the `IContentCmdletProvider` interface methods:

```
public interface IContentCmdletProvider
{
    // clear-content
    void ClearContent(string path);
    object ClearContentDynamicParameters(string path);

    // get-content
    IContentReader GetContentReader(string path);
    object GetContentReaderDynamicParameters(string path);

    // set-content, add-content
    IContentWriter GetContentWriter(string path);
    object GetContentWriterDynamicParameters(string path);
}
```

Here is the `IContentReader` interface:

```
public interface IContentReader : IDisposable
{
    void Close();
    IList Read(long readCount);
    void Seek(long offset, SeekOrigin origin);
}
```

Here is `IContentWriter`:

```
public interface IContentWriter : IDisposable
{
    void Close();
    void Seek(long offset, SeekOrigin origin);
    IList Write(IList content);
}
```

Let's examine what happens when the user executes the `get-content` cmdlet:

```
PS C:\Documents and Settings\Owner>get-content foo.txt
```

1. We're in the `FileSystem` provider here, so `ItemExists()` is invoked to make sure the item exists
2. If the item exists, then the `GetContentWriter()` method is invoked and an object implementing the `IContentReader` interface is returned.
3. `IContentReader.Read(0)` is invoked. When the `readCount` is zero or negative, that indicates to read to the end. In the case of the `FileSystem` provider, it reads CRLF delimited lines from the file until it reaches EOF (End of File). Unless the `-encoding` parameter is specified. What encoding parameter, you ask? Well, the `FileSystem` provider has an `-encoding` dynamic parameter defined for all its `*-content` cmdlets. This controls whether it reads the file as text or as binary, in which case it reads it by blocks rather than lines of text. This is just another example of how providers differ and how dynamic parameters come in handy. The returned `IList` of objects are all then written to the pipeline by the provider infrastructure, so the developer never actually calls `WriteItemObject()` or anything similar. They return an `IContentReader` from `GetContentReader()` with the `Read()` method implemented, which returns a collection of objects that are written to the pipeline.

`Set-content` and `add-content` are similar but they call `GetContentWriter()`, which returns an `IContentWriter`, and the `Write()` method is called on that instance. The difference here, however, is that `set-content` replaces the current content, while `add-content` appends. Following is the order of callbacks for `add-content`:

1. `ItemCmdletProvider.ItemExists()`
2. `IContentCmdletProvider.GetContentWriter()`
3. `IContentWriter.Seek(0,SeekOrigin.End)`
4. `IContentWriter.Write(IList content)`: The content parameter here is whatever the user is specifying as `-value` when calling `add-content`.

Now let's look at the methods for our minimalistic `FileSystem` provider when we execute `get-content` (taken from `SampleFileSystemProvider.cs`). Let's use the following command line to walkthrough the order of callbacks by the provider infrastructure:

PS C:\Documents and Settings\Owner > set-content samplefilesystemprovider::c:\examples \foo.txt "foo"

```
public IContentWriter GetContentWriter(string path)
{
        WriteVerbose(string.Format("SampleFileSystemProvider::
GetContentWriter(path = '{0}')", path));

        // First check if we have a directory, throw terminating error because
        // directories have no content
        // ----------------------------------
        DirectoryInfo dir = new DirectoryInfo(path);
        if (dir.Exists)
        {
            ErrorRecord error = new ErrorRecord(new
InvalidOperationException("Directories have no content!"),
```

```
                "InvalidOperation", ErrorCategory.InvalidOperation, path);
            ThrowTerminatingError(error);
        }

        // now check for file
        // ------------------
        if (File.Exists(path))
        {
            // TODO: handle exceptions thrown from ctore which calls
            // File.CreateText(). Catch them and call WritError()
            // -------------------------------
            return new FileContentWriter(path, this);
        }
        else
            return null;
}
```

The `ItemExists()` method callback from `ItemCmdletProvider` only validates that the item exists. In our `GetContentWriter()` callback, we need to verify that the item has content that can be set. In our case, directories are items that don't support content, so we should produce the appropriate error. Once we're past that, we create a `FileContentWriter` instance and return it. We also pass a reference to the current provider. That way, the writer may use its methods and properties for easily performing its write operations and for error handling.

This sample code shows the constructor and `Write()` method for the `FileContentWriter` class we're creating to support the `set-content` and `get-content` cmdlets.

```
public class FileContentWriter : IContentWriter
{
    string _path;
    TextWriter _writer;
    CmdletProvider _provider;

    public FileContentWriter(string path, CmdletProvider provider)
    {
        _path = path;
        _writer = File.CreateText(_path);
        _provider = provider;
    }

    public System.Collections.IList Write(System.Collections.IList content)
    {
        _provider.WriteVerbose("FileContentWriter.Write()");
        foreach (object obj in content)
        {
            _writer.WriteLine("{0}", obj);
        }
        return content;
    }
}
```

The `Write()` method iterates through the objects and writes them as strings to the file. A more robust write method would handle binary data and not assume that each line should be CRLF delimited.

However, the main point of the example here is to highlight the boilerplate code needed to support the `*-content` cmdlets for a provider.

ISecurityDescriptorCmdletProvider

This interface has methods for setting and retrieving the ACLs (Access Control Lists) on the items in your data store. The `ObjectSecurity` class is a standard .NET class from which the security descriptor for your item must derive. For example, the `FileSystem` provider uses `FileSecurity` and `Directory-Security` objects, which derive from `ObjectSecurity` and are also included in the .NET Framework. `FileInfo` and `DirectoryInfo` objects have methods for getting and setting the `AccessSecurity` for the file or directory they represent.

```
public interface ISecurityDescriptorCmdletProvider
{
        // get-acl
        void GetSecurityDescriptor(string path, AccessControlSections
includeSections);

        ObjectSecurity NewSecurityDescriptorFromPath(string path,
AccessControlSections includeSections);
       ObjectSecurity NewSecurityDescriptorOfType(string type, AccessControlSections
includeSections);

        // set-acl
        void SetSecurityDescriptor(string path, ObjectSecurity
securityDescriptor);
}
```

Design Guidelines and Tips

Here are some guidelines and things to keep in mind when implementing your provider:

- It is most important to determine which base class and optional interfaces to derive from. Trying to shoehorn too much stuff into one of the less feature-rich provider types isn't good, and neither is using a more advanced provider interface but only supporting a small fraction of its operations.
- Path syntax: Make sure you understand how to convert between the Windows PowerShell paths and your provider internal paths.
- If you declare a `ProviderCapability`, make sure you actually implement it. In addition, make sure you support it for *all* the operations to which it applies.
- Remember that dynamic parameters exist. If you're having trouble figuring out how to add extra information via the path syntax, maybe you should keep the path syntax as is and add a dynamic parameter for some extra context.
- The `SessionState` object enables you to interact with the shell via APIs to access things such as variables and functions, and to execute arbitrary scripts and even provider-specific commands. Keep this in mind, explore the APIs of the `SessionState` class and the classes it holds, and you might find an elegant solution when facing a roadblock in developing your provider.

- Deriving from `PSDriveInfo` and adding your own properties to the new class is a good way to persist information for a drive about the data store it represents.
- Use the appropriate methods for error handling, rather than throw exceptions from the callback methods: `ThrowTerminatingError()` for operation ending errors and `WriteError()` for nonfatal errors.
- Look at the methods on `CmdletProvider` to see what other information or useful things exist. Prompting or user feedback can be handy as well. Use `WriteProgress()` for lengthy operations. Use `ShouldContinue()` for a boundary case that you're not sure how to handle. This prompts the user for the course of action.

Summary

We covered a lot of material in this chapter. There are a lot of classes, cmdlets, and concepts associated with PowerShell providers. It is hoped that you now have the knowledge in hand to begin implementing your own providers that do cool and amazing things. Based on the functionality and features you want your provider to support, you will choose one of the following base classes from which to derive your provider:

- **ItemCmdletProvider:** Supports access to items identified by unique paths
- **ContainerCmdletProvider:** Supports the concept of containers
- **NavigationCmdletProvider:** Allows navigation of the provider and keeps track of the user's current location in the provider

Remember that all of the preceding classes derive from `DriveCmdletProvider`, which ultimately inherits from `CmdletProvider`. These two base classes offer essential functionality for your provider, but they aren't very useful by themselves. You really should choose one of the aforementioned three classes to derive from.

In addition to the base provider type, your provider can implement from a set of optional interfaces:

- **IPropertyCmdletProvider/IDynamicPropertyCmdletProvider:** Supports static/runtime properties of the items in your provider
- **IContentCmdletProvider:** Supports stream-based or row-based access to the internal content of the items in your provider
- **ISecurityDescriptorCmdlet:** Controls access/security to the items in your provider

Paths and drives apply to all provider types, and the format of the paths your provider supports is based on the base provider type. You should also determine which "capabilities" your provider supports and be sure to implement support for these if you include them in your provider class declaration. Finally, provide consistent and robust error handling for your provider. If users can't understand why an operation in your provider failed, they will get frustrated and your support calls will increase.

6

Hosting the PowerShell Engine in Applications

Assuming you've tried out Windows PowerShell prior to reading this, you're familiar with PowerShell's console host, which is the user interface that shows you the prompt, accepts your commands, and displays their results. In most command shells, no distinction is visible between the front-end application and the back-end execution engine — to the user, it's all one monolithic executable.

From a command-line user's perspective, the same might seem true of Windows PowerShell. To the .NET developer, however, the PowerShell execution engine exposes a public API that enables it be called independently of the console host, providing a powerful means of integrating PowerShell functionality into .NET applications.

In this chapter, you'll learn how the PowerShell engine's public API can be used for integrating PowerShell into managed code applications. Along the way, you'll be introduced to several classes and concepts that make this possible.

Runspaces and Pipelines

The fundamental component of the engine API is the `Runspace` class. An instance of the `Runspace` class represents an instance of the PowerShell engine, and contains its own set of variables, drive mappings, functions, and so on, which are collectively referred to as the runspace's *session state*. The runspace provides an interface for loading cmdlets, snap-ins, and variables, as well as methods for creating new pipelines in the runspace.

To run a command line in a runspace, you create and then invoke an instance of the `Pipeline` class. You can think of an instance of the `Pipeline` class as an object representation of a PowerShell command line, containing individual commands and their parameters and exposing entry points and a set of input, output, and error pipes.

The engine's public API provides a range of ways to invoke pipelines, from very expedient one-liners to ways that provide you with precise control over the runspace and pipeline. As you'll see, though, there's a trade-off between expedience and efficiency.

Getting Started

To use the PowerShell engine API from a .NET application, you need to reference the `System.Management.Automation` assembly installed by PowerShell and the Windows SDK. If you're not ready to install the Windows SDK, you can find the `System.Management.Automation` assembly in the global assembly cache (GAC) by running the following command from the PowerShell command line:

```
$host.GetType().Assembly.Location
```

Once you've created the reference, add the following "using" directives to your source code file:

```
using System.Management.Automation;
using System.Management.Automation.Runspaces;
using System.Collections.ObjectModel;
```

The `System.Management.Automation` namespace contains fundamental types such as `PSObject` and `RuntimeException`. `System.Management.Automation.Runspaces` contains the public types for runspaces and pipelines, and `System.Collections.ObjectModel` contains the generic collection type that pipelines use to return their results.

Executing a Command Line

Most programming language runtimes include some facility for executing commands as though they were entered on the operating system's command line. You may be familiar with the `system()` function in Perl, or the `SHELL` command in QBasic, for example. This section discusses ways you can use the PowerShell engine API to execute PowerShell commands.

Using RunspaceInvoke

The simplest way to execute a command line in the PowerShell engine is to invoke it directly using the `RunspaceInvoke` class. An instance of `RunspaceInvoke` encapsulates the basic functionality of the `Runspace` and `Pipeline` classes, and eliminates most of the work involved in creating pipelines, managing I/O, and so on.

This comes at a price, however, because the `RunspaceInvoke` class isolates the application from the more flexible API provided by `Runspace` and `Pipeline`. That said, the `RunspaceInvoke` class provides a simple, usable interface when all you want to do is execute a command line and synchronously receive the results.

To run a command via `RunspaceInvoke`, you first need to create an instance of `RunspaceInvoke`. The type has four constructors, which enable you to build your `RunspaceInvoke` object from nothing, a pre-existing runspace, a `RunspaceConfiguration`, or a console file. `RunspaceConfiguration` and console files are discussed later in this chapter. For now, just use the default constructer, which internally creates a runspace with a default configuration:

```
RunspaceInvoke invoker = new RunspaceInvoke();
```

Having created an instance of `RunspaceInvoke`, you now work with it using the `Invoke()` method. There are three overloads of `Invoke()`, which give you varying levels of control over the input and output of the command line. The simplest of the three just accepts a script block as a string parameter and returns a collection of results:

```
Collection<PSObject> results = invoker.Invoke("get-process");
```

The results are provided as a generic collection of `PSObject` instances. In the next section, you'll learn how to use `PSObject`; but for now, let's assume that you just want to display the results to a user on the console, using the text returned by `ToString()`:

```
foreach (PSObject thisResult in invoker.Invoke("get-process"))
{
    Console.WriteLine(thisResult.ToString());
}
```

The other two overloads of the `Invoke` method enable you to pass in an `IEnumerable` collection of input and specify an output parameter of type `IList` to receive the output of the error pipe. These correspond to the input and error pipes you get when you use the PowerShell command line. As an example, you could use the input pipe to pass an array of integers to the `sort-object` cmdlet, and then display the output. Note that a final piece of glue is necessary for the script block to pick up the input, and that's to add `"$input |"` to the beginning:

```
int[] input = {3, 7, 1, 3};
foreach (PSObject thisResult in invoker.Invoke("$input | sort-object", input))
{
    Console.WriteLine(thisResult.ToString());
}
```

The final overload for `Invoke()` enables you to receive the results of the error stream. Non-terminating errors that occur during the execution of the pipeline are accumulated here. Later in this chapter, you'll learn about the structure of these errors and how to use them. For now, as with `PSObject`, you can just use the `ToString()` method to retrieve the messages. In addition, if you need to retrieve the error output but don't want to specify input, you can pass null to the input parameter of the last overload.

The following console application demonstrates the use of the output, input, and error pipes using `RunspaceInvoke` with the default runspace configuration. The strings `"system"`, `"software"`, and `"security"` are passed as input and the `get-item` cmdlet uses the strings to look for an item under `HKLM:\`. The third string, `"security"`, will result in a non-terminating error, as the `HKLM\Security` Registry key is ACLed to prevent reading:

```
using System;
using System.Collections;
using System.Collections.ObjectModel;
using System.Management.Automation;

namespace RunspaceInvokeSample1
```

```
{
    class Program
    {
        static void Main(string[] args)
        {
            RunspaceInvoke invoker = new RunspaceInvoke();
            string[] input = { "system", "software", "security" };
            IList errors;
            string scriptBlock =
                          "$input | foreach {get-item hklm:\\$_}";

            foreach (PSObject thisResult in
                     invoker.Invoke(scriptBlock, input, out errors))
            {
                Console.WriteLine("Output: {0}", thisResult);
            }
            foreach (object thisError in errors)
            {
                Console.WriteLine("Error: {0}", thisError);
            }
        }
    }
}
```

Using Runspace and Pipeline

Another way to execute a command line in the PowerShell engine is to create a `Pipeline` object, and then invoke it. A `Pipeline` object is created by building it programmatically or from a script block. A script block is simply a pipeline in string form, such as what a user would enter on the console, as shown here:

```
"calc"
```

You can't create a pipeline from this script block yet, however, because pipelines are created using the `CreatePipeline` methods of a runspace instance, and we don't have a runspace. To create a runspace, use the static `CreateRunspace()` method of the `RunspaceFactory` class. You can't create an instance using "new"' because `Runspace` is actually a base class that defines the interface, and the object you get back from `CreateRunspace` is an instance of a derived class called `LocalRunspace`. This is to enable future expansion of the engine API, but with PowerShell 1.0 you always deal with `LocalRunspaces`.

`CreateRunspace()` has overloads that enable you to pass in `RunspaceConfiguration` and `Host` objects, but for this example don't pass `CreateRunspace()` any arguments — we'll use the default host and configuration for now:

```
Runspace runspace = RunspaceFactory.CreateRunspace();
```

Now that you have an instance of `Runspace`, the next step is to call `Open()` on the runspace to set it in a state that allows execution. The runspace can actually create pipelines before it's opened, but if you try to execute a pipeline from a runspace that hasn't been opened, an exception will be thrown. Here is the call to `Open()`:

```
runspace.Open();
```

The `Runspace` class has a method called `CreatePipeline()` that creates and returns a `Pipeline` object. For this example, we'll use the overload of `CreatePipeline()`, which accepts a script block as a string.

PowerShell's parser converts the string to a parse tree automatically. Another overload of `CreatePipeline()` is available, which takes no arguments and returns an empty pipeline, and which can be programmatically constructed from `Command` objects, but this is discussed later in the chapter. For now, we'll just create a pipeline from a string:

```
Pipeline pipeline = runspace.CreatePipeline("calc");
```

A second overload of `CreatePipeline()` accepts a script block and a Boolean parameter that indicates whether the script block should be added to the command history of the runspace. If this parameter is omitted or set to `false`, the script block will not be added to the history. Only if it is explicitly specified as `true` will the history be modified. Pipelines created with this parameter set to `true` are recorded in the command history of the runspace when they are invoked and can be retrieved later using the `*-history` cmdlets.

To execute the pipeline, call the pipeline's `Invoke()` method. The `Invoke()` method blocks until execution of the pipeline has completed, after which control returns to the calling program. Another overload of `Invoke()` accepts a collection of input objects, and a nonblocking invoke method called `InvokeAsync()` is also available, but these are discussed later in the chapter. For now, we'll call `Invoke()` with no arguments. If you compile and run this, an instance of `calc.exe` should appear on your desktop:

```
pipeline.Invoke();
```

Because the `"calc"` command is at the end of the pipeline and is a GUI application, the PowerShell engine won't wait for it to finish executing before returning from `Invoke()`. The same behavior can be observed from the PowerShell command line — if you type **calc** and press Enter, `calc.exe` opens but PowerShell immediately returns to the prompt. If you recompile with the script block `"[Threading.Thread]::Sleep(15000)"` instead of `"calc"`, you will see that `Invoke()` takes fifteen seconds to return.

Here is the complete code for this example:

```
using System;
using System.Management.Automation;
using System.Management.Automation.Runspaces;

namespace PSBook.Chapter6
{
    class Sample1
    {
        static void Main(string[] args)
        {
            // Create and open a runspace that uses the default host
            Runspace runspace = RunspaceFactory.CreateRunspace();
            runspace.Open();

            // Create a pipeline that runs the script block "calc"
            Pipeline pipeline = runspace.CreatePipeline("calc");

            // Run it
            pipeline.Invoke();
        }
    }
}
```

Using the Output of a Pipeline

Usually, when you run a command in the shell, it produces output. Commands in traditional shells produce their output as text, and PowerShell commands produce their output as objects. The output of a command is written to one or more *streams* or *pipes* of output. In traditional environments such as DOS and Unix, a command has an output stream and an error stream. PowerShell follows this model, and a PowerShell pipeline has an output pipe and an error pipe.

If you use the PowerShell engine API to invoke a pipeline, in many cases your calling program needs to receive and process the pipeline's output. This section describes how you can retrieve this output from synchronous and asynchronous pipeline invocations.

The Return Value of Invoke()

The `Invoke()` method of the `Pipeline` class has a return type of `Collection<PSObject>`, which means it returns a generic collection of `PSObject` objects. This is where the first and third "using" directives described in the previous section come into play. `PSObject` is declared in the `System.Management.Automation` namespace, and `Collection<T>` comes from `System.Collections.ObjectModel`.

The `Invoke()` method returns a collection of `PSObject` objects, rather than raw .NET objects, because the PowerShell environment allows you to decorate objects with arbitrary properties and methods, and `PSObject` provides an extended interface by which these extensions can be used.

To retrieve the collection returned by `Invoke()`, just define a new variable of type `Collection<PSObject>` and assign `Invoke()`'s return value to it, as shown here:

```
Collection<PSObject> results = pipeline.Invoke();
```

Once the pipeline has finished and the result has been retrieved, you can enumerate it:

```
foreach (PSObject thisResult in results) {...}
```

Using PSObject Objects Returned from a Pipeline

When using the results of `Invoke()`, it's tempting to go straight to the `BaseObject` property of the `PSObject` object and treat everything like a native .NET object. There are a couple of reasons you should avoid this, however.

First, depending on the script block that was executed to produce the set of results, the resulting objects may have been decorated with properties and methods that are inaccessible from the `BaseObject`. To access these members, you need to do so by proxy, through the `Properties` and `Methods` collections of the `PSObject` class.

Second, depending on the implementation of the runspace, the `BaseObject` might not exist, or it might be of a wholly unexpected type. In PowerShell version 1, the only kind of runspace is `LocalRunspace`, but someday your code could find itself parsing a collection of `PSObject` objects from another implementation of `Runspace` that returns deserialized objects, or objects that are completely implemented via `PSObject` methods and properties. Unless your code accesses the members through the interface that `PSObject` exposes, it can malfunction.

Handling Terminating Errors

In the style of traditional Unix and DOS command-line applications, PowerShell pipelines output non-terminating error information through an error pipe. However, terminating errors from commands, parsing failures, and other engine errors are surfaced to the hosting application through managed exceptions during the call to `Invoke()`. In general, errors are wrapped in instances of `System.Management.Automation.RuntimeException`, so the call to `Invoke()` should be wrapped in a `try...catch` block:

```
Collection<PSObject> results = null;
try
{
    results = pipeline.Invoke();
}
catch (RuntimeException e)
{
    ...
}
```

The following example shows a host application that creates a pipeline, retrieves the results of the asynchronous `Invoke()` call, handles `RuntimeExceptions` thrown by the PowerShell engine, and writes the `BaseObject` of each result to the console:

```
using System;
using System.Collections.ObjectModel;
using System.Management.Automation;
using System.Management.Automation.Runspaces;

namespace PSBook.Chapter6
{
    class Sample2
    {
        static void Main(string[] args)
        {
            // Create and open a runspace that uses the default host
            Runspace runspace = RunspaceFactory.CreateRunspace();
            runspace.Open();

            // Create a pipeline that runs a script block
            Pipeline pipeline = runspace.CreatePipeline("dir c:\\");

            // Invoke the pipeline in a try...catch and save the
            // collection returned by Invoke()
            Collection<PSObject> results = null;
            try
            {
                results = pipeline.Invoke();
            }
            catch (RuntimeException e)
            {
                // Display a message and exit if a RuntimeException is thrown
                Console.WriteLine("Exception during Invoke(): {0}, {1}",
                                  e.GetType().Name, e.Message);
                return;
            }
```

```
                // Display the BaseObject of every PSObject returned by Invoke()
                foreach (PSObject thisResult in results)
                {
                    Console.WriteLine("Result is: {0}", thisResult.BaseObject);
                }
            }
        }
    }
```

Input, Output, and Errors for Synchronous Pipelines

The `Pipeline` class provides three properties, `Input`, `Output`, and `Error`, which enable a hosting application to provide input and receive output and non-terminating errors. In addition to the `Input` property, input can be passed as an `IEnumerable` collection to the synchronous `Invoke()` method.

The input pipe is an instance of the `System.Management.Automation.Internal.ObjectWriter` class, and provides a `Write()` method for adding objects to the pipeline. The `Write()` method is type-agnostic regarding the input object, so objects of any type can be passed to it.

The output pipe is an instance of the `System.Management.Automation.Internal.PSObjectReader` class. It provides methods for synchronous and asynchronous reading, peek, and read-to-end operations. Because the output pipe returns its results as `PSObject` objects, rather than native .NET objects, the read methods are strongly typed to return `PSObject` objects and generic collections of `PSObject`.

The error pipe is an instance of the `System.Management.Automation.Internal.ObjectReader` class. Like the input pipe, it is type-agnostic, so its read methods return `Object` and generic collections of `Object`. In practice, however, objects returned by the error pipe will usually be of type `System.Management.Automation.ErrorRecord`.

Passing Input to Your Pipeline

To pass input to a synchronously executed pipeline, you can add the input to a collection that implements `IEnumerable` and pass it to the pipeline's `Invoke()` method. However, if your pipeline was created directly from a script block, as in the previous examples, the input won't be automatically piped into the first command in the script block, but will be provided to the script block as the `$input` variable. Later in the chapter, you will learn how to programmatically build a pipeline from individual commands, in which case the input is sent directly to the first command. Until then, here is the code for sending input to a synchronous pipeline created from a script block:

```
Pipeline pipeline = runspace.CreatePipeline("$input | sort-object");
Collection<int> input = new Collection<int>;
input.Add(3);
input.Add(1);
input.Add(2);
pipeline.Invoke(input);
```

In this example, notice that the input is piped to the `sort-object` cmdlet by adding the `$input` variable to the beginning of the pipeline.

You also can use the `Pipeline` class's `Input` property to individually pipe objects into the pipeline. The utility of this isn't immediately apparent when you're invoking the pipeline synchronously, but when we discuss asynchronous execution later in the chapter, you can see the difference. For now, to use the `Input` property to pass objects to the pipeline, simply use the `Input.Write()` method before the pipeline is invoked:

```
Pipeline pipeline = runspace.CreatePipeline("$input | sort-object");
pipeline.Input.Write(3);
pipeline.Input.Write(1);
pipeline.Input.Write(2);
pipeline.Invoke();
```

The input pipe is an instance of the `PipelineWriter` class. Besides the `Write()` method you've already seen, another overload of `Write` enables you to write a collection and expand it. The following example writes an entire array to the pipe, one element at a time:

```
Pipeline pipeline = runspace.CreatePipeline("$input | sort-object");
int[] numbers = {3, 2, 1};
pipeline.Input.Write(numbers, true);
pipeline.Invoke();
```

The Output Pipe in Synchronous Execution

For synchronously invoked pipelines, all output is collected in the return value of the synchronous `Invoke()` method, so after the call to `Invoke()`, `Output.Read()` never returns anything. The `Read()` methods of the output pipe can be called prior to synchronous invocation as well, but for obvious reasons this also never returns any results. Later in the chapter, you will learn about asynchronous invocation, and you will be able to see how objects can be read from the output pipe while the pipeline is executing.

Retrieving Non-Terminating Errors from the Error Pipe

In contrast to the output pipe, during synchronous invocation, the contents of the error pipe are not aggregated in a collection and must be read using the error pipe's read methods. Non-terminating errors are analogous to messages written to the `stderr` pipe of a console application. PowerShell has expanded on this concept, and returns non-terminating errors as `ErrorRecord` objects, which contain details such as the error message; the exception, if any, that originated the error; and a unique error identifier that can be used during debugging to identify the exact line of code that wrote the error into the error pipe.

After an asynchronous `Invoke()`, non-terminating errors are read from the error pipe using the `Non-BlockingRead()`, `Read()`, `Peek()`, and `ReadToEnd()` methods. Calling `ReadToEnd()` will retrieve all of the available errors in a generic collection, or the `EndOfPipeline` property can be used by a hosting application for iterating through the errors:

```
pipeline.Invoke();
while (!pipeline.Error.EndOfPipeline)
{
    ErrorRecord thisError = pipeline.Error.Read() as ErrorRecord;
    if (thisError != null) {...}
}
```

The ErrorRecord Type

Errors returned from a Pipeline object's error pipe are packaged as instances of ErrorRecord. ErrorRecord contains a great deal of information to help developers and end users diagnose failures. Depending on the needs of your hosting application, you may choose to display only the minimal information provided by the ErrorRecord's ToString() method, you can retrieve detailed information from the object, as provided by the CategoryProperty class, or you can, in some cases, retrieve information as specific as the stack trace of the exception that originated the error.

The following example shows a host application that runs the script block "get-childitem hklm:\". Because the HKEY_LOCAL_MACHINE Registry key contains a subkey called Security, whose default ACL prevents it from being opened by users, running the script block produces a set of PSObject results interrupted by one non-terminating error, which is retrieved and displayed to the user:

```
using System;
using System.Management.Automation;
using System.Management.Automation.Runspaces;

namespace PSBook.Chapter6
{
    class Sample4
    {
        static void Main(string[] args)
        {
            // Create and open a runspace that uses the default host
            Runspace runspace = RunspaceFactory.CreateRunspace();
            runspace.Open();

            // Create a pipeline that enumerates hklm:\
            Pipeline pipeline = runspace.CreatePipeline("get-childitem hklm:\\");

            // Invoke the pipeline
            pipeline.Invoke();
            // Display errors from the error pipe
            while (!pipeline.Error.EndOfPipeline)
            {
                Console.WriteLine("Error: {0}", pipeline.Error.Read());
            }
        }
    }
}
```

Other Pipeline Tricks

The runspace and pipeline object model puts some limitations on host applications. This section demonstrates some ways in which you can work around concurrency and reuse issues you might face while developing your custom host.

Nested Pipelines

One limitation of the PowerShell engine is its inability to execute two pipelines in a runspace concurrently. This stems from the lack of thread safety in the runspace instance's session state. Pipelines running concurrently in one runspace could easily modify the same variables, drive mappings, and so on, and conflict with each other. Rather than take on the expense of ensuring thread safety in session state, a design decision was made to throw an exception when an application attempts to invoke a pipeline while another is already running in the same runspace.

Note a caveat to this, however: If a pipeline is synchronously invoked from an already running pipeline, then the existing pipeline is guaranteed to be blocked until the new one is finished executing. This allows for the new concept of a *nested pipeline*. The `Runspace` type provides two overloads of a method called `CreateNestedPipeline()`, which creates a `Pipeline` object that can be called from the thread of a pipeline that's already running.

A practical example of this is the nested prompt functionality of the PowerShell host. When a cmdlet prompts for user input, it can offer the option of entering a nested prompt. If the user selects this option, they are dropped into a new command prompt; and when they exit this prompt, they return to the cmdlet's prompt. Without the nested pipeline functionality, this behavior would be impossible.

The overloads of `CreateNestedPipeline()` are similar to those of `CreatePipeline()`. You can either create an empty pipeline and programmatically populate it with commands, or you can specify a script block and a Boolean history parameter. Once you've created the nested pipeline, if you try to execute it outside of a running pipeline's thread, then an exception is thrown. An exception is also thrown if you attempt to execute the pipeline asynchronously, via the pipeline's `InvokeAsync()` method. In addition, if a pipeline is created using `CreateNestedPipeline()`, then its `IsNested` property will return `true`.

Reusing Pipelines

Once a pipeline has been invoked, that instance can never be invoked again. However, any pipeline, regardless of its state, can be duplicated using the pipeline type's `Copy()` method. This effectively makes a pipeline reusable, as an endless number of exact copies can be made. The following example creates a pipeline to check whether a filesystem path exists, and invokes it every 100 milliseconds until it returns `true`:

```
Pipeline pipeline = runspace.CreatePipeline("test-path x:\\");
while ($true)
{
    foreach (PSObject thisResult in pipeline.Copy().Invoke())
        if ((bool)thisResult.BaseObject)
            return true;
    Thread.Sleep(100);
}
```

This allows a pipeline to be constructed, stored, passed around by reference, and finally executed from another code block that needn't contain the logic to rebuild the pipeline. For instance, a pipeline could be created, set aside, and then passed to an event handler for execution.

Copying a Pipeline Between Runspaces

The engine API in PowerShell 1.0 doesn't have a built-in mechanism for copying a pipeline from one runspace to another, but an application developer can accomplish this simply by copying the `Commands` collection from one pipeline to another one in a different runspace. The following code performs such a copy operation:

```
Pipeline oldPipeline = oldRunspace.CreatePipeline();
...
Pipeline newPipeline = newRunspace.CreatePipeline();
foreach (Command thisCommand in oldPipeline.Commands)
{
    newPipeline.Commands.Add(thisCommand);
}
```

Because the state of the `Command` objects in the `Commands` collection doesn't change when the runspace is invoked, the new pipeline can be invoked in the new runspace as though it were originally constructed there.

Configuring Your Runspace

Until now, the runspace instances we've created have all used the default set of cmdlets, providers, initialization scripts, and formatting information provided when you call `CreateRunspace()` with no arguments. In the previous section, for example, the runspace we created is pre-configured with the `get-childitem` cmdlet and the Registry Provider. No additional step is required to make the cmdlet or provider available to the script block.

When authoring a custom host application, however, the PowerShell engine gives developers control over the initial configuration of their runspace via the `RunspaceConfiguration` class, which is passed to `CreateRunspace()`. After a runspace has been created, variables in the runspace's session state can be set and retrieved using the `SessionStateProxy` property of the `Runspace` class.

After you create a runspace instance, the runspace's configuration is exposed by its `RunspaceConfiguration` property. While the runspace is in the `BeforeOpen` state, you can still change the configuration, but not all changes to `RunspaceConfiguration` will be reflected in the runspace if the changes are made after the runspace has been opened. Specifically, calls to `AddPSSnapin()` and `RemovePSSnapin()` are honored after the runspace is open, but direct changes to the `Assemblies`, `Cmdlets`, `Formats`, `Scripts`, and `Types` collections are not.

Creating a Runspace with a Custom Configuration

To create a runspace instance with a custom configuration, you must first construct a `RunspaceConfiguration` object. The `System.Management.Automation.Runspaces.RunspaceConfiguration` class provides a static method called `Create()`, whose overloads enable you to create a basic configuration, create a configuration from a snap-in assembly, or create a configuration from a PowerShell console file.

However you choose to create your `RunspaceConfiguration`, the resulting object is always pre-loaded with PowerShell's cmdlets, providers, and other configuration information. These are exposed as collection properties on the `RunspaceConfiguration` class, however, and these collections can be programmatically emptied if need be.

Adding and Removing Snap-Ins

The recommended practice for deploying cmdlets and providers is to package them in PowerShell snap-ins, which are .NET assemblies containing cmdlet and provider classes. For a complete discussion of creating custom snap-ins for PowerShell, refer to Chapter 2.

To load a snap-in in a `RunspaceConfiguration`, use `RunspaceConfiguration.Create()` with no arguments to create a basic configuration. Then, use the `AddPSSnapIn()` method to add a registered snap-in:

```
RunspaceConfiguration configuration = RunspaceConfiguration.Create();
PSSnapInException warning = null;
configuration.AddPSSnapIn("MySnapIn", out warning);
```

The second parameter to `AddPSSnapIn()` is an `out` parameter that returns an instance of `PSSnapInException` if the call partially fails. If the snap-in cannot be found, or some other fatal error occurs, the call to `AddPSSnapin()` throws an exception.

Once the snap-in has been loaded into the `RunspaceConfiguration`, the configuration can be used to create a runspace instance as shown in the previous section. Snap-ins loaded in a runspace can be removed using the `RemovePSSnapin()` method.

Creating RunspaceConfiguration from a Console File

At creation time, a hosting application can specify a PowerShell console file from which to create a `RunspaceConfiguration` instance. A console file is simply an XML file with the extension `.psc1`, which contains a list of registered PowerShell snap-ins to be loaded into the runspace.

To create a `RunspaceConfiguration` from a console file, call the overload of `RunspaceConfiguration.Create()` with two parameters. The first parameter is the filename of the console file to load, and the second is an `out` parameter of type `PSConsoleLoadException`, which returns warnings:

```
PSConsoleLoadException warning = null;
RunspaceConfiguration configuration =
    RunspaceConfiguration.Create("c:\\myconsole.psc1", out warning);
```

As with `AddPSSnapIn`, fatal errors during the call to `Create()` are thrown as exceptions.

Once the console file has been loaded into the `RunspaceConfiguration`, the configuration can be used to create a runspace instance, as described earlier.

Creating RunspaceConfiguration from an Assembly

The `RunspaceConfiguration` type provides a third constructor whose signature is described in the PowerShell SDK documentation, but whose function is not. The constructor takes one parameter — a string containing the strong name of an assembly. This constructor is an artifact of the design churn that occurred when PowerShell was included in and then removed from the Longhorn (now Windows Vista) operating system.

Versioning concerns in Windows Vista required a redesign of the way third-party cmdlets were added to PowerShell, and for a brief period a mechanism was provided for third-party developers to create a "custom shell," a separate console host that would be initialized with a set of cmdlets and providers specified at compile time.

An application called `make-shell.exe` was developed to generate custom shells, and significant effort was invested in developing a serialization system by which objects generated by one custom shell could be converted to XML and reconstituted by another custom shell, resulting in an imperfect, but functional, means of marshalling objects between unrelated third-party cmdlets.

The custom shell design was eventually sidelined and replaced by PowerShell snap-ins, but the plumbing for it was never completely removed. `Make-shell.exe` is still available in the PowerShell SDK, and this third, enigmatic constructor for `RunspaceConfiguration` is part of the custom shell design.

Using SessionStateProxy to Set and Retrieve Variables

After a runspace has been created, a hosting application can use the `SessionStateProxy` property of the runspace to read and set the variables in the runspace instance's session state. The `SessionStateProxy` property is an instance of `System.Management.Automation.Runspaces.SessionStateProxy`, which provides the methods `SetVariable()` and `GetVariable()`.

The `SetVariable()` method accepts a variable name as a string and a value as an object, and uses them to set the value of a variable in `SessionState`. The variable name is provided in the same form as it appears on the PowerShell command line, without the leading `$` character.

The `GetVariable()` method accepts a variable name as a string and returns the value of the variable as an object. If the variable is not defined, the method returns `null`.

Both `SessionStateProxy` methods can accept a variable whose name specifies a scope, such as `global:x`.

The following code illustrates how a hosting application can use `SessionStateProxy` to pass data to and from the session state of a runspace:

```
// Create a Runspace
Runspace runspace = RunspaceFactory.CreateRunspace();
runspace.Open();

// Set two variables in session state
runspace.SessionStateProxy.SetVariable("factorOne", 7);
runspace.SessionStateProxy.SetVariable("factorTwo", 11);

// Run a pipeline to multiply the variables and store the answer in a third
// variable
runspace.CreatePipeline("$answer = $factorOne * $factorTwo").Invoke();

// Retrieve the result
int answer = (int)runspace.SessionStateProxy.GetVariable("answer");
```

Fine-Tuning RunspaceConfiguration

Typically, custom cmdlets and providers are deployed as members of PowerShell snap-in classes. However, for applications that need a more granular level of control, the `RunspaceConfiguration` class provides several collection properties that enable different configuration elements to be added and removed "a la carte." The following table lists the collections and the corresponding configuration entry classes that can be added to them.

Collection	Configuration Entry Class	Description
Assemblies	AssemblyConfigurationEntry	Loaded snap-in assemblies
Cmdlets	CmdletConfigurationEntry	Loaded cmdlets
Formats	FormatConfigurationEntry	Output formatting files
InitializationScripts	ScriptConfigurationEntry	Scripts run when the runspace is opened
Scripts	ScriptConfigurationEntry	Functions to define in the global scope
Providers	ProviderConfigurationEntry	Loaded providers
Types	TypeConfigurationEntry	Extended type data files

Each of these properties returns a `RunspaceConfigurationEntryCollection` object, which contains methods for adding and removing entries, clearing the collection, and committing changes to the collection.

Adding a Configuration Collection Entry

Entries can be added to the configuration collections individually or in groups, and they can be added to the beginning or the end of the list. The four methods for adding entries are as follows:

```
Append(T)
Append(IEnumerable<T>)
Prepend(T)
Prepend(IEnumerable<T>)
```

Before you can add an entry to the collection, however, you have to create an instance of it.

Removing a Configuration Collection Entry

Individual entries or ranges of entries can be removed from a configuration collection. The methods for removing entries are as follows:

```
RemoveItem(int index)
RemoveItem(int index, int count)
```

Indexes or ranges that exceed the bounds of the collection will cause `IndexOutOfRangeException` to be thrown.

Clearing a Configuration Collection

The entire contents of a collection can be cleared by calling the `Reset()` method. This is particularly useful if you want to create a runspace without the default PowerShell configuration elements loaded. The following code demonstrates how to create such a runspace:

```
Runspace runspace = RunspaceFactory.CreateRunspace();
runspace.RunspaceConfiguration.Cmdlets.Reset();
runspace.RunspaceConfiguration.Scripts.Reset();
runspace.RunspaceConfiguration.Providers.Reset();
runspace.RunspaceConfiguration.Types.Reset();
runspace.Open();
```

Committing Changes to a Configuration Collection

Changes to a configuration collection don't take effect in the runspace until the `Update()` method of the collection is called. This method is called automatically when a snap-in is added or removed, or it can be called directly by the hosting application.

Adding a Cmdlet

The constructor for a `CmdletConfigurationEntry` takes three parameters: the name of the cmdlet in verb-noun form, the .NET type that implements the cmdlet, and the name of the help file associated with the cmdlet. If there is no help file, the third parameter can be `null`. The following example shows how to add a cmdlet entry to the `RunspaceConfiguration` of a runspace:

```
runspace.RunspaceConfiguration.Cmdlets.Append(
    new CmdletConfigurationEntry("get-widget",
        typeof(GetWidgetCmdlet), null));
runspace.RunspaceConfiguration.Cmdlets.Update();
```

Once the entry object has been created, the help filename and implementing type are exposed in the `HelpFileName` and `ImplementingType` properties of the class.

Adding a Provider

Adding a provider to a `RunspaceConfiguration` is nearly identical to adding a cmdlet, except that the `ProviderConfigurationEntry` type is used. The constructor for `ProviderConfigurationEntry` takes the name of the provider, the implementing type, and the name of the help file, which can be `null`.

Adding a Formatting File

Formatting files are described in Chapter 8. Adding a formatting file is similar to adding a cmdlet, except you use the `FormatConfigurationEntry` class and you have the choice of two constructors. The first constructor takes a single string that indicates the filename, and the second constructor takes two strings for the filename and the name of the entry, which is exposed in a property inherited from its base class:

```
runspace.RunspaceConfiguration.Formats.Append(
    new FormatConfigurationEntry("c:\\myformats.ps1xml");
runspace.RunspaceConfiguration.Cmdlets.Update();
```

Adding a Type File

Adding a type file is identical to adding a format file, except that the corresponding `TypeConfigurationEntry` class and `Types` collection are used instead of `FormatConfigurationEntry` and `Formats`.

Adding a Function

Global functions can be defined in a `RunspaceConfiguration` before it is used to create a runspace. To define a function, create a `ScriptConfigurationEntry` by passing the name of the function and the function's definition to its constructor, and then add the entry to the `Scripts` collection of the `RunspaceConfiguration`:

```
runspace.RunspaceConfiguration.Scripts.Append(
    new ScriptConfigurationEntry("add", "return $args[0]+$args[1]");
runspace.RunspaceConfiguration.Cmdlets.Update();
```

If a function is added to the `RunspaceConfiguration` of an opened runspace, it will be ignored. In addition, once a `ScriptConfigurationEntry` has been created, its definition can be retrieved from the `Definition` property.

Running a Pipeline Asynchronously

As the complexity of your application increases, it may eventually be necessary to be able to run a pipeline asynchronously while the application's main thread interacts with the user or with other resources. The threading capabilities of the .NET API already make this possible, even if you continue to use the synchronous `Invoke()` method, as you can create a new thread, and then use it to perform all of the runspace interactions.

However, suppose you're performing a time-consuming operation in the pipeline and it produces a steady stream of output objects as it executes. In order for the application to be truly interactive, it must read and render the output objects as they become available from the pipeline's output pipe. It also needs to allow the user to cancel the operation while it is being executed. With the synchronous `Invoke()` method, this isn't possible, as the output objects are accumulated in a collection and returned to the calling method at the end of the operation.

The `Pipeline` class provides another invoke method, `InvokeAsync()`, which is the key to asynchronously executing a pipeline.

Calling InvokeAsync()

The prerequisites for calling `InvokeAsync()` are identical to those for calling `Invoke()`. You must first create a runspace, and then open the runspace and create a pipeline. The `Runspace` class has an asynchronous counterpart to `Open()` called `OpenAsync()`; however, the runspace state that results from calling either of these methods is the same, so you needn't open your runspace with `OpenAsync()` in order to use `InvokeAsync()`. The following code will create a pipeline and invoke it asynchronously:

```
Runspace runspace = RunspaceFactory.CreateRunspace();
runspace.Open();
Pipeline pipeline = runspace.CreatePipeline(
                                "gps | foreach {sleep 1; $_}");
pipeline.InvokeAsync();
```

The script block in this example runs the `get-process` cmdlet and pauses for one second after each object it produces.

Closing the Input Pipe

If you compile and execute the preceding example, you'll find a counterintuitive quirk of the API: No matter how long you leave the pipeline running, no objects will appear in the output pipe. That's because after you call `InvokeAsync()`, execution of the pipeline is actually suspended until you close the input pipe. If you modify the code as follows, the pipeline will execute:

```
Runspace runspace = RunspaceFactory.CreateRunspace();
runspace.Open();
Pipeline pipeline = runspace.CreatePipeline(
                            "gps | foreach {sleep 1; $_}");
pipeline.InvokeAsync();
pipeline.Input.Close();
```

Calling `Close()` on the input pipe while it's already closed won't throw an exception, but you can check the state of the pipe using the `PipelineWriter` class's `IsOpen` property.

Reading Output and Error from an Asynchronous Pipeline

At this point, if the script block you're running in the pipeline has some effect other than writing objects, then you'll be able to see it, but you still haven't received the output of the pipeline. The next step is to read objects from the running pipeline's output and error pipes.

The `Output` and `Error` properties of the pipeline are instances of the generic `PipelineReader<T>` class, which contains methods for detecting when objects are available and for reading the available objects in several different ways. The following table lists the methods you can use to read objects from `PipelineReader`.

Method	Description
Read()	Reads one object and blocks if it isn't available
Read(count)	Reads "count" objects and blocks until all are read
ReadToEnd()	Reads until the pipe is closed
Peek()	Checks whether any objects are available to read
NonBlockingRead()	Reads one object and returns immediately if there isn't one
NonBlockingRead(count)	Reads "count" objects and returns immediately if there aren't enough

`PipelineReader` also provides a `WaitHandle` property, which can be used to wait for output, and an event, `DataReady`, which is raised when output is available.

Reading from Multiple Pipes with WaitHandle

If your application can spare a thread, or if it's implemented in a language (like PowerShell script) that can't manage event handling, then you can use the `WaitHandle` property of `PipelineReader` to wait for data from one or more `PipelineReader` instances.

The `System.Threading.WaitHandle` class provides a static method, `WaitAny()`, that waits for data on one or more `WaitHandle` objects. The following sample invokes a pipeline asynchronously and uses `WaitHandle` to read from its output and error pipes in the same thread:

```
using System;
using System.Collections.ObjectModel;
using System.Management.Automation;
using System.Management.Automation.Runspaces;
using System.Threading;
namespace CustomHostConsoleApp1
{
    class Program
    {
        static void Main(string[] args)
        {
            // Create a runspace
            Runspace runspace = RunspaceFactory.CreateRunspace();
            runspace.Open();
            // Create a pipeline
            Pipeline pipeline = runspace.CreatePipeline("1..10 | foreach {$_; write-
error $_; start-sleep 1}");

            // Read output and error until the pipeline finishes
            pipeline.InvokeAsync();
            WaitHandle[] handles = new WaitHandle[2];
            handles[0] = pipeline.Output.WaitHandle;
            handles[1] = pipeline.Error.WaitHandle;
            pipeline.Input.Close();
            while (pipeline.PipelineStateInfo.State == PipelineState.Running)
            {
                switch (WaitHandle.WaitAny(handles))
                {
                    case 0:
                        while (pipeline.Output.Count > 0)
                        {
                            Console.WriteLine("Output: {0}", pipeline.Output.Read());
                        }
                        break;
                    case 1:
                        while (pipeline.Error.Count > 0)
                        {
                            Console.WriteLine("Error: {0}", pipeline.Error.Read());
                        }
                        break;
                }
            }
        }
    }
}
```

Using this approach avoids the thread synchronization issues the application will face during truly asynchronous, event-driven operation. For example, if the output of two pipelines is being aggregated into one collection, then you don't have to worry about two event threads touching the collection at the same time. However, the trade-off is that you have to dedicate a thread to reading the output.

Reading from PipelineReader with the DataReady Event

Output from `PipelineReader` also can be read by subscribing to the `PipelineReader`'s `DataReady` event. To do this, the hosting application should create a delegate, and then add the delegate to the event. The following example behaves identically to the previous example, except it uses the `DataReady` event. Note that the same delegate can subscribe to events from both pipes as long as it has a means of differentiating between them:

```
using System;
using System.Collections.ObjectModel;
using System.Management.Automation;
using System.Management.Automation.Runspaces;
using System.Threading;
namespace MultiplePipeReader2
{
    class Program
    {
        static void Main(string[] args)
        {
            // Create a runspace
            Runspace runspace = RunspaceFactory.CreateRunspace();
            runspace.Open();
            // Create a pipeline
            Pipeline pipeline = runspace.CreatePipeline("1..10 | foreach {$_; write-
error $_; start-sleep 1}");

            // Subscribe to the DataReady events of the pipes
            pipeline.Output.DataReady += new EventHandler(HandleDataReady);
            pipeline.Error.DataReady += new EventHandler(HandleDataReady);

            // Start the pipeline
            pipeline.InvokeAsync();
            pipeline.Input.Close();

            // Do important things in the main thread
            do
            {
                Thread.Sleep(1000);
                Console.Title = string.Format("Time: {0}", DateTime.Now);
            } while (pipeline.PipelineStateInfo.State == PipelineState.Running);
        }

        static void HandleDataReady(object sender, EventArgs e)
        {
            PipelineReader<PSObject> output = sender as PipelineReader<PSObject>;
```

```
                if (output != null)
                {
                    while (output.Count > 0)
                    {
                        Console.WriteLine("Output: {0}", output.Read());
                    }
                    return;
                }

                PipelineReader<object> error = sender as PipelineReader<object>;
                if (error != null)
                {
                    while (error.Count > 0)
                    {
                        Console.WriteLine("Error: {0}", error.Read());
                    }
                    return;
                }
            }
        }
    }
```

The pipeline's error pipe provides nearly the same interface as the output pipe and can be read in the same manner; the only difference is the type of the objects returned from the pipe. Output always returns instances of `PSObject`, whereas error can return any type of object.

Until the event handler returns, pipeline execution is blocked. In addition, when the pipeline completes and the pipe is closed, a final event is raised, which doesn't correspond to an object being written to the pipe. Because of this, the event handler should verify that an object is available from the pipe before reading it.

Monitoring a Pipeline's StateChanged Event

In the asynchronous examples presented so far, the pipeline has been executing independently of the application's main thread, but the main thread has still been servicing the pipeline while it executes. For true asynchronous operation, you need to completely divorce the pipeline from the application's main thread.

As you've seen, the output and error pipes provide events that are raised when objects are written to the pipes. The pipeline also provides an event that is raised when pipeline state changes occur. A hosting application that subscribes to all of these events can process them completely independently of the main thread.

The pipeline's `StateChanged` event is raised immediately after the pipeline's state changes. The pipeline's state can be read from the `PipelineStateInfo` property, which is an instance of the `PipelineStateInfo` type. This type exposes a property called `Reason`, which contains the exception, if any, that caused the last state change, and a `State` property, which is a value of the `PipelineState` enum. The following table lists the members of this enum.

PipelineState enum Members	Description
NotStarted	The pipeline has been instantiated but not invoked
Running	The pipeline has been invoked and is still running
Stopping	Either `Stop()` or `StopAsync()` was called, and the pipeline is stopping
Stopped	The pipeline was programmatically stopped
Completed	The pipeline finished without error
Failed	A terminating error occurred

When the pipeline is invoked, its state changes to `Running`. If the pipeline succeeds, the state will eventually change to `Completed`; and if a terminating error occurs, it will change to `Failed`. The following example illustrates how an application can subscribe to the `StateChanged` event of a pipeline:

```
Pipeline pipeline = runspace.CreatePipeline("dir");
pipeline.StateChanged +=
       new EventHandler<PipelineStateEventArgs>(pipeline_StateChanged);
pipeline.InvokeAsync();
...
static void pipeline_StateChanged(object sender,
                                  PipelineStateEventArgs e)
{
    Pipeline pipeline = sender as Pipeline;
    Console.WriteLine("State: {0}", pipeline.PipelineStateInfo.State);
}
```

In an application where multiple pipelines are in use, a single event handler can register for the `StateChanged` event and differentiate between the pipelines using the `InstanceId` property of the `Pipeline` type. This is a long integer that is guaranteed to be unique within the pipeline's runspace. In addition, the runspace to which the pipeline belongs can be retrieved from the `Runspace` property.

Reading Terminating Errors via PipelineStateInfo.Reason

When you call the synchronous `Invoke()` method, terminating errors such as parsing errors, pipeline state errors, exceptions thrown by cmdlets, and explicit cmdlet calls to the `ThrowTerminatingError()` method are surfaced to the hosting application by an exception thrown during the call. When an application calls the pipeline's `InvokeAsync()` method, returning terminating errors this way isn't possible because they can occur at any point after the call to `InvokeAsync()` has returned.

When a terminating error occurs in an asynchronous pipeline, the pipeline's state is changed to `Failed` and the pipeline's `StateChanged` event is raised. The Reason property of the `PipelineStateInfo` object contains an `ErrorRecord` with information about the terminating error, which can be retrieved by the event handler.

The following code shows a `StateChanged` event handler that retrieves and displays a terminating error from an asynchronously invoked pipeline:

```
static void pipeline_StateChanged(object sender,
                                  PipelineStateEventArgs e)
{
    Pipeline pipeline = sender as Pipeline;
    if (pipeline.PipelineStateInfo.State == PipelineState.Failed)
    {
        MessageBox.Show(
                pipeline.PipelineStateInfo.Reason.ToString(), "Error");
    }
}
```

Stopping a Running Pipeline

Occasionally, a hosting application that is running an asynchronous pipeline will need to stop the pipeline before it completes by itself. To allow for this, `Pipeline` has methods called `Stop()` and `StopAsync()`. The `Stop()` method blocks until the pipeline finishes stopping, and the `StopAsync()` method initiates a stop, but returns immediately.

When `Stop()` or `StopAsync()` are called, the pipeline's state is changed to `Stopping` and the `StateChanged` event is raised. If the pipeline's thread is in a callout to external code, such as a .NET method, the pipeline remains in the `Stopping` state indefinitely, waiting for the call to return. Once the pipeline is successfully stopped, the state moves to `Stopped`.

Asynchronous Runspace Operations

The `Runspace` type exposes asynchronous functionality similar to that of the `Pipeline` class. Runspaces can be opened without blocking, and the `Runspace` type provides a host application with events to signal state changes, so the life cycle of a runspace can be managed in an asynchronous manner.

The OpenAsync() Method

At the beginning of this chapter, you were introduced to the `Open()` method of the `Runspace` class. You may have wondered why, if every runspace needs to be opened before it can be used, doesn't `RunspaceFactory` simply produce instances of `Runspace` that are already open? The answer to this is two-fold.

First, as discussed at the beginning of the chapter, `CreateRunspace()` actually returns an instance of the `LocalRunspace` class, which derives from the `Runspace` base class. A `LocalRunspace` instance in the `BeforeOpen` state contains all of the information required to set up the runspace, but much of the heavy lifting involved in loading snap-ins and initializing providers hasn't been done. Creating a `LocalRunspace` in the `BeforeOpen` state is relatively lightweight in terms of CPU time and memory, compared to setting it to the `Opened` state. In the `Opened` state, the memory footprint of `LocalRunspace` with the default host and configuration is larger than the same in the `BeforeOpen` state by a factor of about 30. By deferring your call to `Open()`, you can create runspaces containing a full set of configuration information, but avoid allocating resources until you're ready to use them.

In future versions of PowerShell, another derivation of `Runspace` might contain information for connection to a remote computer or process in the `BeforeOpen` state, for example, but not actually establish the connection until it moves to the `Opened` state.

The second reason for not returning opened runspaces from `RunspaceFactory` is to support the `OpenAsync()` method, which allows a hosting application's main thread to open a runspace with a non-blocking call and monitor the progress of the call and any errors via the runspace's `StateChanged` event.

Handling the Runspace's StateChanged Event

Like the pipeline's `StateChanged` event, the runspace's `StateChanged` event is raised immediately after the state of the runspace changes. An event handler that subscribes to the event can retrieve the new state of the runspace from the runspace's `RunspaceStateInfo` property.

The `RunspaceStateInfo` property is an instance of the `RunspaceStateInfo` class. `RunspaceStateInfo` provides the current state of the runspace via its `State` property, which is of type `RunspaceState`, as well as an exception in the `Reason` property. Constructors for `RunspaceStateInfo` will most likely not be used by application developers, but variants allow creation from an existing `RunspaceStateInfo`, a `RunspaceState`, or a `RunspaceState` and an `Exception`. `RunspaceStateInfo` also implements `ICloneable`, so an instance of it can be duplicated using the `Clone()` method.

The following list shows the possible states of a `Runspace` instance, which are defined in the `RunspaceState` enum:

- **BeforeOpen:** The runspace has been instantiated but not opened.
- **Broken:** An error has occurred and the runspace is no longer functional. In this case, the `Reason` property of `RunspaceStateInfo` will be populated.
- **Closed:** The runspace has been explicitly closed by the application.
- **Closing:** The `CloseAsync()` method has been called and the runspace is in the process of closing.
- **Opened:** The runspace is opened and ready to execute commands.
- **Opening:** The `OpenAsync()` method has been called and the runspace is opening, but it is not yet ready to execute commands.

An intermediate state, Opening, occurs after the call to `Open()` or `OpenAsync()` but before the runspace ultimately reaches the Opened state. Attempting to invoke a pipeline while the runspace is in the Opening state will result in an error, so a hosting application must verify that the state has reached Opened before invoking a pipeline.

Each instance of `Runspace` is assigned a GUID, which is exposed in the runspace's `InstanceId` property. If a `Runspace.StateChanged` event handler subscribes to events from multiple `Runspace` objects, this property can be used to differentiate between them.

Constructing Pipelines Programmatically

The logic provided in the PowerShell engine should be treated as the authoritative "expert" on PowerShell language syntax. Hosting applications should not attempt to replicate this logic outside of the engine; and by extension, hosting applications should never do the work of translating programmatic data to or from PowerShell script.

For example, imagine a .NET application with a WinForms GUI that takes a string via a text box control and passes it as a parameter to a cmdlet invoked in a runspace. A quick-and-dirty way to do this would be to use `String.Format()` to embed the string in a script block, and then execute the script block, as shown here:

```
// *** Never Use This Example ***
// String scriptBlock = String.Format("dir {0}", pathTextBox.Text);
// Pipeline pipeline = runspace.CreatePipeline(scriptBlock);
```

This works well with a simple input case like "`c:\`," but problems arise when the user enters any special characters, such as quotation marks, semicolons, and so on. The wrong sequence of characters can result in anything from a parsing error to unintended execution of a command. The problem becomes much worse if the string comes from an untrusted source, such as a Web page form, as a malicious user could use this to execute arbitrary commands.

Because of this, the PowerShell engine API provides two ways of constructing a pipeline. The first, which you've already used extensively, is to convert a script block directly into a pipeline and execute it. This method is appropriate if you're using a constant string as the script block, or the string comes from the user in whole form, such as in a command-line shell.

The second method is to programmatically build a pipeline from instances of `Command` and `Parameter` objects. Using this method, user input can be received as fully qualified .NET objects and then passed to commands without an intermediate translation into and out of PowerShell script.

Creating an Empty Pipeline

The first step in programmatically building a pipeline is to create an empty instance of the `Pipeline` class. To do this, call the overload of the `CreatePipeline()` method that takes no parameters:

```
Pipeline pipeline = runspace.CreatePipeline();
```

At this point, if you try to invoke the pipeline, either through `Invoke()` or `InvokeAsync()`, a `MethodInvocationException` is thrown. The pipeline must contain at least one command before it can be invoked.

Creating a Command

The `System.Management.Automation.Runspaces.Command` class is instantiated with `new` in C#, and provides three constructors. The first constructor takes a single string parameter, which is analogous to the command token at the beginning of a PowerShell command. The string can be a cmdlet name, the path to a document or executable, an alias, or a function name, and it undergoes the same command discovery sequence that it would if it were being processed in a script block:

```
Command command = new Command("get-childitem");
```

Command discovery does not occur until the pipeline is invoked, however, so the hosting application doesn't need to catch exceptions while creating the `Command` instance.

The other two constructors of `Command` take one and two Boolean parameters, respectively, which indicate that the command is a script, and whether to run the command in the local scope. The SDK documentation touches on this subject rather lightly, so it is expanded on here.

The second and third `Command` constructors, like `CreatePipeline()`, can accept a full script block when they are constructed. In the following example, the first line will successfully create a command from a script block. The second line will create a `Command` instance, but `CommandNotFoundException` will be thrown when the pipeline is invoked because PowerShell will attempt to resolve the entire string as a command name:

```
Command command1 = new Command("get-childitem c:\\", true);
Command command2 = new Command("get-childitem c:\\", false);
```

The third constructor takes an additional Boolean parameter, which indicates whether the command will be run in the local scope. This is analogous to "dot-sourcing" a script on the command line. If `true` is passed to this third parameter, session state changes, such as setting variables, mapping drives, and defining functions, will occur in a temporary local scope and will be lost when the pipeline finishes executing. By default, session state changes are applied to the global scope. The following code illustrates how to create a command whose session state effects only apply to the local scope:

```
Command command = new Command("$myLocalVariable = 1", true, true);
```

Once a command has been created, its text, parameters, whether it is a script, and whether the script should use the local or global scope are exposed in the `Command` object's `CommandText`, `Parameters`, `IsScript`, and `UseLocalScope` properties, respectively.

Merging Command Results

When you construct a pipeline, by default the output of each command goes to the next command's input stream, and the error output of all commands is aggregated in the pipeline's error stream. The `Command` type provides a mechanism by which a command can accept the previous command's error output as input. To do this, set the command's `MergeUnclaimedPreviousCommandResults` property before invoking the pipeline, as shown here:

```
Command commandOne = new Command("dir");
Command commandTwo = new Command("out-file MyLog.txt");
commandTwo.MergeUnclaimedPreviousPropertyResults =
    PipelineResultTypes.Error | PipelineResultTypes.Output;
```

When these commands are added to a pipeline and invoked, the error and output streams of the first command are merged as input for the second command. The property is an instance of the `PipelineResultTypes` enum. The enum contains values `None`, `Error`, and `Output`, but in PowerShell version 1, an error will occur if you specify anything other than one of the following:

- `PipelineResultTypes.None`
- `(PipelineResultTypes.Error | PipelineResultTypes.Output)`

Another mechanism is provided for doing the same from the perspective of the first command in the pipeline. By calling the first command's `MergeMyResults` method, you can merge the first command's error output into the input of the second command, as shown here:

```
Command commandOne = new Command("dir");
commandOne.MergeMyResults(PipelineResultTypes.Error,
    PipelineResultTypes.Output);
Command commandTwo = new Command("out-file MyLog.txt");
```

Again, the only supported values in PowerShell 1.0 are to merge or not merge the error output of one command into the input of the other. When using either of these approaches, the effects can be reversed by passing `PipelineResultTypes.None` as the target value:

```
commandOne.MergeMyResults(PipelineResultTypes.Error,
    PipelineResultTypes.None);
commandTwo.MergeUnclaimedPreviousPropertyResults =
    PipelineResultTypes.None;
```

Adding Command Parameters

Parameters are passed to an instance of a `Command` as a collection of `CommandParameter` objects stored in the `Parameters` property of the `Command`. Commands created from command tokens and from script blocks both expose a `Parameters` collection, although parameters added to a `Command` created from a script block will be ignored.

The `Parameters` collection contains an `Add()` method that enables you to add parameters, either by directly specifying their names and values, or by constructing them as instances of `CommandParameter`, and then passing the `CommandParameter` instances to `Add()`. When calling `Add()` with the name of a parameter, you can pass just the name for Boolean parameters, or the name and an object. If an object is passed to a parameter but it is of a type that is incompatible with the parameter's definition of the command, then a `ParameterBindingException` will be thrown when the pipeline is invoked.

The following sample illustrates how a hosting application adds the `"recurse"` and `"path"` parameters to the `"get-childitem"` command. The `"recurse"` parameter is Boolean:

```
Command command = new Command("get-childitem");
command.Parameters.Add("recurse");
command.Parameters.Add("path", textPath.Text");
```

`CommandParameter` provides two constructors. The first takes a single string and produces a `Command-Parameter` that represents a Boolean parameter. The second takes a string and an object, and can be used to pass an argument of any type to the command. The following example shows how to create the `CommandParameter` objects independently and then pass them to the `Add()` method:

```
Command command = new Command("get-childitem");
CommandParameter recurse = new CommandParameter("recurse");
CommandParameter path = new CommandParameter("path", textPath.Text");
command.Parameters.Add(recurse);
command.Parameters.Add(path);
```

After a `CommandParameter` has been constructed, its name and value can be retrieved using the `Name` and `Value` properties.

Adding Commands to the Pipeline

Once a command has been created and its parameters have been populated, it can be added to the pipeline's `Commands` collection, which is an instance of `CommandCollection`. Each subsequent command added to the collection is appended to the pipeline, so the output of the first command becomes the input for the second command, and so on, as shown in the following example:

```
pipeline.Commands.Add(dirCommand);
pipeline.Commands.Add(sortCommand);
```

The `Commands` collection also provides two shorthand ways of adding commands to the pipeline when no parameters are provided, without the overhead of creating the `Command` objects. The `Add()` method of the `Commands` collection can take a string, which is interpreted as a command token. Additionally, a separate method called `AddScript()` is available, which takes a script block. An overload of this method accepts a flag to specify local or global scope. The following calls add a command, a script block, and a local scope script block to the pipeline, respectively:

```
pipeline.Commands.Add("get-childitem");
pipeline.Commands.AddScript("$a = 1");
pipeline.Commands.AddScript("$a = 1", true);
```

This next code sample is a complete host application, which executes a programmatically constructed pipeline:

```
using System;
using System.Collections.ObjectModel;
using System.Management.Automation;
using System.Management.Automation.Runspaces;

namespace MonadSamples2
{
    class Program
    {
        static void Main(string[] args)
        {
            // Create and open a runspace
            Runspace runspace = RunspaceFactory.CreateRunspace();
            runspace.Open();

            // Create an empty pipeline
            Pipeline pipeline = runspace.CreatePipeline();

            // Create a get-childitem command and add the
            // 'path' and 'recurse' parameters
            Command dirCommand = new Command("get-childitem");
            dirCommand.Parameters.Add("path",
                  "hklm:\\software\\microsoft\\PowerShell");
            dirCommand.Parameters.Add("recurse");

            // Add the command to the pipeline
            pipeline.Commands.Add(dirCommand);

            // Append a sort-object command using the shorthand method
            pipeline.Commands.Add("sort-object");
```

```
                // Invoke the command
                Collection<PSObject> results = pipeline.Invoke();
                foreach (PSObject thisResult in results)
                {
                    Console.WriteLine(thisResult.ToString());
                }
            }
        }
    }
```

Cmdlets as an API Layer for GUI Applications

One of the driving reasons that led to the development of Windows PowerShell was the lack of parity between the GUI experience in Windows and the command-line experience. Systems administrators lamented to Microsoft that whereas they could do nearly anything in the GUI, they could do almost nothing in the default command line. This wasn't just an inconvenience for veteran command-line users — it meant that without investing in a high-level language, it was impossible to automate most administrative tasks.

To close this gap, and achieve one-to-one parity between the GUI experience and the command-line experience, several Microsoft products are moving to a model whereby PowerShell cmdlets serve as an underlying API, on top of which the GUI is built. A notable example of this is the latest version of Microsoft Exchange, which shipped with several hundred custom cmdlets and an MMC-based GUI layer built on top of them.

This section of the chapter discusses the techniques (and challenges) of building such a GUI layer.

High-Level Architecture

If you've read this far in the chapter, you already know everything you need to know in order to implement a basic integration of a GUI application with the PowerShell engine API. The following example shows a GUI application that accepts a button click, calls the `get-date` cmdlet using a `RunspaceInvoke` object, and displays it in a WinForms message box:

```
using System;
using System.Collections.Generic;
using System.ComponentModel;
using System.Data;
using System.Drawing;
using System.Text;
using System.Windows.Forms;
using System.Collections.ObjectModel;
using System.Management.Automation;

namespace AbsoluteBasicGuiApp1
{
    public partial class GetDateForm : Form
    {
        public GetDateForm()
```

```
            {
                InitializeComponent();
            }

            private void button1_Click(object sender, EventArgs e)
            {
                foreach (PSObject thisDate in new RunspaceInvoke().Invoke("get-date"))
                {
                    MessageBox.Show(thisDate.ToString(), "Today's Date");
                }
            }
        }
    }
```

Although this example runs, it lacks several design considerations that prevent it from scaling into a useful application when more functionality is added.

Keys to Successful GUI Integration

PowerShell provides a rich public interface that exposes the execution environment to the hosting application in several flexible ways. The drawback to this is that when you're building a GUI application on top of this interface, it's easy to over-integrate and end up with a host implementation that's difficult to debug and maintain. Here are some points to keep in mind when creating your initial design.

Isolate Your Business Logic

The key to achieving parity between your GUI and command line is to isolate your business logic at or below the cmdlet level. If business logic is implemented above the cmdlet layer, it will be inaccessible from the command line.

Prepare to Decouple the Engine

By the time you finish developing a clean GUI layer for your application, you will have invested a significant amount of effort in it, and you should plan to preserve that investment if you decide that you no longer want to use PowerShell cmdlets as your API layer. The more PowerShell-specific code you have in the GUI layer, the more work it will take to decouple it from the engine. Therefore, you should abstract out as much of the PowerShell-specific work as you can into its own set of classes, and then call these from your GUI.

Don't Waste Resources

In the example from the last section, every time the "get-date" button is clicked, an entire runspace and pipeline are created, initialized, and thrown away. This is inefficient in terms of both memory and time. You should create your `Runspace` and `Pipeline` objects up front, and do as little work as possible when it comes time to execute a command.

Providing a Custom Host

If you're developing a GUI application to host the PowerShell engine, you have the option to provide a custom implementation of PowerShell's host interfaces, which will allow cmdlets and scripts to interact directly with your GUI. Implementing a custom host is described in detail in Chapter 7.

Once you've implemented the host interfaces in your application, you can tell the PowerShell engine to use your host by passing an instance of it to the `CreateRunspace()` method on `RunspaceFactory`. In previous examples, we called `CreateRunspace()` with a `RunspaceConfiguration` or with no arguments. The following example instantiates a custom host, creates a `Runspace`, and executes a script block that displays a message on the host:

```
MyCustomHost customHost = new MyCustomHost();
Runspace runspace = RunspaceFactory.CreateRunspace(customHost);
runspace.Open();
runspace.CreatePipeline("$host.UI.WriteLine('Hello, Host!')").Invoke();
runspace.Close();
```

Summary

This chapter introduced you to the PowerShell Engine API, and showed you how to incorporate it into your custom host applications. You can use the techniques in this chapter to add PowerShell script-processing functionality to most .NET environments, bringing together the power of .NET and the versatility of a user-modifiable scripting language.

In the next chapter, you learn about the PowerShell host interfaces in detail. They can be extended to give the PowerShell engine direct access to your host application's user interface.

7

Hosts

As you saw in Chapter 6, the Windows PowerShell hosting engine provides access to output, error, and input streams of a pipeline. The Windows PowerShell engine also provides a way for cmdlet and script writers to generate other forms of data such as verbose, debug, warning, progress, and prompts. In this chapter, you will learn how a hosting application can register with the Windows PowerShell engine and get access to these and other forms of data.

An application can host Windows PowerShell using the `Pipeline`, `Runspace`, and `RunspaceInvoke` API, as shown in Chapter 6. However, to get the other aforementioned data, the hosting application has to provide an implementation of `System.Management.Automation.Host.PSHost`. In fact, `powershell.exe`, the Windows PowerShell startup application, implements one such host, `Microsoft.PowerShell.ConsoleHost`.

This chapter begins by explaining how the Windows PowerShell engine interacts with a host, and then describes different built-in cmdlets that interact with a host. It also explores different classes such as `PSHost`, `PSHostUserInterface`, and `PSHostRawUserInterface` that make up a host.

Host-Windows PowerShell Engine Interaction

A hosting application typically constructs a runspace and uses this runspace to execute a command line (or script). A runspace is a representation of a Windows PowerShell engine instance and contains information specific to the engine, such as cmdlets, providers and their drives, functions, variables, aliases, and so forth. When a runspace is loaded, all the built-in cmdlets, providers, functions, and variables are loaded. The following example demonstrates the different ways to create a runspace (from the factory class `System.Management.Automation.Runspaces.RunspaceFactory`):

```
        public static Runspace CreateRunspace();
        public static Runspace CreateRunspace(PSHost host);
        public static Runspace CreateRunspace(RunspaceConfiguration
runspaceConfiguration);
        public static Runspace CreateRunspace(PSHost host, RunspaceConfiguration
runspaceConfiguration);
```

Refer to Chapter 6 for more details about `Runspace` and `RunspaceConfiguration`. One interesting thing to notice here is the `host` parameter passed to the `CreateRunspace()` factory method. Every instance of a runspace is associated with a host. The Windows PowerShell engine is capable of generating forms of data other than just output and errors. For example, a cmdlet or script developer can generate verbose, debug, warning, and progress data along with output and errors. (You will learn more about these later in this chapter.) However, a pipeline supports only output and error streams (see Figure 7-1). It is the host that enables the Windows PowerShell engine to support different forms of data other than output and error. Note that `Runspace` can be bound to a host only when the runspace is created. After a runspace is created, it cannot be rebound to a different host.

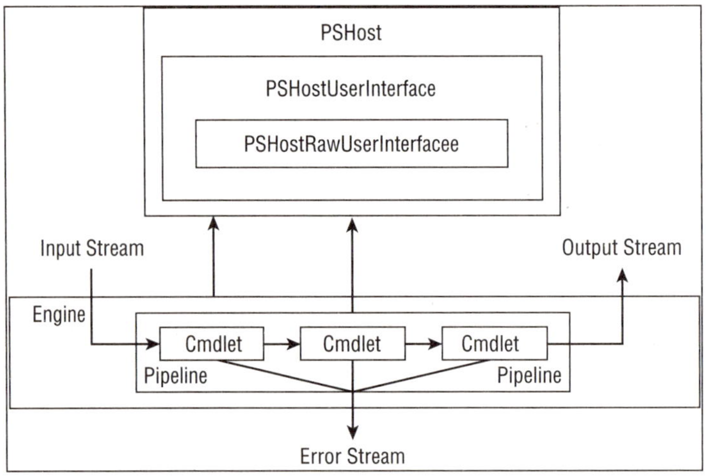

Figure 7-1: How the Windows PowerShell engine interacts with a host on behalf of a pipeline.

Every pipeline takes input through an input stream, and writes output objects to an output stream, and error objects to an error stream. Every cmdlet or script in the pipeline has access to a host, and they can call the host whenever needed, according to certain rules that you'll see later. The instance of the host that is passed to a runspace is exposed by the runspace to the cmdlets, scripts, and providers that are executed in that runspace. Scripts access the host instance through the `$Host` built-in variable. Cmdlets access the host through the `Host` property of the `PSCmdlet` base class. Members of the host instance can be called by the runspace or any cmdlet or script executed in that runspace, in any order and from any thread.

It is the responsibility of a host developer to define the host in a thread-safe fashion. An implementation of the host should not depend on method execution order. It is recommended that you maintain a 1:1 relationship between a host instance and a runspace. Binding the same instance of a host to multiple runspaces is not supported and might result in unexpected behavior.

`PSHost` is designed to let the Windows PowerShell engine notify hosting applications whenever a cmdlet/script enters or exits a nested prompt, whenever a legacy application is launched or ended, and so on. `PSHostUserInterface` is designed to be the UI for the Windows PowerShell engine. `PSHostRawUserInterface` is designed to support low-level character-based user interactions for cmdlets and scripts. At the time of designing these interfaces, the only host the development team considered supporting is a console-based host. Hence, `PSHostUserInterface` and `PSHostRawUserInterface` classes have members such as `Write()`, `WriteLine()`, `WriteErrorLine()`, `WriteDebugLine()`, and so on. Windows PowerShell built-in format cmdlets such as `format-list` and `format-table` use these `PSHostUserInterface` members to display data to the user.

Let's look at the built-in Windows PowerShell cmdlets that take advantage of the `PSHost`.

Built-In Cmdlets That Interact with the Host

A scripter can provide information to a host using the built-in cmdlets `Write-Debug`, `Write-Progress`, `Write-Verbose`, `Write-Warning`, `Write-Host`, `Read-Host`, and `Out-Host`. These cmdlets directly call the host API according to the value of certain engine variables. Apart from these cmdlets, every cmdlet in Windows PowerShell has access to the ubiquitous parameters `-Debug` and `-Verbose`.

The following sections illustrate how these cmdlets interact with the host and how different session variables such as `DebugPreference`, `VerbosePreference`, `WarningPreference`, and `ProgressPreference` control the behavior of these cmdlets.

Write-Debug

The `Write-Debug` cmdlet writes a debug message to the host. The built-in variable `DebugPreference` controls the behavior of this cmdlet. `DebugPreference` can be one of the following values:

Value	Description
SilentlyContinue	Ignore debug messages.
Stop	Write the debug message and stop the pipeline.
Continue	Write the debug message and continue.
Inquire	Write the debug message and ask the host whether to continue or stop.

Here is an example of how this cmdlet works:

```
PS D:\psbook> write-debug "This is a debug message"
PS D:\psbook>
```

By default, `DebugPreference` is set to `SilentlyContinue` when the Windows PowerShell engine is created; as a result, the `write-debug` cmdlet does not write the debug message to the host.

```
PS D:\psbook> $DebugPreference
SilentlyContinue
PS D:\psbook>
```

A user can control the value of `DebugPreference` in two ways: by changing the value of the variable or by calling the cmdlet with the `-Debug` parameter:

```
PS D:\psbook> $DebugPreference
```

```
SilentlyContinue
PS D:\psbook> $DebugPreference = "Continue"
PS D:\psbook> write-debug "This is a debug message"
DEBUG: This is a debug message
PS D:\psbook> $DebugPreference
Continue
PS D:\psbook>
```

Changes to the value of a variable persist until the variable is changed again or the PowerShell session is closed. In the preceding example, because we changed the value of `DebugPreference`, running the `Write-Debug` cmdlet again will show the debug message.

Every cmdlet in Windows PowerShell has access to the ubiquitous parameter `Debug`. This is a `Switch-Parameter`, i.e., the parameter specifies `on` or `off` behavior. If the `Debug` parameter is set to `on`, then the cmdlet behaves as if `DebugPreference` were set to `Inquire` and it ignores the actual value of the `DebugPreference` variable. The following example shows how this works:

```
PS D:\psbook> $DebugPreference
SilentlyContinue
PS D:\psbook> Write-Debug "This is a debug message" -Debug
DEBUG: This is a debug message

Confirm
Continue with this operation?
[Y] Yes  [A] Yes to All  [H] Halt Command  [S] Suspend  [?] Help (default is "Y"): y
PS D:\psbook>
```

In this case, there are two calls to the host (this will be explained in detail later in this chapter). For the time being assume that the Windows PowerShell engine calls the host for writing the debug message and for prompting.

Write-Verbose

The `Write-Verbose` cmdlet writes a verbose message to the host. The variable `VerbosePreference` controls the behavior of this cmdlet. `VerbosePreference` can be one of the following values:

Value	Description
SilentlyContinue	Ignore verbose messages.
Stop	Write the verbose message and stop the pipeline.
Continue	Write the verbose message and continue.
Inquire	Write the verbose message and ask the host whether to continue or stop.

Here's an example showing how this cmdlet works:

```
PS D:\psbook> Write-Verbose "This is a verbose message"
PS D:\psbook>
```

By default, `VerbosePreference` is set to `SilentlyContinue` when the Windows PowerShell engine is created. As a result, the `Write-Verbose` cmdlet does not write the verbose message to the host:

```
PS D:\psbook> $VerbosePreference
SilentlyContinue
PS D:\psbook>
```

A user can control the value of `VerbosePreference` in two ways, just like `DebugPreference`, i.e., by changing the value of variable or by calling the cmdlet with the `-Verbose` parameter:

```
PS D:\psbook> $VerbosePreference
SilentlyContinue
PS D:\psbook> $VerbosePreference="Continue"
PS D:\psbook> Write-Verbose "This is a verbose message"
VERBOSE: This is a verbose message
PS D:\psbook> $VerbosePreference
Continue
PS D:\psbook>
```

Changes to the value of a variable persist until the variable is changed again or the PowerShell session is closed. Because the value of `VerbosePreference` is changed in the preceding example, running the `Write-Verbose` cmdlet again shows the verbose message.

Every cmdlet in Windows PowerShell has access to the ubiquitous parameter `Verbose`. This is a `Switch-Parameter`, i.e., the parameter specifies `on` or `off` behavior. If the `Verbose` parameter is set to `on`, then the cmdlet behaves as if `VerbosePreference` were set to `Continue` and ignores the actual value of the `VerbosePreference` variable. The following example shows how this works:

```
PS D:\psbook> $VerbosePreference
SilentlyContinue
PS D:\psbook> Write-Verbose "This is a verbose message" -Verbose
VERBOSE: This is a verbose message
PS D:\psbook>
```

The ubiquitous parameter `-Debug` has an effect on this preference. If `-Debug` is `on` and the `-Verbose` parameter is not used, the cmdlet behaves as if `VerbosePreference` were set to `Inquire`. Let's see this in action:

```
PS D:\psbook> $VerbosePreference
SilentlyContinue
PS D:\psbook> Write-Verbose "This is a verbose message"
PS D:\psbook> Write-Verbose "This is a verbose message" -Debug
VERBOSE: This is a verbose message

Confirm
Continue with this operation?
[Y] Yes  [A] Yes to All  [H] Halt Command  [S] Suspend  [?] Help (default is "Y"): y
PS D:\psbook>
```

Notice how the use of the `-Debug` parameter changed the behavior of the `Write-Verbose` cmdlet. Even though `VerbosePreference` is set to `SilentlyContinue`, the `Write-Verbose` cmdlet behaves as if `VerbosePreference` were set to `Inquire`. This is because the default behavior of `-Debug` is to `Inquire`.

Write-Warning

The `Write-Warning` cmdlet writes a warning message to the host. The variable `WarningPreference` controls the behavior of this cmdlet. `WarningPreference` can be one of the following values:

Value	Description
SilentlyContinue	Ignore warning messages.
Stop	Write the warning message and stop the pipeline.
Continue	Write the warning message and continue.
Inquire	Write the warning message and ask the host whether to continue or stop.

Here's an example of how this works:

```
PS D:\psbook> Write-Warning "This is a warning message"
WARNING: This is a warning message
PS D:\psbook>
```

By default, `WarningPreference` is set to `Continue` when the Windows PowerShell engine is created. As a result, the `write-warning` cmdlet writes the warning message to the host:

```
PS D:\psbook> $WarningPreference
Continue
PS D:\psbook>
```

`WarningPreference` is different from `DebugPreference` and `VerbosePreference` in that individual cmdlets cannot control this preference using a ubiquitous parameter. However, the ubiquitous parameters `–Debug` and `–Verbose` do have an effect on this preference. If the `-Debug` parameter is `on`, the `WarningPreference` behaves as if its value were set to `Inquire`. If the `–Verbose` parameter is `on`, the `WarningPreference` behaves as if its value were set to `Continue`. The following example illustrates how this works:

```
PS D:\psbook> $WarningPreference
Continue
PS D:\psbook> write-warning "This is a warning message" -Debug
WARNING: This is a warning message

Confirm
Continue with this operation?
[Y] Yes  [A] Yes to All  [H] Halt Command  [S] Suspend  [?] Help (default is "Y"): y
PS D:\psbook> $WarningPreference="Stop"
PS D:\psbook> $WarningPreference
Stop
PS D:\psbook> write-warning "This is a warning message" -Verbose
WARNING: This is a warning message
PS D:\psbook>
```

Notice how the use of `–Debug` and `–Verbose` control the behavior of the `Write-Warning` cmdlet.

Write-Progress

The `Write-Progress` cmdlet writes a progress message to the host. The variable `ProgressPreference` controls the behavior of this cmdlet. `ProgressPreference` can be one of the following values:

Value	Description
SilentlyContinue	Ignore progress messages.
Stop	Write the progress message and stop the pipeline.
Continue	Write the progress message and continue.
Inquire	Write the progress message and ask the host whether to continue or stop.

Here's an example of how this works:

```
PS D:\psbook> for($i=0;$i -lt 100;$i++) { write-progress "Writing Progress" "%
Complete:" -perc $i}
PS D:\psbook>
```

By default, `ProgressPreference` is set to `Continue` when the Windows PowerShell engine is created. As a result, the `Write-Progress` cmdlet writes the progress message to the host (see Figure 7-2).

Figure 7-2: Because of the nature of the default host provided with powershell.exe, progress messages appear at the top of the console window.

This behavior exists only in powershell.exe and is not enforced on every custom host. A custom host developer can choose to display progress in any format according to the application's requirements.

Write-Host and Out-Host

The `Write-Host` and `Out-Host` cmdlets call the host API `Write()` and `WriteLine()`, which you will learn about later in this chapter. The `Write-Host` cmdlet provides support for customizing foreground and background colors of the data that is displayed (see Figure 7-3).

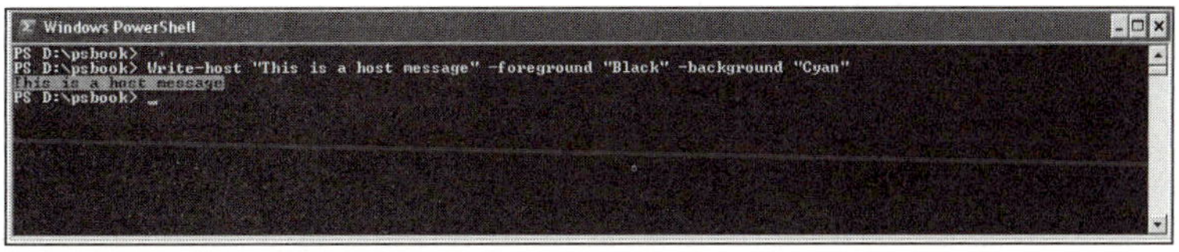

Figure 7-3: The host supplied with powershell.exe changes the console's foreground and background colors as specified by the cmdlet.

The `Out-Host` cmdlet supports paging. The Windows PowerShell engine handles all the logic required to page data. The host only needs to implement the `Write()` and `WriteLine()` methods.

Read-Host

The `Read-Host` cmdlet calls the `ReadLine()` and `ReadLineAsSecureString()` host API and writes the read data to the output stream. You will learn more about this API later in the chapter. The host supplied with `powershell.exe` reads data from the console window.

The following example shows this cmdlet in action:

```
PS D:\psbook> read-host | % { write-host $_}
Input to read-host cmdlet
Input to read-host cmdlet
PS D:\psbook>
```

In the preceding example, the `Read-Host` cmdlet read the data from the console window and wrote the data to the output stream. The `Foreach-Object` cmdlet (`%`) read this data from its input stream and supplied the data to the `Write-Host` cmdlet, which wrote the data back to the console window.

The preceding sections described how different cmdlets interact with the host. Although you looked at the behavior of session variables such as `DebugPreference`, `VerbosePreference`, `WarningPreference`, and `ProgressPreference` in the context of `Write-Debug`, `Write-Verbose`, `Write-Warning`, and `Write-Progress`, these preference variables come into play for any cmdlets that call the base `Cmdlet` methods `WriteDebug()`, `WriteVerbose()`, `WriteWarning()`, and `WriteProgress()`, respectively. The same is true with the ubiquitous parameters `-Debug` and `-Verbose`. These parameters are available to every cmdlet in Windows PowerShell.

The following sections discuss the interfaces a host provides. All the cmdlets discussed so far will interact with one or more of these host interfaces.

Cmdlet and Host Interaction

Every cmdlet in Windows PowerShell has access to base Cmdlet methods `WriteDebug()`, `WriteVerbose()`, `WriteWarning()`, and `WriteProgress()`. Calling any of these methods from inside the cmdlet will call the host API depending on certain variables and state of ubiquitous parameters `-Debug` and `-Verbose`.

`WriteDebug` method call is dependent on `DebugPreference` variable and `-Debug` ubiquitous parameter (just like `Write-Debug` cmdlet). If `-Debug` is switched `on`, the `WriteDebug` method call behaves as if `DebugPreference` is set to `Inquire` and ignores the actual value of the `Debugpreference` variable. If `-Debug` is switched `off`, the `WriteDebug` method call depends on the value of `DebugPreference` variable. By default `DebugPreference` is set to `SilentlyContinue`. `Write-Debug` cmdlet is just a wrapper around `WriteDebug` method.

`WriteVerbose()` method call is dependent on `VerbosePreference` variable and `-Debug`, `-Verbose` ubiquitous parameters. If `-Verbose` parameter is `on`, the `WriteVerbose()` method call behaves as if `VerbosePreference` is set to `Continue` and ignores the actual value of the `VerbosePreference` variable. If `-Debug` is `on` and `-Verbose` parameter is not used, the cmdlet behaves as if `VerbosePreference` is set to `Inquire`. By default `VerbosePreference` is set to `SilentlyContinue`. `Write-Verbose` cmdlet is just a wrapper around `WriteVerbose()` method.

`WriteWarning()` method call is dependent on `WarningPreference` variable and `-Debug`, `-Verbose` ubiquitous parameters. If `-Debug` or `-Verbose` is switched `on`, then the `WarningPreference` variable is ignored. If `-Debug` is switched `on`, the `WriteWarning()` method call behaves as if `WarningPreference` were set to `Inquire`. If `-Verbose` is switched `on`, the `WriteWarning()` method call behaves as if `WarningPreference` were set to `Continue`. By default, `WarningPreference` is set to `Continue`. The `Write-Warning` cmdlet is just a wrapper around the `WriteWarning()` method.

The `WriteProgress()` method call is dependent on `ProgressPreference` variable. By default, `ProgressPreference` is set to `Continue`.

Here's a simple cmdlet to understand the `WriteDebug()` base Cmdlet method:

```
// Save this to a file using filename: PSBook-7-WriteDebugSample.cs


using System;
using System.ComponentModel;
using System.Management.Automation;


namespace PSBook.Chapter7
{
    [RunInstaller(true)]
    public class PSBookChapter7WriteDebugSnapIn : PSSnapIn
    {
        public PSBookChapter7WriteDebugSnapIn()
            : base()
        {
        }
        // Name for the PowerShell snap-in.
        public override string Name
        {
            get
            {
                return "Wiley.PSProfessional.Chapter7.WriteDebug";
            }
        }
        // Vendor information for the PowerShell snap-in.
        public override string Vendor
        {
            get
            {
                return "Wiley";
            }
        }
        // Description of the PowerShell snap-in
        public override string Description
        {
            get
            {
                return "This is a sample PowerShell snap-in";
```

```
            }
        }
    }

    [Cmdlet(VerbsCommunications.Write, "DebugSample")]
    public sealed class WriteDebugSampleCommand : Cmdlet
     {
         [Parameter(Position = 0, Mandatory = true, ValueFromPipeline = true)]
         [AllowEmptyString]
         public string Message
         {
             get { return message;}
             set { message = value;}
         }
         private string message = null;
         protected override void ProcessRecord()
         {
              base.WriteDebug(Message);
         }
     }
}
```

The preceding code sample creates a `Write-DebugSample` cmdlet by deriving from the `System.Management.Automation.Cmdlet` class. This cmdlet accepts a string message as a parameter value and writes the message to the Debug interfaces of the host using the `WriteDebug()` method. Because this is a custom cmdlet, I created a `PSBookChapter7WriteDebugSnapIn` class to register and load the cmdlet in a Windows PowerShell session (refer to Chapter 2 for more details about Windows PowerShell snap-ins). Compile the preceding file and install the snap-in dll that's generated.

```
PS D:\psbook> & $env:windir\Microsoft.NET\Framework\v2.0.50727\csc.exe
/target:library /r:System.Management.Automation.d
ll D:\psbook\Chapter7_WriteDebug\psbook-7-WriteDebugSample.cs
Microsoft (R) Visual C# 2005 Compiler version 8.00.50727.42
for Microsoft (R) Windows (R) 2005 Framework version 2.0.50727
Copyright (C) Microsoft Corporation 2001-2005. All rights reserved.

PS D:\psbook> & $env:windir\Microsoft.NET\Framework\v2.0.50727\installutil.exe
PSBook-7-WriteDebugSample.dll
Microsoft (R) .NET Framework Installation utility Version 2.0.50727.832
Copyright (c) Microsoft Corporation.  All rights reserved.

Running a transacted installation.

Beginning the Install phase of the installation.
See the contents of the log file for the D:\psbook\PSbook-7-WriteDebugSample.dll
assembly's progress.
The file is located at D:\psbook\PSbook-7-WriteDebugSample.InstallLog.
Installing assembly 'D:\psbook\PSbook-7-WriteDebugSample.dll'.
Affected parameters are:
   logtoconsole =
   assemblypath = D:\psbook\PSbook-7-WriteDebugSample.dll
   logfile = D:\psbook\PSbook-7-WriteDebugSample.InstallLog

The Install phase completed successfully, and the Commit phase is beginning.
```

```
See the contents of the log file for the D:\psbook\PSbook-7-WriteDebugSample.dll
assembly's progress.
The file is located at D:\psbook\PSbook-7-WriteDebugSample.InstallLog.
Committing assembly 'D:\psbook\PSbook-7-WriteDebugSample.dll'.
Affected parameters are:
   logtoconsole =
   assemblypath = D:\psbook\PSbook-7-WriteDebugSample.dll
   logfile = D:\psbook\PSbook-7-WriteDebugSample.InstallLog

The Commit phase completed successfully.

The transacted install has completed.
```

The preceding steps installed our `PSBookChapter7WriteDebugSnapIn` snap-in on the system. Now we should add this snap-in to a Windows PowerShell session to see how it works. Let's add the snap-in to a `PowerShell.exe` session and run the cmdlet. Notice how the session variable `DebugPreference` controls the behavior of our `Write-DebugSample` cmdlet:

```
PS D:\psbook> asnp Wiley.PSProfessional.Chapter7.WriteDebug
PS D:\psbook> Write-DebugSample "This a message from debug sample cmdlet"
PS D:\psbook> $DebugPreference
SilentlyContinue
PS D:\psbook> $DebugPreference = "Continue"
PS D:\psbook> Write-DebugSample "This a message from debug sample cmdlet"
DEBUG: This a message from debug sample cmdlet
PS D:\psbook> $DebugPreference = "SilentlyContinue"
PS D:\psbook> Write-DebugSample "This a message from debug sample cmdlet" -Debug
DEBUG: This a message from debug sample cmdlet

Confirm
Continue with this operation?
[Y] Yes  [A] Yes to All  [H] Halt Command  [S] Suspend  [?] Help (default is "Y"): Y
PS D:\psbook>
```

As shown in the preceding example, the `Write-DebugSample` cmdlet behaves exactly like the `Write-Debug` cmdlet. All we did is call the `base.WriteDebug()` method from inside the `ProcessRecord()` of our cmdlet. The `WriteDebug()` method call takes care of querying the `DebugPreference` variable and the `–Debug SwitchParameter` of the cmdlet, and takes care of invoking the host API depending on the rules described earlier.

`WriteDebug()`, `WriteVerbose()`, `WriteWarning()`, and `WriteProgress()` result in a host call, whereas `WriteObject()` and `WriteError()` write to the output and error streams, respectively. Therefore, a hosting application might receive debug, verbose, warning, and progress messages before it actually receives the output and error data.

PSHost Class

The Windows PowerShell engine generates different kinds of data other than just output and errors, as shown until now. However, a pipeline supports only input, output, and error. If a hosting application needs more information from the executing pipeline, the hosting application must supply an implementation of the `PSHost` interface to the runspace at the time the runspace is created. The purpose of this class is to enable the hosting application to register for different notifications that the Windows

PowerShell engine raises while executing a command (in the runspace). The `PSHost` abstract base class is defined in `System.Management.Automation.dll` under the `System.Management.Automation.Host` namespace. The abstract `PSHost` base class looks like the following:

```
namespace System.Management.Automation.Host
{
   public abstract class PSHost
   {
       protected PSHost();
       public abstract CultureInfo CurrentCulture { get; }
       public abstract CultureInfo CurrentUICulture { get; }
       public abstract Guid InstanceId { get; }
       public abstract string Name { get; }
       public virtual PSObject PrivateData { get; }
       public abstract PSHostUserInterface UI { get; }
       public abstract Version Version { get; }
       public abstract void EnterNestedPrompt();
       public abstract void ExitNestedPrompt();
       public abstract void NotifyBeginApplication();
       public abstract void NotifyEndApplication();
       public abstract void SetShouldExit(int exitCode);
   }
}
```

The hosting application must derive from this class and pass an instance of the derived class to the `RunspaceFactory.CreateRunspace()` method to bind Runspace to the host. Windows PowerShell engine can call any of the methods defined in the host after the host is bound to the Runspace. Windows PowerShell engine uses this host instance to notify any non-fatal errors that may occur while opening the Runspace through `Runspace.Open()` method. `Runspace.Open()` is not executed in the context of a pipeline, so it is not possible to notify non-fatal errors that may occur opening the Runspace without a host instance. Once a host instance is bound to a Runspace, the instance must not be destroyed until the Runspace is closed. The Host instance attached to the Runspace is not directly available to Cmdlets and Scripts as Windows PowerShell engine internally wraps the supplied host. Windows PowerShell engine exposes this wrapped host to scripts through `$Host` built-in variable and to cmdlets through the `Host` property of the `PSCmdlet` base class. Windows PowerShell engine will not provide the Runspace ID or the pipeline ID for which the host method is called. Hence the host developer should make sure only 1 Runspace is bound to the host. A Runspace can execute only 1 pipeline. This way the host method call can be traced back to the Runspace and Pipeline.

The following sections describe each member in the `PSHost` class, how Windows PowerShell engine interacts with these members and guidelines to developer implementing these members.

InstanceId

The `InstanceId` property uniquely identifies an instance of a host. This property is defined as follows:

```
public abstract Guid InstanceId { get; }
```

The value of this property should remain invariant for the lifetime of the instance. Typically, this field is initialized during the construction time of the host instance in the constructor. It is recommended that you use `System.Guid.NewGuid()` to create a unique GUID for each host instance. Such an identifier has a very low probability of being duplicated.

The Windows PowerShell engine uses this identifier while logging data to event logs. Thus, each event log entry can be uniquely identified and correlated to a particular host instance. A simple test shows this:

```
PS D:\psbook> $host.InstanceId.ToString()
9194b492-c96a-4972-9bc0-19d8a13a3076
PS D:\psbook> get-eventlog "Windows PowerShell" -newest 1 | select message  | fl

Message : Engine state is changed from None to Available.

          Details:
             NewEngineState=Available
             PreviousEngineState=None

             SequenceNumber=8

             HostName=ConsoleHost
             HostVersion=1.0.0.0
             HostId=9194b492-c96a-4972-9bc0-19d8a13a3076
             EngineVersion=1.0.0.0
             RunspaceId=87eea710-e959-460c-889a-5502b1cd7cc2
             PipelineId=
             CommandName=
             CommandType=
             ScriptName=
             CommandPath=
             CommandLine=
```

Name

The `Name` property identifies a host instance in some user-friendly fashion. This property is defined as follows:

```
public abstract string Name { get; }
```

This property can be referenced by scripts and cmdlets to identify the host that is executing them. The format of the value is not defined, but a short simple string is recommended. For the default console host shipped by Microsoft, this is set to "`ConsoleHost`".

The Windows PowerShell engine uses this identifier while logging data to event logs. A simple test shows this:

```
PS D:\psbook> $host.Name.ToString()
ConsoleHost
PS D:\psbook> get-eventlog "Windows PowerShell" -newest 1 | select message  | fl

Message : Engine state is changed from None to Available.

          Details:
             NewEngineState=Available
             PreviousEngineState=None

             SequenceNumber=8
```

```
HostName=ConsoleHost
HostVersion=1.0.0.0
HostId=9194b492-c96a-4972-9bc0-19d8a13a3076
EngineVersion=1.0.0.0
RunspaceId=87eea710-e959-460c-889a-5502b1cd7cc2
```

Version

The `Version` property identifies the version of the host. This property is defined as follows:

```
public abstract Version Version { get; }
```

The value of this property should remain invariant for a particular build of the host. If you plan to develop multiple versions of the host, use this member to distinguish each version. It is generally not a good practice to create a dependency on this host member in a script or cmdlet. Scripts and cmdlets should be developed independently of the host. This way, they can be run in any application hosting the Windows PowerShell engine. The Windows PowerShell engine uses this property while logging data to event logs.

CurrentCulture

The `CurrentCulture` property represents the host's culture. This property is defined as follows:

```
public abstract CultureInfo CurrentCulture { get; }
```

The runspace uses this to set the execution thread's `CurrentCulture` property each time it starts a pipeline. Cmdlets and scripts execute in the context of the pipeline thread, so this value affects the cmdlet and script execution and their results.

`Culture`, which is indicated by the `Thread.CurrentCulture` property, corresponds to the Regional and Language Options in the Control Panel by default. `CurrentCulture` affects how numbers, dates, and times are formatted. This is also what determines which sorting and casing rules to use.

CurrentUICulture

The `CurrentUICulture` property represents the host's `UICulture`. This property is defined as follows:

```
public abstract CultureInfo CurrentUICulture { get; }
```

The runspace uses this to set the execution thread's `CurrentUICulture` property each time it starts a pipeline. Cmdlets and scripts execute in the context of the pipeline thread, so this value affects the cmdlet and script execution and their results.

`UICulture`, which is indicated by the `Thread.CurrentUICulture` property, corresponds to the language of the operating system by default, or the selected language on a multi-language version of Windows. This affects which resources are loaded, thus determining which strings and pictures the user sees.

PrivateData

The `PrivateData` property is used to enable the host to pass private data through a runspace to cmdlets or scripts running inside that runspace. This property is defined as follows:

```
public virtual PSObject PrivateData { get; }
```

The type and nature of this private data is entirely defined by the host. Notice that `PrivateData` is a read-only property. Hence, scripts or cmdlets cannot modify it. The value of this property is totally controlled by the host. It's up to the host to ensure the thread safety and state of the object. If the `ImmediateBaseObject` (of this property's returned instance) is a `reference` type, then scripts or cmdlets can modify the object's members. Therefore, it is recommended that the returned instance of this property has *value semantics*, i.e., changes to the state of the returned instance will not be visible across multiple cmdlets or scripts.

`Runspace` supports a session state. Session state has a global variable store that is visible to every cmdlet and script executing in that runspace. A host developer can choose to pass private data to scripts or cmdlets using the runspace's session state. Note that a variable in a runspace's session state can be removed or modified by scripts or cmdlets unless it is a `Constant` variable. If a variable is created as a `Constant`, then it cannot be modified or deleted by the owner either (assuming the variable has value semantics).

In general, scripts and cmdlets should not depend on this host property, as they will not be compatible with other applications hosting the Windows PowerShell engine. Consider passing the private data as an input or as a parameter to the script or cmdlet instead of depending on the host's `PrivateData` property or the runspace's session state. This way, the script or cmdlet user does not need to depend on the environment in which the script or cmdlet executes.

EnterNestedPrompt

The `EnterNestedPrompt()` method is called by the Windows PowerShell engine to instruct the host to interrupt the currently running pipeline and start a new *nested* pipeline using the currently running pipeline's runspace. This method is defined as follows:

```
public abstract void EnterNestedPrompt();
```

This method is called by the Windows PowerShell engine in response to some user action that suspends the currently running pipeline, such as choosing the Suspend option of a `Confirm()` call, as shown in the following example:

```
PS D:\psbook> get-process powershell | stop-process -confirm

Confirm
Are you sure you want to perform this action?
Performing operation "Stop-Process" on Target "powershell (320)".
[Y] Yes  [A] Yes to All  [N] No  [L] No to All  [S] Suspend  [?] Help (default is "Y"):
```

Notice the `[S] Suspend` option displayed in the preceding code. The Windows PowerShell engine calls the `EnterNestedPrompt()` method if user chooses this option. The Windows PowerShell `ConsoleHost` uses this method call to create a nested pipeline and execute a new command. This is a useful feature, as it allows the user to monitor system state like environment variables, session state variables, and so on before deciding whether to really go ahead with the operation. The currently running pipeline is suspended until the `EnterNestedPrompt()` method returns. In fact, `EnterNestedPrompt()` is called from the currently running pipeline thread.

A runspace can allow at most one pipeline at any given time. This is because the Windows PowerShell engine's session state and other subsystems can allow only one thread to use them. Because the pipeline is suspended when the `EnterNestedPrompt()` method is called, the Windows PowerShell engine allows a specialized nested pipeline to use a different engine's subsystems. As a result, a host developer can only invoke nested pipelines in the `EnterNestedPrompt()` method. A nested pipeline is created using the runspace's `CreateNestedPipeline()` method, as discussed in Chapter 6. Only `Invoke()` method is allowed on a nested pipeline.

Typically, a host runs in a `User Input- > Create Nested Pipeline- > Invoke` loop inside the `EnterNestedPrompt()` method. The Windows PowerShell engine informs the host to exit from this loop by calling the `ExitNestedPrompt()` method.

The `EnterNestedPrompt()` method is called in response to a prompt and some user action. Prompting requires the host to support the UI. Hence, if the `UI` property of the host is `null`, then the `EnterNestedPrompt()` method will never be called. Before calling the `EnterNestedPrompt()` method, the Windows PowerShell engine will do the following:

- Increment the `NestedPromptLevel` session state variable
- Set the `CurrentlyExecutingCommand` session state variable with information about the currently running cmdlet, such as `CommandInfo` and `StackTrace`

These session-state variables are available to the nested pipeline. Let's look at an example:

```
PS D:\psbook> $nestedpromptlevel
0
PS D:\psbook> $CurrentlyExecutingCommand
PS D:\psbook> get-process powershell | stop-process -confirm

Confirm
Are you sure you want to perform this action?
Performing operation "Stop-Process" on Target "powershell (304)".
[Y] Yes  [A] Yes to All  [N] No  [L] No to All  [S] Suspend  [?] Help (default is
"Y"): S
PS D:\psbook>>> $nestedpromptlevel
1
PS D:\psbook>>> $CurrentlyExecutingCommand | fl CommandInfo

CommandInfo : Stop-Process
```

ExitNestedPrompt

The `ExitNestedPrompt()` method is called by the Windows PowerShell engine to instruct the host to exit from a nested prompt. This method is defined as follows:

```
public abstract void ExitNestedPrompt();
```

Typically, a host runs in a `User Input- > Create Nested Pipeline- > Invoke` loop inside the `EnterNestedPrompt()` method. The Windows PowerShell engine informs the host to exit from this loop by calling the `ExitNestedPrompt()` method.

After the host returns from the `ExitNestedPrompt()` method, the Windows PowerShell engine resets the `NestedPromptLevel` and `CurrentlyExecutingCommand` session state variables and displays the original prompt that took the host to the nested prompt state. The following code shows an example of this:

```
PS D:\psbook> $nestedPromptLevel
0
PS D:\psbook> $currentlyExecutingCommand
PS D:\psbook> get-process powershell | stop-process -confirm

Confirm
Are you sure you want to perform this action?
Performing operation "Stop-Process" on Target "powershell (304)".
[Y] Yes  [A] Yes to All  [N] No  [L] No to All  [S] Suspend  [?] Help (default is
"Y"): S
PS D:\psbook>>> exit

Confirm
Are you sure you want to perform this action?
Performing operation "Stop-Process" on Target "powershell (304)".
[Y] Yes  [A] Yes to All  [N] No  [L] No to All  [S] Suspend  [?] Help (default is
"Y"):n
PS D:\psbook> $nestedPromptLevel
0
PS D:\psbook> $currentlyExecutingCommand
PS D:\psbook>
```

Notice that the original prompt is displayed after `exit` is called from the nested prompt. A session-state variable `LastExitCode` is set, which holds the value passed with `exit`. This variable is set before the `ExitNestedPrompt()` method is called.

```
PS D:\psbook> $lastexitcode
0
PS D:\psbook> write-debug "This is a debug message" -debug
DEBUG: This is a debug message

Confirm
Continue with this operation?
[Y] Yes  [A] Yes to All  [H] Halt Command  [S] Suspend  [?] Help (default is "Y"):
s
PS D:\psbook>>> exit 5

Confirm
Continue with this operation?
[Y] Yes  [A] Yes to All  [H] Halt Command  [S] Suspend  [?] Help (default is "Y"):
y
```

```
PS D:\psbook> $lastexitcode
5
PS D:\psbook>
```

Application Notification Methods

`NotifyBeginApplication` and `NotifyEndApplication` are used by the Windows PowerShell engine to notify the host when it is about to start and close a legacy application, respectively. These methods are defined as follows:

```
public abstract void NotifyBeginApplication()
public abstract void NotifyEndApplication()
```

`NotifyBeginApplication` is called by the Windows PowerShell engine to notify the host that it is about to execute a "legacy" application. Such an application can read from `stdin`, write to `stdout`, write to `stderr`, or call any Win32 console API, and so on. Notifying the host before executing such an application allows the host to do such things as save any state that might need to be restored when the legacy application terminates. The engine always calls this method and the `NotifyEndApplication()` method in matching pairs. These API are designed to support console-based shells. Legacy applications change the console window title and hence affect the console hosting Windows PowerShell. To revert back to the original window title before calling the legacy application, a console-based host developer can take advantage of the `NotifyBeginApplication()` and `NotifyEndApplication()` methods. These methods are called only when the application is run standalone, i.e., input, output and error are not redirected.

SetShouldExit

The `SetShouldExit()` method is called by the Windows PowerShell engine to request the host to shut down the engine. This method is defined as follows:

```
public abstract void SetShouldExit(int exitCode)
```

This is initiated by running the `exit` Windows PowerShell command. The `exitCode` accompanying the `exit` command is passed as an argument to the method. The host is expected to stop accepting and submitting pipelines to the runspace and to close the runspace after this method is called.

The following example creates a simple host to illustrate these concepts. This example creates a GUI-based application hosting Windows PowerShell. It defines an implementation of `PSHost` and uses an instance of this implementation to create a runspace. An input text box, invoke button, and output text box are used to take input, invoke commands, and show results, respectively:

```
// Save this to a file using filename: PSbook-7-GUIHost.cs
using System;
using System.Collections;
using System.Collections.ObjectModel;
using System.Collections.Generic;
using System.Text;
using System.Threading;
using System.Globalization;
using System.Management.Automation;
using System.Management.Automation.Host;
using System.Management.Automation.Runspaces;
```

```
using System.Windows.Forms;

namespace PSBook.Chapter7
{
    public sealed class GUIPSHost : PSHost
    {
        // private data
        private Guid instanceId;
        private Version version;
        private const string privateData = "gui host private data";
        private PSGUIForm gui;
        private Runspace runspace;

        public GUIPSHost(PSGUIForm form) : base()
        {
            gui = form;
            gui.InvokeButton.Click += new EventHandler(InvokeButton_Click);
            instanceId = Guid.NewGuid();
            version = new Version("0.0.0.1");
        }

        public void Initialize()
        {
            runspace = RunspaceFactory.CreateRunspace(this);
            runspace.Open();
        }

        private void InvokeButton_Click(object sender, EventArgs e)
         {
           // disable invoke button to make sure only 1
           // command is running
           gui.InvokeButton.Enabled = false;
           Pipeline pipeline = runspace.CreatePipeline(gui.InputTextBox.Text);
           pipeline.Commands[0].MergeMyResults(PipelineResultTypes.Error,
PipelineResultTypes.Output);
           pipeline.Commands.Add("out-string");
           pipeline.Input.Close();
           pipeline.StateChanged +=
               new EventHandler<PipelineStateEventArgs>(pipeline_StateChanged);
           pipeline.InvokeAsync();
         }

         private void pipeline_StateChanged(object sender, PipelineStateEventArgs e)
         {
             Pipeline source = sender as Pipeline;
             // if the command completed update GUI.
             bool updateGUI = false;
             StringBuilder output = new StringBuilder();
             if (e.PipelineStateInfo.State == PipelineState.Completed)
             {
                 updateGUI = true;
                 Collection<PSObject> results = source.Output.ReadToEnd();
                 foreach (PSObject result in results)
                 {
                    string resultString =
```

```
(string)LanguagePrimitives.ConvertTo(result, typeof(string));
                    output.Append(resultString);
                }
            }
            else if ((e.PipelineStateInfo.State == PipelineState.Stopped) ||
                     (e.PipelineStateInfo.State == PipelineState.Failed))
            {
                updateGUI = true;
                string message = string.Format("Command did not complete
successfully. Reason: {0}",
                    e.PipelineStateInfo.Reason.Message);
                MessageBox.Show(message);
            }
            if (updateGUI)
            {
                PSGUIForm.SetOutputTextBoxContentDelegate optDelegate =
                    new
PSGUIForm.SetOutputTextBoxContentDelegate(gui.SetOutputTextBoxContent);
                gui.OutputTextBox.Invoke(optDelegate, new object[] {
output.ToString()} );
                PSGUIForm.SetInvokeButtonStateDelegate invkBtnDelegate =
                    new
PSGUIForm.SetInvokeButtonStateDelegate(gui.SetInvokeButtonState);
                gui.InvokeButton.Invoke(invkBtnDelegate, new object[] { true} );
            }
        }

        public override Guid InstanceId
        {
            get { return instanceId; }
        }

        public override string Name
        {
            get { return "PSBook.Chapter7.Host"; }
        }

        public override Version Version
        {
            get { return version; }
        }

        public override CultureInfo CurrentCulture
        {
            get { return Thread.CurrentThread.CurrentCulture; }
        }

        public override CultureInfo CurrentUICulture
        {
            get { return Thread.CurrentThread.CurrentUICulture; }
        }

        public override PSObject PrivateData
        {
            get
```

```
            {
                return PSObject.AsPSObject(privateData);
            }
        }

        public override void EnterNestedPrompt()
        {
            throw new Exception("The method or operation is not implemented.");
        }

        public override void ExitNestedPrompt()
        {
            throw new Exception("The method or operation is not implemented.");
        }

        public override void NotifyBeginApplication()
        {
            throw new Exception("The method or operation is not implemented.");
        }

        public override void NotifyEndApplication()
        {
            throw new Exception("The method or operation is not implemented.");
        }

        public override void SetShouldExit(int exitCode)
        {
            string message = string.Format("Exiting with exit code: {0}",
exitCode);
            MessageBox.Show(message);
            runspace.CloseAsync();
            Application.Exit();
        }

        public override PSHostUserInterface UI
        {
            get { return null; }
        }


        [STAThread]
        public static void Main()
        {
            Application.EnableVisualStyles();
            Application.SetCompatibleTextRenderingDefault(false);

            // attach form to the host and start message loop
            // of the form
            PSGUIForm form = new PSGUIForm();
            GUIPSHost host = new GUIPSHost(form);
            host.Initialize();
            Application.Run(form);
        }
    }
}
```

```
// Save this to a file using filename: PSBook-7-GUIForm.cs
using System;
using System.Windows.Forms;

namespace PSBook.Chapter7
{
    public sealed class PSGUIForm : Form
    {
        public PSGUIForm()
        {
            InitializeComponent();
        }

        #region Public interfaces

        public TextBox OutputTextBox
        {
            get { return outputTextBox; }
        }

        public TextBox InputTextBox
        {
            get { return inputTextBox; }
        }

        public Button InvokeButton
        {
            get { return invokeBtn; }
        }

        public void SetInvokeButtonState(bool isEnabled)
        {
            invokeBtn.Enabled = isEnabled;
            inputTextBox.Focus();
        }

        public void SetOutputTextBoxContent(string text)
        {
            outputTextBox.Clear();
            outputTextBox.AppendText(text);
        }

        public delegate void SetInvokeButtonStateDelegate(bool isEnabled);
        public delegate void SetOutputTextBoxContentDelegate(string text);

        #endregion

        protected override void Dispose(bool disposing)
        {
            if (disposing && (components != null))
            {
                components.Dispose();
            }
            base.Dispose(disposing);
```

```
        }

        private void InitializeComponent()
        {
           this.outputTextBox = new System.Windows.Forms.TextBox();
           this.invokeBtn = new System.Windows.Forms.Button();
           this.inputTextBox = new System.Windows.Forms.TextBox();
           this.SuspendLayout();
           //
           // outputTextBox
           //             this.outputTextBox.BackColor = System.Drawing.Color.White;
           this.outputTextBox.Font = new System.Drawing.Font("Courier New", 8.25F,
System.Drawing.FontStyle.Regular, System.Drawing.GraphicsUnit.Point, ((byte)(0)));
           this.outputTextBox.Location = new System.Drawing.Point(8, 41);
           this.outputTextBox.Multiline = true;
           this.outputTextBox.Name = "outputTextBox";
           this.outputTextBox.ReadOnly = true;
           this.outputTextBox.ScrollBars = System.Windows.Forms.ScrollBars.Both;
           this.outputTextBox.Size = new System.Drawing.Size(365, 272);
           this.outputTextBox.TabIndex = 2;
           this.outputTextBox.WordWrap = false;
           //
           // invokeBtn
           //
           this.invokeBtn.Location = new System.Drawing.Point(298, 12);
           this.invokeBtn.Name = "invokeBtn";
           this.invokeBtn.Size = new System.Drawing.Size(75, 23);
           this.invokeBtn.TabIndex = 1;
           this.invokeBtn.Text = "Invoke";
           this.invokeBtn.UseCompatibleTextRendering = true;
           this.invokeBtn.UseVisualStyleBackColor = true;
           //
           // inputTextBox
           //
           this.inputTextBox.Font = new System.Drawing.Font("Arial", 9F,
System.Drawing.FontStyle.Regular, System.Drawing.GraphicsUnit.Point, ((byte)(0)));
           this.inputTextBox.Location = new System.Drawing.Point(8, 12);
           this.inputTextBox.Name = "inputTextBox";
           this.inputTextBox.Size = new System.Drawing.Size(284, 21);
           this.inputTextBox.TabIndex = 0;
           //
           // PSGUIForm
           //
           this.AutoScaleDimensions = new System.Drawing.SizeF(6F, 13F);
           this.AutoScaleMode = System.Windows.Forms.AutoScaleMode.Font;
           this.ClientSize = new System.Drawing.Size(394, 325);
           this.Controls.Add(this.inputTextBox);
           this.Controls.Add(this.invokeBtn);
           this.Controls.Add(this.outputTextBox);
           this.Name = "PSGUIForm";
           this.Text = "PSBook Chapter 7";
           this.ResumeLayout(false);
           this.PerformLayout();

       }
```

```
            private System.Windows.Forms.TextBox outputTextBox;
            private System.Windows.Forms.Button invokeBtn;
            private System.Windows.Forms.TextBox inputTextBox;
            private System.ComponentModel.IContainer components = null;
        }
    }
```

The preceding example creates an instance of a `GUIPSHost` and attaches a .NET form to the host. `GUIPSHost` creates a runspace and attaches a `click` event handler to monitor click events of the Invoke button in the form. When the Invoke button is clicked, this handler creates a pipeline, taking the text from the form's input textbox as the command and then invoking the pipeline asynchronously. A pipeline `StateChanged()` handler listens to the pipeline state change events and notifies the form when the output is ready. If the command execution fails, then a message box displays the reason for the failure. When the `exit` command is invoked, the host exits gracefully, displaying the exit code, closing the runspace, and exiting the application.

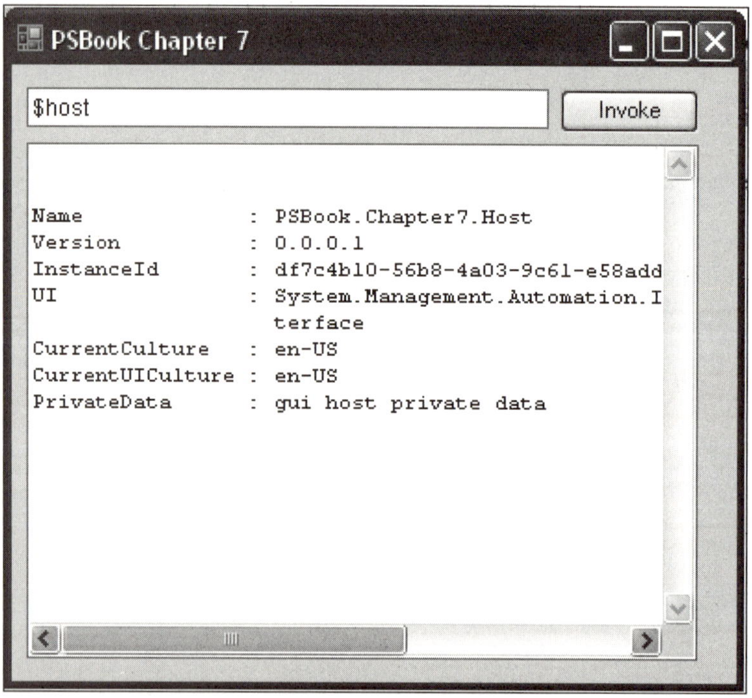

Figure 7-4: Notice the `Name`, `Version`, and `PrivateData` property values of the `$host` variable. These are the properties defined by our `GUIPSHost`.

The Windows PowerShell pipeline actually performs the `InvokeAsync` asynchronous operation in a different thread called a *Pipeline Execution Thread*. This keeps the UI thread of the form unblocked while Windows PowerShell executes the command. However, when the command completes, the pipeline state change notifications arrive in the pipeline execution thread. Hence, the pipeline `StateChanged()` handler cannot directly modify the UI controls such as output textbox, input textbox, and so on.

Controls created by the UI thread can only be modified from the UI thread. Therefore, the changes are sent to the GUI form by posting a message to the UI thread's message loop, using the `Invoke()` method ofthe control.

Compile and run the executable generated:

```
PS D:\psbook> & $env:windir\Microsoft.NET\Framework\v2.0.50727\csc.exe
/target:exe /r:system.drawing.dll /r:system.windo
ws.forms.dll /r:System.Management.Automation.dll
D:\psbook\Chapter7_GUIHost_Sample1\GuiForm.cs D:\psbook\Chapter7_GUIHos
t_Sample1\psbook-7-GUIHost.cs
Microsoft (R) Visual C# 2005 Compiler version 8.00.50727.42
for Microsoft (R) Windows (R) 2005 Framework version 2.0.50727
Copyright (C) Microsoft Corporation 2001-2005. All rights reserved.

PS D:\psbook> .\psbook-7-GUIHost.exe
```

The application will look like what is shown in Figure 7-4.

This application gets only the output and error messages from the pipeline. It's not yet capable of displaying messages such as verbose, debug, warning, progress, and so on. In the following section, you'll learn how to get this data into your application.

PSHostUserInterface Class

The `PSHostUserInterface` class is designed to enable hosting applications to register for user-interface-related notifications that the Windows PowerShell engine raises. The Windows PowerShell engine supports cmdlets and scripts that generate different kinds of data that should be made available to the user immediately. Some cmdlets and scripts require user input, such as passwords, which may not be passed directly as a parameter. The Windows PowerShell engine routes these notifications on behalf of the cmdlets and scripts to the host using an instance of the `PSHostUserInterface` class.

The hosting application must register an instance of this class through the `PSHost.UI` property at the time the runspace is created. If the value of the `PSHost.UI` property is `null`, then the Windows PowerShell engine will not route the UI-related notifications to the host. The `PSHostUserInterface` abstract class is defined in `System.Management.Automation.dll` under the `System.Management.Automation.Host` namespace. The abstract `PSHostUserInteface` base class looks like the following:

```
namespace System.Management.Automation.Host
{
    public abstract class PSHostUserInterface
    {
        protected PSHostUserInterface();

        public abstract void WriteDebugLine(string message);
        public abstract void WriteVerboseLine(string message);
        public abstract void WriteWarningLine(string message);
        public abstract void WriteProgress(long sourceId, ProgressRecord record);
        public abstract void WriteErrorLine(string value);
        public abstract void Write(string value);
        public abstract void Write(ConsoleColor foregroundColor, ConsoleColor
```

```
backgroundColor, string value);
        public virtual void WriteLine();
        public abstract void WriteLine(string value);
        public virtual void WriteLine(ConsoleColor foregroundColor, ConsoleColor
backgroundColor, string value);

        public abstract PSHostRawUserInterface RawUI { get; }

        public abstract Dictionary<string, PSObject> Prompt(string caption, string
message, Collection<FieldDescription> descriptions);
       public abstract int PromptForChoice(string caption, string message,
Collection<ChoiceDescription> choices, int defaultChoice);
       public abstract PSCredential PromptForCredential(string caption, string
message, string userName, string targetName);
       public abstract PSCredential PromptForCredential(string caption, string
message, string userName, string targetName, PSCredentialTypes
allowedCredentialTypes, PSCredentialUIOptions options);
       public abstract string ReadLine();
       public abstract SecureString ReadLineAsSecureString();
    }
}
```

There are some *write* methods and some *read/prompt* methods, all of which are intended to interact with the user. Write methods are used to provide users with informational messages, whereas *read/prompt* methods are used to take input from the user. Write methods are divided into different categories such as debug, verbose, warning, progress, and so on. This offers more flexibility to the cmdlet/script developer and hosting application developer. For example, cmdlet/script developers may choose to provide *verbose* messages when the cmdlet/script completes an action, and *debug* messages to display the state of a variable. In addition, a hosting application developer can choose to display verbose messages and debug messages differently, thereby giving the end user more control over what is displayed and how.

Scripts access the host instance through `$Host` built-in variable. Cmdlets access the host through the `Host` property of the `PSCmdlet` base class.

The following sections describe each member in the `PSHostUserInterface` class, including how the Windows PowerShell engine interacts with these members, and offers guidelines for developers implementing these members.

WriteDebugLine

The `WriteDebugLine()` method is called by the Windows PowerShell engine (on behalf of the cmdlet) to send a debug message to the host. This method is defined as follows:

```
public abstract void WriteDebugLine(string message)
```

It is up to the host to handle the message in the manner it wants. The Windows PowerShell console host writes the message immediately to the console window. Displaying debug messages by default may annoy users, especially when the cmdlet generates huge amounts of debug data. In the Windows PowerShell console window, debug and output messages are shown in the same window as they arrive. If the cmdlet generates huge amounts of debug data and less output data, then the user may have to dig through the console window to find the actual output.

To improve the experience, Windows PowerShell enables users to decide what to do with the debug messages through the `$DebugPreference` variable. Every cmdlet in Windows PowerShell has access to a base cmdlet method `WriteDebug()`. The `$DebugPreference` variable can control debug messages only if the cmdlet calls the `WriteDebug()` method of the base cmdlet. If the cmdlet chooses to call the host directly, then `$DebugPreference` has no effect on such a message. Hence, it is recommended that you use the `WriteDebug()` method of the base `Cmdlet` class instead of calling the `WriteDebugLine()` method of the host. Scripts should use the `Write-Debug` cmdlet as described earlier in the chapter.

WriteVerboseLine

The `WriteVerboseLine` method is called by the Windows PowerShell engine (on behalf of the cmdlet) to notify a verbose message to the host. This method is defined as follows:

```
public abstract void WriteVerboseLine(string message)
```

Again, it is up to the host to handle the message in the manner it wants. The Windows PowerShell console host writes the message immediately to the console window. Windows PowerShell enables the user to decide what to do with the verbose messages through the `$VerbosePreference` variable. Every cmdlet in Windows PowerShell has access to a base cmdlet method `WriteVerbose()`. The `$VerbosePreference` variable can control verbose messages only if the cmdlet calls the `WriteVerbose()` method of the base cmdlet. If the cmdlet chooses to call host directly, then `$VerbosePreference` has no effect on such a message. Hence, it is recommended that you use the `WriteVerbose()` method of the base `Cmdlet` class instead of calling the `WriteVerboseLine()` method of the host. Scripts should use the `Write-Verbose` cmdlet as described earlier in the chapter.

WriteWarningLine

The `WriteWarningLine()` method is called by the Windows PowerShell engine (on behalf of the cmdlet) to send a warning message to the host. This method is defined as follows:

```
public abstract void WriteWarningLine(string message)
```

Windows PowerShell enables the user to decide what to do with the warning messages through the `$WarningPreference` variable. Like the `WriteDebugLine()` and `WriteVerboseLine()` methods, this method should not be called directly. Instead, the cmdlet developer should call the `WriteWarning()` method of the base `Cmdlet` class, and script developers should use the `Write-Warning` cmdlet.

WriteProgress

The `WriteProgress()` method is called by the Windows PowerShell engine (on behalf of the cmdlet) to notify a progress message to the host. This method is defined as follows:

```
public abstract void WriteProgress(long sourceId, ProgressRecord record)
```

Debug, verbose, and warning messages typically do not include additional information other than the message. Progress usually includes information such as percent completed, time remaining, and so on. A hosting application can choose this more granular information to display a sophisticated UI to the user. This granular information comes through a `ProgressRecord` object. It is up to the cmdlet or script developer to generate the `ProgressRecord` object. Cmdlet/script developers should not call this host method directly. Instead, developers should call the `WriteProgress()` method of the base `Cmdlet` class or use the Write-Progress cmdlet from a script. This way, the variable $ProgressPreference controls whether the host receives the progress message or not. ProgressRecord has members such as PercentComplete, SecondsRemaining, StatusDescription, and so on, which enable the host to display a sophisticated UI, such as a progress bar.

WriteErrorLine

The WriteErrorLine() method is a special method that Windows PowerShell engine calls to notify an error message. This method is defined as follows:

```
public abstract void WriteErrorLine(string value);
```

You might wonder why this is needed when a pipeline already has an error stream. When a pipeline is running, all errors are routed through the error stream. However, when the Windows PowerShell engine is starting up (Runspace.Open()) there is no pipeline associated with it and hence no error stream. All the nonfatal errors that occur during engine startup are sent through this host method. These nonfatal errors include errors generated from parsing types files, parsing format files, loading assemblies, providers, cmdlets specified in RunspaceConfiguration, and so on.

Write Methods

The following write methods are designed to notify a host to display a message immediately:

```
public abstract void Write(string value)
public abstract void Write(ConsoleColor foregroundColor, ConsoleColor
backgroundColor, string value)
public virtual void WriteLine();
public abstract void WriteLine(string value)
public virtual void WriteLine(ConsoleColor foregroundColor, ConsoleColor
backgroundColor, string value)
```

All these methods are called by the Windows PowerShell engine's Format and Output (F&O) subsystem. The methods were designed with the assumption that Windows PowerShell is hosted in a console-based application. The F&O subsystem needs more control over what the output looks like in a console window. For example, F&O needs to display a table with the Format-Table cmdlet, a list with the Format-List cmdlet, and so on. These Write() and WriteLine() methods assist the F&O subsystem in achieving this task. Instead of directly using the Console.Write and Console.WriteLine() methods, these methods are designed to make Windows PowerShell hostable in any application, not just console-based applications.

A WriteLine() method variant is called to notify the host to display a message in the current line and display future messages in a new line, following the current line. A Write() method variant is called to notify the host to just display the message in the current line. The foregroundColor and backgroundColor parameters specify what colors to use as the foreground and background of a message, respectively. However, the F&O subsystem does not take advantage of these foregroundColor and backgroundColor parameters. See Figure 7-5 for an example.

Prompt Method

The Prompt() method is called by the Windows PowerShell engine whenever missing data is needed from the user. This method is defined as follows:

```
public abstract Dictionary<string, PSObject> Prompt(string caption, string message,
Collection<FieldDescription> descriptions);
```

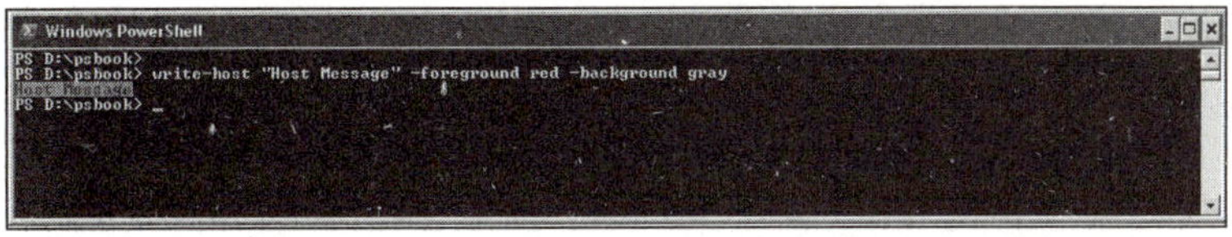

Figure 7-5: The F&O subsystem does not support message coloring in version 1 of Windows PowerShell. The write-host cmdlet addresses this by providing two parameters: ForegroundColor and BackgroundColor.

This method is called in situations where the user forgets to supply a value for a mandatory parameter, as shown in the following example:

```
PS D:\psbook> stop-process

cmdlet stop-process at command pipeline position 1
Supply values for the following parameters:
Id[0]:
```

Here, the cmdlet parameter binder calls the `Prompt()` method. The hosting application is expected to take input from the user based on the supplied *descriptions* and return the results. A *caption* and a *message* are provided as hints to be displayed to the user. The results must be of type `System.Collections.Generic.Dictionary` with the key being the name supplied with the *descriptions* parameter. For example, if *descriptions* contain three entries with the names `FirstParameter`, `SecondParameter`, and `ThirdParameter`, then the results should also contain three entries, with the key names being `FirstParameter`, `SecondParameter`, and `ThirdParameter`, respectively. This ensures that the Windows PowerShell engine's cmdlet parameter binder correctly binds a parameter to its value. `FieldDescription` has the following members:

```
namespace System.Management.Automation.Host
{
    public class FieldDescription
    {
        public FieldDescription(string name);
        public Collection<Attribute> Attributes { get; }
        public PSObject DefaultValue { get; set; }
        public string HelpMessage { get; set; }
        public bool IsMandatory { get; set; }
        public string Label { get; set; }
        public string Name { get; }
        public string ParameterAssemblyFullName { get; }
        public string ParameterTypeFullName { get; }
        public string ParameterTypeName { get; }

        public void SetParameterType(Type parameterType);
    }
}
```

`Name` is used to uniquely identify the parameter field. `HelpMessage` is a message specific to the field, used as a tip to the user to supply an appropriate value for the field. `DefaultValue` is the default value for this parameter field. This can be used to populate the UI with a default value. This is an instance of type `PSObject`, so that it can be serialized and manipulated just like any pipeline object. `IsMandatory` indicates whether or not a value should be supplied for this field. `Attributes` will contain a set of attributes that are attached to a cmdlet parameter declaration. The `ParameterAssemblyFullName`, `ParameterTypeFullName`, and `ParameterTypeName` identify the parameter type and its assembly.

A cmdlet developer can take advantage of this method and call it directly without depending on the Windows PowerShell engine's cmdlet parameter binder in some cases where a parameter may not be mandatory. This may be necessary in situations where user input is needed in the middle of processing a command.

PromptForCredential

The `PromptForCredential()` methods are used to get credentials, i.e., username and password, from the user. These methods are defined as follows:

```
public abstract PSCredential PromptForCredential(string caption, string message,
string userName, string targetName)

public abstract PSCredential PromptForCredential(string caption, string message,
string userName, string targetName, PSCredentialTypes allowedCredentialTypes,
PSCredentialUIOptions options)
```

These methods must return a `PSCredential` object holding username and password credentials. The `caption` parameter provides a header to be displayed to the user. The `message` parameter provides a short message describing what is expected. The `username` parameter provides the username for which the credential is required. This may be null or empty, in which case the hosting application may need to get the username along with the password from the user. The `target` parameter describes a target for which the credential is needed. The `options` parameter provides additional context regarding whether the `username` parameter is read-only, whether username syntax must be validated, and whether to prompt for username and password even if the password is cached. Depending on the cmdlet's needs, a cmdlet developer may call this method differently.

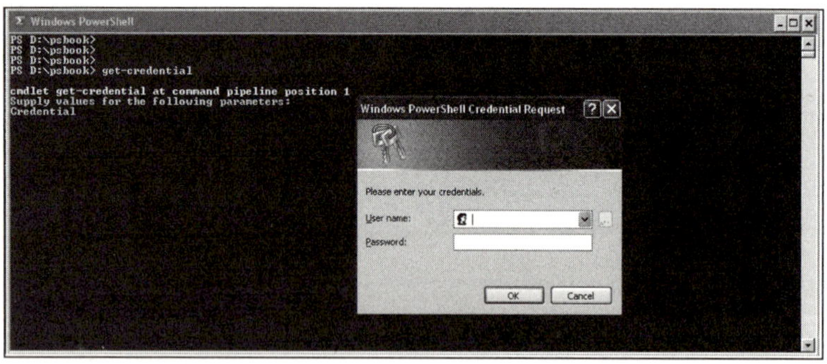

Figure 7-6: Windows PowerShell's console host displays a UI like this to collect credentials in a secure manner.

Because this is sensitive information, the hosting application must do everything necessary to protect the data. While taking password input from the user, make sure the display is secured (i.e., not showing user-typed characters on the screen). Figure 7-6 shows a typical dialog for entering credentials. The `PromptForCredential()` method is called by the Windows PowerShell engine to populate a cmdlet parameter declared with the `Credential` attribute. For example, the `Get-Credential` cmdlet has a parameter declared with the `Credential` attribute.

A hosting application is encouraged to deploy similar methods to collect credentials in a secure manner from the user.

Read Methods

These methods are used to take user input other than parameter values, choice selections, and credentials:

```
public abstract string ReadLine()
public abstract SecureString ReadLineAsSecureString()
```

`ReadLine` is used to get regular input from the user. `ReadLineAsSecureString()`, as the name suggests, is used to get user input in a secure fashion. The host developer is expected to protect such data just like the `PromptForCredential()` method. The `Read-Host` cmdlet calls these methods:

```
PS D:\psbook> $unsecureString = read-host
This is unsecured data
PS D:\psbook> $unsecureString
This is unsecured data
PS D:\psbook> $secureString = read-host -assecurestring
********************
PS D:\psbook> $securestring
System.Security.SecureString
PS D:\psbook> $bstr =
[System.Runtime.InteropServices.marshal]::SecureStringToBSTR($securestring)
PS D:\psbook> $convertedString =
[System.Runtime.InteropServices.marshal]::PtrToStringAuto($bstr)
PS D:\psbook> [System.Runtime.InteropServices.marshal]::ZeroFreeBSTR($bstr)
PS D:\psbook> $convertedString
This is secured data
PS D:\psbook>
```

Notice how Windows PowerShell's `ConsoleHost` protects the user input with `read-host -assecurestring`. The preceding example also shows how to decrypt data from an instance of type `System.Security.SecureString`.

The `PSHostUserInterface` class is designed to notify the host about certain messages, such as debug, warning, prompt, and so on. The internal host's display layout is not exposed to the Windows PowerShell engine using this interface. As shown in the next section, in some circumstances the Windows PowerShell engine needs to access the host's display. The following section discusses the `PSHostRawUserInterface` class, which exposes the host's display layout.

PSHostRawUserInterface Class

The Windows PowerShell engine needs minute details about how the UI is structured. This is to support paging for the `Out-Host` cmdlet, to effectively compute the width of the UI window for the `Out-String` cmdlet, and so on. This way, every hosting application may not need to implement similar functionality to support various behaviors. The Windows PowerShell engine assumes that the UI is represented as a two-dimensional array of cells, with each cell holding a single character.

The `PSHostRawUserInterface` class is designed to represent the raw user interface of the UI as viewed by the Windows PowerShell engine. This interface was designed with the assumption that Windows PowerShell is hosted only in console-based applications. Hence, some of the members may not make sense for GUI-based applications, such as .NET forms-based applications. The hosting application must register an instance of this class through the `PSHost.UI.RawUI` property when the runspace is created. If the value of the `PSHost.UI.RawUI` property is `null`, then the Windows PowerShell's F&O subsystem may not be able to format certain data effectively.

For example, paging with the `Out-Host` cmdlet may not work properly. The `PSHostUserInterface` abstract class is defined in `System.Management. Automation.dll` under the `System.Management.Automation.Host` namespace. The abstract `PSHostRawUserInteface` base class looks like the following:

```
namespace System.Management.Automation.Host
{
    public abstract class PSHostRawUserInterface
    {
        protected PSHostRawUserInterface();
        public abstract ConsoleColor BackgroundColor { get; set; }
        public abstract Size BufferSize { get; set; }
        public abstract Coordinates CursorPosition { get; set; }
        public abstract int CursorSize { get; set; }
        public abstract ConsoleColor ForegroundColor { get; set; }
        public abstract bool KeyAvailable { get; }
        public abstract Size MaxPhysicalWindowSize { get; }
        public abstract Size MaxWindowSize { get; }
        public abstract Coordinates WindowPosition { get; set; }
        public abstract Size WindowSize { get; set; }
        public abstract string WindowTitle { get; set; }

        public abstract void FlushInputBuffer();
        public abstract BufferCell[,] GetBufferContents(Rectangle rectangle);
        public virtual int LengthInBufferCells(char source);
        public virtual int LengthInBufferCells(string source);
        public BufferCell[,] NewBufferCellArray(Size size, BufferCell contents);
        public BufferCell[,] NewBufferCellArray(int width, int height, BufferCell
contents);
        public BufferCell[,] NewBufferCellArray(string[] contents, ConsoleColor
foregroundColor, ConsoleColor backgroundColor);
        public KeyInfo ReadKey();
        public abstract KeyInfo ReadKey(ReadKeyOptions options);
        public abstract void ScrollBufferContents(Rectangle source, Coordinates
destination, Rectangle clip, BufferCell fill);
        public abstract void SetBufferContents(Coordinates origin, BufferCell[,]
contents);
        public abstract void SetBufferContents(Rectangle region, BufferCell fill);
    }
}
```

As shown in the preceding definition, the interface represents different metadata of the UI, such as `CursorSize`, `CursorPosition`, `WindowSize`, `MaxWindowSize`, `BufferSize`, and so on. Using this metadata, the Windows PowerShell `Out-Host` cmdlet effectively pages data. The following table describes the purpose of each of the properties in the `PSHostRawUserInterface` class:

Property	Purpose
BackgroundColor	Gets or sets the background color that is used to render each character
ForegroundColor	Gets or sets the foreground color that is used to render each character
BufferSize	Gets or sets the current size of the screen buffer, measured in buffer cells
CursorSize	Gets or sets the cursor size. The value must be in the range 0–100.
CursorPosition	Gets or set the cursor position
WindowSize	Gets or sets the current window size. The window size must not be greater than `MaxWindowSize`.
MaxWindowSize	Gets the size of the largest window possible for the current buffer, current font, and current display hardware
WindowPosition	Gets or sets the position of the view relative to the screen buffer, in characters. (0,0) is the upper-left corner of the screen buffer.
WindowTitle	Gets or sets the title bar text of the current UI window
KeyAvailable	A non-blocking call to examine whether a keystroke is waiting

The Windows PowerShell engine depends on the `BackgroundColor`, `ForegroundColor`, `BufferSize`, and `WindowSize` properties directly to format output. The rest of the members are not directly called by the Windows PowerShell engine. A host developer should keep in mind that scripts may also depend on some or all of these properties, so in order to provide script compatibility, it is recommended that you properly support these interfaces as described above.

The `ReadKey()` method is intended to read keystrokes from the keyboard device. This method should block until a keystroke is pressed. Scripts may use this to handle actual keypad keystrokes other than traditional characters and to get granular details, such as whether the key is pressed down or up. For example, to identify a Ctrl + A message, a scripter will call the `ReadKey()` method, as shown in the following example:

```
PS D:\psbook> $option =
[System.Management.Automation.Host.ReadKeyOptions]"IncludeKeyUp"
PS D:\psbook> $keyInfo = $host.UI.RawUI.ReadKey($option)
PS D:\psbook> $keyInfo | fl VirtualKeyCode,ControlKeyState

VirtualKeyCode  : 65
ControlKeyState : LeftCtrlPressed, NumLockOn
```

VirtualKeyCode 65 indicates that key "A" is pressed on the keypad. ControlKeyState indicates that the left Ctrl key is pressed and Num Lock is on.

The rest of the methods support cell manipulation. For example, a BufferCell looks like the following:

```
namespace System.Management.Automation.Host
{
    public struct BufferCell
    {
        public BufferCell(char character, ConsoleColor foreground, ConsoleColor
background, BufferCellType bufferCellType);

        public static bool operator !=(BufferCell first, BufferCell second);
        public static bool operator ==(BufferCell first, BufferCell second);

        public ConsoleColor BackgroundColor { get; set; }
        public BufferCellType BufferCellType { get; set; }
        public char Character { get; set; }

        public ConsoleColor ForegroundColor { get; set; }
        public override bool Equals(object obj);
        public override int GetHashCode();
        public override string ToString();
    }
}
```

Effectively, a BufferCell represents a single character and its associated background color, foreground color, and cell type. A cell type can be either *complete, leading,* or *trailing.* A *leading* cell type represents the leading cell of a character that occupies two cells, such as an East Asian character. A *trailing* cell type represents the trailing cell of a character that occupies two cells. The conditional operators handle BufferCell comparisons. Two BufferCells are considered equal when the values of the individual properties in each of the BufferCells are equal.

The GetBufferContents() method extracts the BufferCells for the identified screen coordinates:

```
public abstract BufferCell[,] GetBufferContents(Rectangle rectangle);
```

If the screen coordinates are completely outside of the screen buffer, a BufferCell array of zero rows and columns should be returned. The resulting array should be organized in row-major order.

The SetBufferContents() method copies the *contents* of the BufferCell array into the screen buffer at the given origin, clipping it such that cells in the *contents* of the BufferCell array that would fall outside the screen buffer are ignored:

```
public abstract void SetBufferContents(Coordinates origin, BufferCell[,] contents)
```

The following method copies the given character (identified by the fill parameter) to all of the character cells identified by the region rectangle parameter:

```
public abstract void SetBufferContents(Rectangle region, BufferCell fill);
```

If all four elements of the `region` parameter are set to 'all', then the entire screen buffer should be filled with the given character.

All of the following methods are supposed to create a two-dimensional array of `BufferCells`:

```
public BufferCell[,] NewBufferCellArray(Size size, BufferCell contents);
public BufferCell[,] NewBufferCellArray(int width, int height, BufferCell
contents);
public BufferCell[,] NewBufferCellArray(string[] contents, ConsoleColor
foregroundColor, ConsoleColor backgroundColor);
```

The first two variants create a two-dimensional `BufferCells` array and fill the array with the supplied `contents` character. *size* represents the width and height of the resulting array. The third variant constructs the result array using the supplied `contents` string array. In this case, each string in the array is observed and broken into multiple characters if needed.

The next two methods should return the number of `BufferCells` needed to fit the character or string specified through the `source` parameter:

```
public virtual int LengthInBufferCells(char source)
public virtual int LengthInBufferCells(string source)
```

Remember that each `BufferCell` can hold at most one character. An East-Asian character might occupy more than one `BufferCell`.

Summary

In this chapter you saw how a hosting application can take advantage of the `PSHost`, `PSHostUserInterface`, and `PSHostRawUserInterface` classes to get different forms of data from the Windows PowerShell engine. The Windows PowerShell's pipeline supports only input, error, and output data. Other forms of data such as debug, verbose, warning, and so on, are notified through the host. A hosting application must register an instance of `PSHost` to the runspace at runspace creation time to access these different forms of data.

Cmdlet developers should take advantage of the `WriteDebug()`, `WriteWarning()`, `WriteVerbose()`, and `WriteProgress()` methods defined in the base `cmdlet` class instead of calling host methods directly. Script developers should take advantage of the `Write-Debug`, `Write-Warning`, `Write-Verbose`, and `Write-Progress` cmdlets. The hosting application must ensure thread safety of the `PSHost`, `PSHostUserInterface`, and `PSHostRawUserInterface` members. It is a good practice to maintain a 1:1 mapping between a host and a runspace.

8

Formatting & Output

Formatting & Output is a single component of PowerShell that determines how objects are displayed to the console. PowerShell enables users to provide custom formatting for types they create or types that already exist in .NET or PowerShell. This custom formatting is controlled via several configuration files, with the file naming convention of `*.format.ps1xml`. These configuration files are used by the format cmdlets (`format-table`, `format-list`, `format-custom`, `format-wide`) to display text to the screen for the default console host (`powershell.exe`). The best way to ensure that objects are displayed in a consistent manner is to add your own "views" by creating your own format configuration file and adding them to the current session. Adding your configuration file to the current session is done by using the `update-formatdata` cmdlet or by including your file(s) with a snap-in.

This chapter provides an introduction to creating your own views for the different view types. Included are several examples of format configuration, which can be used as a baseline for your own custom formatting.

The Four View Types

Four view types are available when displaying objects to the console:

- Table
- List
- Wide
- Custom

The table view displays the properties of each object in a single row using tabbed columns to separate the text for each. Each column has a column header that is the property name or something similar. The list view displays properties for an object on a separate line using a name-value syntax. Each object is thus one or more lines depending on how many properties are to be displayed for each object. Blank lines are used to separate objects on the console for the list view. The wide view displays a single value for each object and formats them in columns. The wide view is the same as using the **dir /w** command in `cmd.exe`. Unlike using **dir** in `cmd.exe`, however, the wide view can be used for any object, not just files and directories. The custom view enables developers and users to create more complex formatting for their objects than what is provided by the list, table, or wide views.

Each object type can have multiple views defined but only one view can be the "default" view. The default view is the view that is used when no `format-*` cmdlet is explicitly specified. The default view for each object is the first view encountered when reading the formatting configuration files. See the section "Loading Your Formatting File(s)" for more details on how to order your views to control the default for your object types.

Table: format-table

The most popular view type for `powershell.exe` is the table view. If the default view for the object being displayed is not the table view, it can be explicitly selected with the `format-table` cmdlet. See the section "Formatting without *.format.ps1xml" for more information about how to use `format-table` to override the default view settings.

The following example console output shows the default table view for all file or directory objects:

```
PS C:\Documents and Settings\Owner> dir

    Directory: Microsoft.PowerShell.Core\FileSystem::C:\Documents and Settings\Owner

Mode                LastWriteTime     Length Name
----                -------------     ------ ----
d----         7/10/2007   4:12 AM            Desktop
d-r--         6/17/2007  10:03 PM            Favorites
d-r--         7/10/2007   3:39 AM            My Documents
d-r--         2/19/2007  11:39 PM            Start Menu
d----         8/20/2003   5:04 AM            VSWebCache
d----          6/9/2003   6:54 AM            WINDOWS
-a---         7/16/2007  11:28 AM    6291456 ntuser.dat
-a---         8/28/2003   6:52 AM        921 reglog.txt
```

List: format-list

The list view displays properties in a sequential list format. The list view can be explicitly selected by using the `format-list` cmdlet. It supports many of the same parameters as `format-table` to enable users to specify what properties to display. The properties displayed in the following example console output are different from the table view because a separate list view is defined for files and directory objects:

```
PS C:\Documents and Settings\Owner> dir | format-list

    Directory: Microsoft.PowerShell.Core\FileSystem::C:\Documents and Settings\Owner

Name           : Desktop
CreationTime   : 1/9/2003 6:58:58 AM
LastWriteTime  : 7/10/2007 4:12:22 AM
LastAccessTime : 7/16/2007 3:06:42 PM
```

```
Name           : My Documents
CreationTime   : 1/9/2003 6:58:58 AM
LastWriteTime  : 7/10/2007 3:39:44 AM
LastAccessTime : 7/16/2007 3:07:54 PM

Name           : Start Menu
CreationTime   : 1/9/2003 6:58:57 AM
LastWriteTime  : 2/19/2007 11:39:49 PM
LastAccessTime : 7/16/2007 1:20:54 PM

Name           : ntuser.dat
Length         : 6291456
CreationTime   : 5/1/2005 4:16:41 PM
LastWriteTime  : 7/16/2007 11:28:04 AM
LastAccessTime : 7/16/2007 11:44:53 AM
VersionInfo    :

Name           : reglog.txt
Length         : 921
CreationTime   : 8/28/2003 6:52:35 AM
LastWriteTime  : 8/28/2003 6:52:35 AM
LastAccessTime : 11/5/2006 1:04:04 AM
VersionInfo    :
```

Custom: format-custom

Users can specify a custom view that is defined in the `*.format.ps1xml` config file. For process objects (`System.Diagnostics.Process`), the custom view creates a class declaration syntax-like view. The custom view should be used when you want to display information for an object in a way other than the rigid table, list, or wide view structures. A good example of the custom view is the help information for a cmdlet. The help objects have a custom view defined that enables them to be displayed in an easy to read format with a lot of text.

```
PS C:\Documents and Settings\Owner> get-process powershell | format-custom

class Process
{
  Id = 3916
  Handles = 500
  CPU = 30.734375
  Name = powershell
}
```

Wide: format-wide

The wide view picks one property from the object to display and formats it in two tabular columns by default. If no wide view is defined for the object type, the first property of the object to be found via reflection is used (the first property alphabetically). The `-autosize` parameter creates as many columns as the width of the output will allow without clipping text.

```
PS C:\Documents and Settings\Owner> dir | format-wide

    Directory: Microsoft.PowerShell.Core\FileSystem::C:\Documents and Settings\Owner
```

```
[Desktop]                                                   [Favorites]
[My Documents]                                              [Start Menu]
[VSWebCache]                                                [WINDOWS]
ntuser.dat                                                  reglog.txt

PS C:\Documents and Settings\Owner> dir | format-wide -autosize

    Directory: Microsoft.PowerShell.Core\FileSystem::C:\Documents and Settings\Owner

[Desktop]          [Favorites]       [My Documents]    [Start Menu]      [VSWebCache]
[WINDOWS]         ntuser.dat        reglog.txt
```

Due to formatting in the book, the actual number of columns in the preceding output example might not match what you see on your screen.

Formatting without *.format.ps1xml

Before we create an XML format file for displaying objects, let's take a quick walk through some examples of what you can accomplish by simply using the `format-*` cmdlets. This is important because you will occasionally want to create a custom look and feel without the overhead of creating an XML config file and adding it to the session. In these examples, `format-list` can be used interchangeably with `format-table` to display the properties in list view format. The only difference is that `format-list` doesn't accept an `-autosize` parameter because it only displays one item per line.

Example 1: Display specific properties for `format-table` or `format-list`. "ft" is the alias for `format-table`.

```
PS C:\Documents and Settings\Owner> dir | ft name,length

Name                                                        length
----                                                        ------
Desktop
Favorites
My Documents
Start Menu
VSWebCache
WINDOWS
ntuser.dat                                                  6291456
reglog.txt                                                  921
```

Example 2: Use wildcard matching to select which properties to display. This example displays the name and any properties that end in `time` (e.g., `CreationTime`, `LastAccessTime`, `LastWriteTime`).

```
PS C:\Documents and Settings\Owner> dir | ft name,*time
Name                     CreationTime              LastAccessTime            LastWriteTime
----                     ------------              --------------            -------------
Desktop                  1/9/2003 6:58:58 AM       7/18/2007 8:48:06 PM      7/18/2007
8:47:50 PM
Favorites                1/9/2003 6:58:58 AM       7/18/2007 8:45:07 PM      6/17/2007
10:03:57 PM
My Documents             1/9/2003 6:58:58 AM       7/18/2007 8:48:59 PM      7/10/2007
```

```
3:39:44 AM
Start Menu          1/9/2003 6:58:57 AM     7/18/2007 1:51:28 PM     2/19/2007
11:39:49 PM
VSWebCache          8/20/2003 5:04:09 AM    7/14/2007 1:26:19 AM     8/20/2003
5:04:09 AM
WINDOWS             6/9/2003 6:54:05 AM     7/14/2007 1:26:20 AM     6/9/2003
6:54:05 AM
ntuser.dat          5/1/2005 4:16:41 PM     7/18/2007 9:49:14 AM     7/18/2007
9:34:46 AM
reglog.txt          8/28/2003 6:52:35 AM    11/5/2006 1:04:04 AM     8/28/2003
6:52:35 AM
```

Example 3: Use a `ScriptBlock` token to display a column with an expression, rather than a property, for every object. Here, I want to display the day on which each file or directory was last written to. The `-autosize` parameter is used to display results as compactly as possible, rather than splitting the screen in half.

```
PS C:\Documents and Settings\Owner> dir | ft -auto name,{$_.LastWriteTime.DayOfWeek}

Name            $_.LastWriteTime.DayOfWeek
----            --------------------------
Desktop                          Wednesday
Favorites                           Sunday
My Documents                       Tuesday
Start Menu                          Monday
VSWebCache                       Wednesday
WINDOWS                             Monday
ntuser.dat                       Wednesday
reglog.txt                        Thursday
```

The preceding examples show how you can explicitly control the properties to be displayed for the table and list views using the `format-table` and `format-list` cmdlets. Similar control can be achieved with `format-wide` but only a single property can be specified per object.

Format Configuration File Example

Now let's create a simple format configuration file to display `Process` objects. The following listing contains all the text necessary for a simple configuration file that adds another table view for `Process` objects. This sample file is also on the `www.wrox.com` website for this book as file `figure8_1.format.ps1xml`. You can download the file from the website or type the following text and save it:

```
<?xml version="1.0" encoding="utf-8" ?>
<Configuration>
  <ViewDefinitions>
    <View>
      <Name>MyProcessView</Name>
      <ViewSelectedBy>
        <TypeName>System.Diagnostics.Process</TypeName>
      </ViewSelectedBy>
      <TableControl>
        <TableHeaders>
          <TableColumnHeader>
            <Label>Name:ID</Label>
```

```
          </TableColumnHeader>
          <TableColumnHeader>
            <Label>Threads</Label>
          </TableColumnHeader>
        </TableHeaders>
        <TableRowEntries>
          <TableRowEntry>
            <TableColumnItems>
              <TableColumnItem>
                <ScriptBlock>$_.ProcessName + ":" + $_.Id</ScriptBlock>
              </TableColumnItem>
              <TableColumnItem>
                <PropertyName>Threads</PropertyName>
              </TableColumnItem>
            </TableColumnItems>
          </TableRowEntry>
        </TableRowEntries>
      </TableControl>
    </View>
  </ViewDefinitions>
</Configuration>
```

After we add our format file to the session, we can use it by explicitly specifying the table view defined in the XML. Note the column headers and how they match the values in the `<TableColumnHeader>` nodes in the XML configuration file. In addition, note the output that results from the `ScriptBlock` command for the `<TableColumnItem>` nodes.

```
PS C:\Documents and Settings\Owner> update-formatdata figure8_1.format.ps1xml
PS C:\Documents and Settings\Owner> gps | ft -view myprocessview

Name:ID                                Threads
-------                                -------
alg:544                                {584, 720, 3748, 3752...}
CCEVTMGR:628                           {812, 904, 1036, 1040...}
cmd:1940                               {504}
cmd:3040                               {1164}
csrss:500                              {508, 512, 516, 520...}
ctfmon:2084                            {2028}
```

Loading Your Format File(s)

Before we dissect the file and examine its individual elements, let's look at the different mechanisms for adding your format configuration file to the existing format configuration. There are three ways to make your format files available for use:

- Use the `update-formatdata` cmdlet.
- Add a snap-in that has the format files included.
- Use the public API of the `RunspaceConfiguration` class.

The first two are the easiest and most common ways to add your files. The last one should only be used when you are implementing your own custom host. This section provides details about these three mechanisms.

Technically, there is a fourth method, editing the built-in format configuration files included with the PowerShell installation, but it is not recommended. It's easy enough to add your own views and ensure that they are used by default or by specifying them using the `-view` parameter without editing the built-in files directly.

Update-formatdata

The `update-formatdata` cmdlet loads the files specified by its `-prependPath` and `-appendPath` parameters. The `prependPath` parameter loads the configuration files and places them before the currently loaded configuration. The `appendPath` parameter loads them after. The reason this distinction must be made is because the default view for an object is the first view encountered for a given type name. Using `-prependPath` places the views in your format file(s) *before* the built-in format files. This enables you to override the default views for objects such as `Process` or `FileSystem` because regardless of the view's name, the first view found in the format configuration files is the one used for the output of that type. This applies to all view types.

If the first view for an object happens to be a list view, then that will be the default output if no `format-*` cmdlet is explicitly specified. If you use `-appendPath` to add your configuration file to the current session, the existing default process view remains the default and you will have to explicitly specify your view with the `-view` parameter. Because you can include multiple views in a single format configuration file, be sure to place your default views for list, wide, and table near the top of the file.

When searching views by type name, PowerShell also takes into account object inheritance. If a view is defined for a base class that has children classes derived from it, objects of the children's type will use the view defined for the parent class. The `ViewSelectedBy` lookup will match the view as closely to the child class's actual type as possible. Thus, an exact type name match would override the base class type match. The following example changes the default process view by prepending the sample format configuration file:

```
PS C:\Dev\games\SampleContentPipeline\SampleContentPipeline> gps powershell

Handles  NPM(K)    PM(K)      WS(K) VM(M)   CPU(s)     Id ProcessName
-------  ------    -----      ----- -----   ------     -- -----------
    240       5    27284      23412   135     0.61   3084 powershell

PS C:\Dev\games\SampleContentPipeline\SampleContentPipeline> update-formatdata
-prependPath figure8-1_table.format.ps1xml

PS C:\Dev\games\SampleContentPipeline\SampleContentPipeline> gps powershell

Name:ID                                                      Threads
-------                                                      -------
powershell:3084                                           {1780, 1052, 356, 2004}. . .
```

For more information on `update-formatdata` type **PSH > help update-formatdata -full**.

Snap-ins

As discussed in Chapter 2, snap-ins are ways of packaging cmdlets, providers, and configuration files for distribution and installation with PowerShell. Snap-ins usually add their own object types via the cmdlets or providers included. If this is the case, it makes sense to include your format configuration files in the same manner. This way, when you add a snap-in to the PowerShell session, those new types are added, including information about how to display them; and no extra step using `update-formatdata` is needed.

RunspaceConfiguration API

Because the `RunspaceConfiguration` object is where the information from the format files is stored, you can add your format files directly via the public `RunspaceConfiguration` API. Add your files to the existing list of format configuration files and call the `Update()` method. The same logic applied for the use of `update-formatdata` applies here for view ordering.

Using the public `RunspaceConfiguration` APIs should be reserved for cases where you want to avoid using `update-formatdata`. One example that comes to mind is a graphical shell that limits the cmdlets to be used such that `update-formatdata` isn't available. Though this is possible, it is recommended that you use `update-formatdata`. Or, if your format file is included with other cmdlets/providers, package your format files as part of a snap-in.

Anatomy of a Format Configuration File

Each format configuration file must start with the `<Configuration>` and `< ViewDefinitions >` XML nodes. One or more views are defined in a single format file and they are each enclosed within the `<View>` node. Remember that the ordering of the views determines which views are used by default, so plan which views should be placed earlier in the file.

Each view declaration consists of two areas. The first area has metadata about the view, such as the view's name, the type(s) it applies to, and optional *group by* information. The second area has the formatting information, which indicates the type of view and what text is to be displayed to the console for each object. This second area contains the entries that define exactly what is displayed for each object.

The following sections cover different aspects of the format configuration file in further detail. For the table view discussion, refer to the format file in `figure8_1.format.ps1xml`. Each view type has a complete, valid configuration file that we will use for analysis purposes. These sample format files can be found on the website as well. They could just as easily be combined into a single format file, but for discussion purposes it is easier to look at them separately.

In addition to looking at the following examples, the reader is encouraged to examine the format configuration files included with the installation of PowerShell. They are located in `\%windir\%\system32\windowspowershell\v1.0`. The following is a command to list the format files included with PowerShell:

```
PS C:\Documents and Settings\Owner> dir $env:windir\system32\windowspowershell\v
1.0\*.format.ps1xml

    Directory: Microsoft.PowerShell.Core\FileSystem::C:\WINNT\system32\windowsp
    owershell\v1.0
```

```
Mode                LastWriteTime     Length Name
----                -------------     ------ ----
-----          9/8/2006  12:28 AM      22120 certificate.format.ps1xml
-----          9/8/2006  12:28 AM      60703 dotnettypes.format.ps1xml
-a---         7/20/2007   7:50 PM      19730 filesystem.format.ps1xml
-----          9/8/2006  12:28 AM     250197 help.format.ps1xml
-----          9/8/2006  12:28 AM      65283 powershellcore.format.ps1xml
-----          9/8/2006   1:28 AM      13394 powershelltrace.format.ps1xml
-----          9/8/2006  12:28 AM      13540 registry.format.ps1xml
```

View

Multiple views can be defined in a single configuration file, and each of them is defined inside the `<View>` node, which is directly under the `<ViewDefinitions>` node. The view has several properties, indicated by its children XML nodes, including `Name`, `ViewSelectedBy`, `GroupBy` (optional), and one of the following, which indicates the type of view that is defined (the names are self-explanatory):

- <TableControl>
- <ListControl>
- <WideControl>
- <CustomControl>

Name

This node specifies the name of the view. This name is what the user can supply to the `-view` parameter for the `format-list` and `format-table` cmdlets. This name must be unique for all views of the same type of display. Otherwise, an error will occur when trying to add the view to the format configuration. If you have multiple views defined for the same type name and the same view type (e.g., table), it is important to understand that the default one to be used is the first one encountered when reading your format configuration file. The section "Adding Your Format Configuration Files" provides more information about how to control the ordering of format files if you have multiple views in separate format config files.

ViewSelectedBy

This child node of `<View>` indicates the objects by the type for which this view is defined. Typically, this node will have a child node of `<Typename>`, and the object's type is used as the lookup to find the correct view. The full `TypeName` (displayed by `get-member` for a given object), which includes `Namespace`, must be specified.

For example, the following view would be used for the `Process` objects that `get-process` returns:

```
. . .
   <ViewSelectedBy>
      <TypeName>System.Diagnostics.Process</TypeName>
   </ViewSelectedBy>
. . .
```

If the type in question happens to be an inner class, then the syntax of the `TypeName` is as follows:

```
. . .
   <ViewSelectedBy>
      <TypeName>Namespace.OuterClass+InnerClass</TypeName>
   </ViewSelectedBy>
. . .
```

The following example illustrates the `TypeName` for a generic type. Note that you need to supply the fully qualified name of the type that the generic type was created with. In this specific example, the type is `SomeGenericClass<int>`:

```
. . .
   <ViewSelectedBy>
      <TypeName>Namespace.SomeGenericClass'1[[System.Int32, mscorlib,
Version=2.0.0.0, Culture=neutral, PublicKeyToken=b77a5c561934e089]]</TypeName>
   </ViewSelectedBy>
. . .
```

GroupBy

The `GroupBy` node causes similar objects to be grouped together in the resulting output. Some criteria is specified via a `propertyName` or a `scriptBlock` expression, which is used to determine whether objects are in the same group. When an object is encountered that doesn't belong to same group as the previous object, a new group is created and some text is displayed to indicate that there is a new group. The `groupBy` feature does *not* gather all the objects and then put them in unique groups. It simply creates a new group for an object if the object is different than the previous object displayed according to the grouping criteria. This means the objects are still displayed in the same exact order in which they are piped to the `format-*` cmdlet. The `format-list` and `format-table` cmdlets also have a `-groupby` parameter that accomplishes the same thing.

Here's some example output of the `GroupBy` feature that uses the file extension to group similar files from the `get-childitem` cmdlet. This output clearly demonstrates that multiple groups for the same extension were created because the file objects are in alphabetical order, not in order by extension:

```
PS C:\Documents and Settings\Owner\Desktop> dir | ft -view GroupByFileExtension

   Extension:

Name                                    Size
----                                    ----
funny_stuff
MIDI_files
music_stuff
what_is_this

   Extension: .lnk

Name                                    Size
----                                    ----
Audacity.lnk                            630
Bicycle Card Collection.lnk             1801
```

```
   Extension: .txt

Name                                   Size
----                                   ----
blues_piano_DVD_notes.txt              589

   Extension: .lnk

Name                                   Size
----                                   ----
Reason.lnk                             1425
```

Determining whether objects are in the same "group" can be controlled by a property on the objects or a script block. There's also an optional `<Label>` that can be used to add more context to the text displayed before each group.

What follows here is grouping by `PropertyName` with an optional `<Label>` tag. This example could be applied to an additional view for `FileSystem` objects (files and directories), and would create groups based on extension:

```
. . .
   <Name>. . .</Name>
   <GroupBy>
      <PropertyName>Extension</PropertyName>
      <Label>FileExtension</Label>
   </GroupBy>
   <ViewSelectedBy>. . .</ViewSelectedBy>
. . .
```

The next snippet shows an example of grouping by a script block that uses the object type. This might be useful if you want to group similar objects that all derive from a single base class.

```
. . .
   <GroupBy>
      <ScriptBlock>$_.GetType()</ScriptBlock>
   </GroupBy>
. . .
```

TableControl

The `<TableControl>` node indicates a table view. The table view has headers and rows that control the label and display for each object. It is the only view that has a separate "headers" section.

TableHeaders

The `<TableHeaders>` node has zero or more `<TableHeaderColumn>` nodes. If no `TableHeaderColumn` entries are present, then the column headers will be labeled according to the property name or script block entries in the `<TableRowEntry>` section. Omitting the table headers is basically the same as explicitly setting values for the `–properties` parameter of the `format-list` or `format-table` cmdlet. The property or script block specified is what is used to display for the header.

When you want to control the text to display for each header, or you want to adjust the width or alignment of the columns for your view, you should add `TableHeaderColumn` entries to your view:

```
. . .
<TableHeaders>
   <TableColumnHeader>
      <Label>col1</Label>
      <Alignment>left</Alignment>
      <Width>10</Width>
   </TableColumnHeader>
   <TableColumnHeader>
      <Label>col2</Label>
   </TableColumnHeader>
</TableHeaders>
. . .
```

The `<Label>` entry controls what is displayed for the column header. The `<Alignment>` node indicates whether the text is left, right, or center justified. The `<Width>` node indicates how many characters wide the column should be.

TableRowEntries

The `<TableRowEntries>` section controls what is displayed for each individual object. Only one `<TableRowEntry>` can be displayed for a given object. The `<TableRowEntry>` node has a `<TableColumnItems>` node that defines one or more `<TableColumnItem>` nodes. The `<TableColumnItem>` entries contain either a `<PropertyName>` node, which indicates the property of the object to display, or a `<ScriptBlock>`, which contains an expression that produces a string to display for that column. Typically, the script block will combine or use properties from the object (via the underbar variable "`$_`") to create a more meaningful result to display. The first full format config file example contains examples of both the property name and the script block, and here they are again in isolation:

```
. . .
<TableRowEntries>
   <TableRowEntry>
      <TableColumnItems>
         <TableColumnItem>
            <ScriptBlock>$_.ProcessName + ":" + $_.Id</ScriptBlock>
         </TableColumnItem>
         <TableColumnItem>
            <PropertyName>Threads</PropertyName>
          </TableColumnItem>
      </TableColumnItems>
   </TableRowEntry>
</TableRowEntries>
. . .
```

ListControl

The `<Name>`, `<ViewSelectedBy>`, and `<GroupBy>` nodes are defined and used in the same manner for a list view as in a table view, as indicated in `figure8_1.format.ps1xml`. The `<ListControl>` node indicates this is a list view. The list view includes <ListEntries> that correspond to rows. Each row consists of a label and the value to display for the object:

```
<?xml version="1.0" encoding="utf-8" ?>
<Configuration>
   <ViewDefinitions>
      <View>
         <Name>MyProcessView</Name>
         <ViewSelectedBy>
            <TypeName>System.Diagnostics.Process</TypeName>
         </ViewSelectedBy>
         <ListControl>
            <ListEntries>
               <ListEntry>
                  <ListItems>
                     <ListItem>
                        <Label>Name:ID</Label>
                        <ScriptBlock>$_.ProcessName + ":" + $_.Id</ScriptBlock>
                     </ListItem>
                     <ListItem>
                     <!-- this label is redundant since it
                          matches propertyname -->
                        <Label>Threads</Label>
                        <PropertyName>Threads</PropertyName>
                     </ListItem>
                  </ListItems>
               </ListEntry>
            </ListEntries>
         </ListControl>
      </View>
   </ViewDefinitions>
</Configuration>
```

Following is the output that would result from using the preceding list view. This example assumes that you've added the format file to the session configuration via `update-formatdata`:

```
PS C:\Documents and Settings\Owner> gps | fl -view myprocessview

Name:ID : alg:544
Threads : {584, 720, 3748, 3752...}

Name:ID : CCEVTMGR:628
Threads : {812, 904, 1036, 1040...}
Name:ID : cmd:1940
Threads : {504}
```

ListEntries

Each <ListItem> under <ListItems> indicates a row to be displayed for the object. An optional <Label> can be supplied. If a label is not supplied, then the default is to use the `PropertyName` or `ScriptBlock` text as the left-hand-side label. The value to be displayed for that <listitem> is either the value of the `PropertyName` property of the object or the result of the `ScriptBlock` expression.

Wide Control

The <WideControl> XML node indicates a wide view. The wide view displays only a single value for each object. This can be the value of a single property (indicated by <PropertyName>) or the result of a script block expression (<scriptblock>). It is usually a good idea to keep the text displayed for each object as short as possible so that multiple columns can be displayed. Otherwise, the wide view loses its usefulness and is nothing more than a list view with a single value for each object.

```
<?xml version="1.0" encoding="utf-8" ?>
<Configuration>
   <ViewDefinitions>
      <View>
         <Name>MyProcessView</Name>
         <ViewSelectedBy>
            <TypeName>System.Diagnostics.Process</TypeName>
         </ViewSelectedBy>
         <WideControl>
            <WideEntries>
               <WideEntry>
                  <WideItem>
                     <ScriptBlock>$_.ProcessName + ":" + $_.Id + ", #Threads: "
+ $_.Threads.Count</ScriptBlock>
                  </WideItem>
               </WideEntry>
            </WideEntries>
         </WideControl>
      </View>
   </ViewDefinitions>
</Configuration>
```

Following is the output after using update-formatdata to load the wide view format file:

```
PS C:\Documents and Settings\Owner> gps | fw -view myprocessview

alg:544, #Threads: 5                  CCEVTMGR:628, #Threads: 17
cmd:1940, #Threads: 1                 cmd:3040, #Threads: 1
csrss:500, #Threads: 11               ctfmon:2084, #Threads: 1
CTSVCCDA:936, #Threads: 2             EvoInst:1064, #Threads: 2
explorer:3296, #Threads: 13           hpobnz08:3368, #Threads: 8
```

WideEntries

Unlike the other view types, for wide views only a single item is displayed for each object. There is no label or header for wide views. The value to be displayed for the object is either the value of the PropertyName property of the object or the result of a ScriptBlock expression. The <WideEntries> node has one or more <WideEntry> nodes, each of which has a single <WideItem> node.

Custom Control

The <CustomControl> XML node indicates a custom view. The <Name>, <ViewSelectedBy>, and <GroupBy> nodes are defined and used in the same manner for the custom view as they are for the other views. The custom view allows greater flexibility in displaying objects. It doesn't conform to the rigid table, list, or view structure, and allows more fine-grained control over how the output is formatted. The following example is the included on the website as `Figure8-4_custom.format.ps1xml`:

```
<?xml version="1.0" encoding="utf-8" ?>
<Configuration>
   <ViewDefinitions>
      <View>
         <Name>MyProcessView</Name>
         <ViewSelectedBy>
            <TypeName>System.Diagnostics.Process</TypeName>
         </ViewSelectedBy>
         <CustomControl>
            <CustomEntries>
               <CustomEntry>
                  <CustomItem>
                     <Text>Process:</Text>
                     <NewLine/>
                     <Text>[</Text>
                     <NewLine/>
                     <Text>    </Text>
                     <ExpressionBinding>
                        <ScriptBlock>$_.Name + ":" + $_.ID</ScriptBlock>
                     </ExpressionBinding>
                     <NewLine/>
                     <Text>    </Text>
                     <ExpressionBinding>
                        <ScriptBlock>[int]($_.WorkingSet/1024)</ScriptBlock>
                     </ExpressionBinding>
                     <Text> MB</Text>
                     <NewLine/>
                     <Text>]</Text>
                  </CustomItem>
               </CustomEntry>
            </CustomEntries>
         </CustomControl>
      </View>
   </ViewDefinitions>
</Configuration>
```

The following example output assumes that the format file is in the current directory:

```
PS C:\Documents and Settings\Owner> Update-FormatData figure8-4_custom.format.ps1xml

PS C:\Documents and Settings\Owner> gps svchost | fc -view MyProcessview

Process:
[
    svchost:756
    4024MB
]
Process:
[
    svchost:836
    4532MB
```

```
]
Process:
[
   svchost:868
   28604MB
]
```

CustomEntries

<CustomEntries> indicates the beginning of the <CustomEntry> nodes. The <CustomEntry> has a single <CustomItem> node that controls how each object is formatted. The <Text> and <NewLine> nodes allow more precise placement of text. The <ScriptBlock> and <PropertyName> nodes must be placed inside the <ExpressionBinding> nodes. The <CustomItem> definition can have an arbitrary number of text, new line, or expression binding nodes defined within it.

Note that the white space inside <Text> nodes is preserved and can be used for indentation purposes.

Miscellaneous Configuration Entries

This section discusses two separate format configuration entries that can be used to "hard-code" the formatting behavior of your objects. The <wrap> and <autosize> nodes can be used to control text wrapping for table views, and autosizing for table and list views.

Wrap

This entry in the format configuration file indicates that text that would cause the row to exceed the width of the console display should be wrapped to the next line, as opposed to being truncated. The default behavior is to truncate the line. To indicate text wrapping, the <Wrap> node is placed inside the <TableRowEntry> for which it is to be used. This is generally used in the table view because the list view wraps text by default and the wide view avoids wrapping altogether.

```
. . .
   <TableRowEntry>
      <Wrap/>
      <TableColumnItems>
         <!-- insert TableColumnItems here -->
      </TableColumnItems>
   </TableRowEntry>
. . .
```

AutoSize

The table and wide views can specify autosizing as part of the view. Place the <AutoSize> node directly under the <TableControl> or <WideControl> node:

```
. . .
<TableControl>
   <AutoSize/>
```

```
        <TableHeaders>
            . . .
         </TableHeaders>
         <TableRowEntries>
            . . .
         </TableRowEntries>
    </TableControl>
    . . .
```

Scenarios

This section discusses some typical user scenarios that warrant specific examples. The example format files presented here may not be complete, but they contain enough of the configuration file to demonstrate each scenario. For each of the scenarios covered here, you can find the full format configuration file on the book's website. In cases where source code is necessary, those files are included as well.

Format Strings

A discussion of custom formatting objects wouldn't be complete without mentioning formatting strings. Format strings can be used within a script block expression to accomplish specific formatting of an object, such as `DateTime`; or a specific `FormatString` XML node can be declared to do this.

The following example uses a `FormatString` entry to display the start time of a `Process` object in table view:

```
. . .
   <TableColumnItem>
      <PropertyName>StartTime</PropertyName>
      <FormatString>{0:MMM} {0:dd} {0:HH}:{0:mm}</FormatString>
   </TableColumnItem>
. . .
```

This next example, from the `filesystem.format.ps1xml` file, shows how the `LastWriteTime` is formatted for all file and directory objects:

```
. . .
   <TableColumnItem>
      <ScriptBlock>
          [String]::Format("{0,10}  {1,8}", $_.LastWriteTime.ToString("d"), $_.Last-
WriteTime.ToString("t"))
       </ScriptBlock>
   </TableColumnItem>
. . .
```

In a `ScriptBlock` expression, you can call any method on the object. Therefore, if it has overloads of `ToString()` that take format string parameters, you can call that method as well to create your output string.

Formatting Deserialized Objects

Deserialized objects are created from serialized XML that results from `export-clixml`. `Import-clixml` creates deserialized objects from the intermediate XML (usually in file format). What's important to understand is that the deserialized objects differ from the original objects in a number of ways.

First, the object is considered *dead*. This means that instead of having an instance of the original object, the deserialized object is really a `PSObject` object with properties. For example, calling methods on a deserialized `Process` object won't work. The methods don't exist and there is no instance of a `Process` object to invoke them against.

Second, all the properties that existed for the original "live" object may not be present in the deserialized object. The properties that are serialized to XML are controlled via the serialization properties in the type's configuration file.

Lastly, the type of the object is different. For example, if the original object's type name was `System.Diagnostics.Process`, the deserialized object's type name is `Deserialized.System.Diagnostics.Process`.

The different type names enable PowerShell to treat deserialized objects differently from their original "live" counterparts if desired. For formatting purposes, you can choose to use the same view for deserialized objects, create different views, or not provide any view for them at all and let default formatting take place. When defining a view, it is possible to add multiple type names to the `ViewSelectedBy` node. Here's an example of what the `ViewSelectedBy` node would look like for live and deserialized `Process` objects:

```
. . .
   <ViewSelectedBy>
      <TypeName>System.Diagnostics.Process</TypeName>
      <TypeName>Deserialized.System.Diagnostics.Process</TypeName>
   </ViewSelectedBy>
. . .
```

Make sure that if a single view is formatting deserialized objects, it doesn't access any methods in the script block that rely on a live instance of the object. Stick to properties and you should be OK.

Class Inheritance

The `<ViewSelectedBy>` type name for a view takes into account inheritance and will be used for objects of derived types if no view is defined for that explicit type. Some scenarios may require more fine-grained control, and in this section you will learn about the available options and trade-offs involved in creating useful views for class hierarchies.

The simplest way of handling objects that inherit from each other is to define a view for the base class type. The view lookup will match derived types against the base class type view. This works great if you want to display the same properties for all the objects in the hierarchy. However, when you need to display different properties based on the derived type from the base class, it gets tricky.

The type of the first object to be displayed is used to determine which view to use. If all the objects to be displayed are of the same type, then this causes no problems. For example, assume you have the class hierarchy included on the website as `Figure8-5.cs`, which can be compiled into an assembly and installed as a snap-in using `InstallUtil.exe`. Make sure the `figure8-5_inheritance.format.ps1xml` format file is in the same directory as the compiled assembly. The directory of the assembly becomes the `ApplicationBase` setting in the Registry, which is used as the base path when searching for configuration files.

Here is the example class hierarchy:

```
public abstract class Employee
{  . . .  }

public class Tester : Employee
{  . . .  }

public class Developer : Employee
{  . . .  }

public class Manager : Employee
 {  . . .  }
```

The format configuration file included has a table view defined for `CustomFormatting.Employee` and `CustomFormatting.Manager`. The view for the `Manager` type has an extra column for the `DirectReports` property. Consider the following output:

```
PS C:\Documents and Settings\Owner> get-employees

Name                      Role                         Level
----                      ----                         -----
John Tester               Test                           61
Jane Tester               Test                           62
Frankie Dev               Dev                            61
Vinny Dev                 Dev                            61
Joey Dev                  Dev                            62
George Manager            Dev Mgr                        63
Jeff Manager              Test Mgr                       63

PS C:\Documents and Settings\Owner> get-employees -emp manager

Name                      Role                Level         # Reports
----                      ----                -----         ---------
George Manager            Dev Mgr              63           3
Jeff Manager              Test Mgr             63           2
```

The manager view is only selected if the first object from the `get-employees` cmdlet is of type `Manager`. Recall that with the table view, only one view can be selected, and the same columns for each object are displayed. If the `Manager` objects were first, then non-`Manager` objects would simply display blank text for the `# Reports` column, as the `DirectReports` property doesn't exist for those types.

There is not much more you can do with the table view in this case. The first view wins and sets the column headers. With list, custom, and wide views, however, you can display different results based on type within the view. For the list view, this is accomplished by adding extra `<ListEntry>` nodes under `<ListControl>`. You can key on the type name and decide to display the extra property for `Manager` types. This is done by adding an `<EntrySelectedBy>` node under the `<ListEntry>` node. The first

<ListEntry> is used for Manager objects, and all other objects that derive from Employee use the second ListEntry, which doesn't include the DirectReports property. Here's an excerpt that shows this:

```
. . .
<View>
   <Name>Employee</Name>
   <ViewSelectedBy>
      <TypeName>CustomFormatting.Employee</TypeName>
   </ViewSelectedBy>
   <ListControl>
      <ListEntries>
         <ListEntry>
            <EntrySelectedBy>
               <TypeName>CustomFormatting.Manager</TypeName>
            </EntrySelectedBy>
            <ListItems>
               <ListItem>
                  <PropertyName>Name</PropertyName>
               </ListItem>
               <ListItem>
                  <PropertyName>Role</PropertyName>
               </ListItem>
               <ListItem>
                  <PropertyName>Level</PropertyName>
               </ListItem>
               <ListItem>
                  <PropertyName>DirectReports</PropertyName>
               </ListItem>
            </ListItems>
         </ListEntry>
         <ListEntry>
            <ListItems>
               <ListItem>
                  <PropertyName>Name</PropertyName>
               </ListItem>
               <ListItem>
                  <PropertyName>Role</PropertyName>
               </ListItem>
               <ListItem>
                  <PropertyName>Level</PropertyName>
               </ListItem>
            </ListItems>
         </ListEntry>
      </ListEntries>
   </ListControl>
</View>
. . .
```

The same concept applies to wide and custom views. The same example format file includes multiple <WideEntry> definitions. One of them uses the <EntrySelectedBy> node to display manager names inside square brackets, while other objects display just the name with no brackets.

Selection Sets

When you have a group of objects that are related (through inheritance or in other similar ways) and you want them to use the same view, it is possible to create a *selection set*. A selection set is indicated by the `<SelectionSet>` XML node. This node can contain multiple type names, which are used to determine what view is to be selected for an object. This is handy in cases where you might be defining multiple views for that same set of objects. Rather than enter the type names in every view's `<ViewSelectedBy>` node, you can simply refer to the selection set. This also makes it easier to add or remove types from that set that will trickle down to all the views using it.

The `<SelectionSet>` definition is outside the `<ViewDefinitions>` node but under the `<Configuration>` node. The following example shows how to create a selection set for all the file and directory objects, as well as their deserialized counterparts. In fact, this example is plucked directly from the `filesystem.format.ps1xml` file included with PowerShell:

```
<Configuration>
   <SelectionSets>
      <SelectionSet>
         <Name>FileSystemTypes</Name>
         <Types>
            <TypeName>System.IO.DirectoryInfo</TypeName>
            <TypeName>System.IO.FileInfo</TypeName>
            <TypeName>Deserialized.System.IO.DirectoryInfo</TypeName>
            <TypeName>Deserialized.System.IO.FileInfo</TypeName>
         </Types>
      </SelectionSet>
   </SelectionSets>
   <ViewDefinitions>
      <View>
         <Name>Files</Name>
         <ViewSelectedBy>
            <SelectionSetName>FileSystemTypes</SelectionSetName>
         </ViewSelectedBy>
         <TableControl>
         . . .
         </TableControl>
      </View>
   </ViewDefinition>
</Configuration>
```

Colors

Because format files may contain script blocks, those script blocks may access the host APIs directly (via the built-in variable `$host`) to change the color of the foreground or background text. This makes it possible to customize the text colors of your environment to your heart's content. This also means that you can use the information from an object to change the color of text for that object as it is being displayed. This involves adding your own format file, as well as a little trickery regarding the `out-default` cmdlet.

For example, suppose that you want to display `Process` objects in different colors based on the amount of memory they are currently using (via `WorkingSet`). The following format configuration file displays the process information in red if `WorkingSet` is greater than 20MB, in yellow if between 10 and 20MB, and in green if less than 10MB:

```
<?xml version="1.0" encoding="utf-8" ?>
<Configuration>
   <ViewDefinitions>
      <View>
         <Name>ProcessViewWithColors</Name>
         <ViewSelectedBy>
            <TypeName>System.Diagnostics.Process</TypeName>
         </ViewSelectedBy>
         <TableControl>
            <TableHeaders>
               <TableColumnHeader>
                  <Label>Name:ID</Label>
               </TableColumnHeader>
               <TableColumnHeader>
                  <Label>WorkingSet</Label>
               </TableColumnHeader>
            </TableHeaders>
            <TableRowEntries>
               <TableRowEntry>
                  <TableColumnItems>
                     <TableColumnItem>
                        <ScriptBlock>$_.ProcessName + ":" + $_.Id</ScriptBlock>
                     </TableColumnItem>
                     <TableColumnItem>
                        <ScriptBlock>
          if ( $_.workingset -gt 20MB ) { $host.ui.rawui.foregroundcolor = "red"}
      elseif ($_.workingset -gt 10MB) { $host.ui.rawui.foregroundcolor = "yellow"}
          else { $host.ui.rawui.foregroundcolor = "green"}
        [int]($_.WorkingSet/1024)
                        </ScriptBlock>
                     </TableColumnItem>
                  </TableColumnItems>
               </TableRowEntry>
            </TableRowEntries>
         </TableControl>
      </View>
   </ViewDefinitions>
</Configuration>
```

After adding this format file to the configuration via `update-formatdata` and using it to display `Process` objects from `get-process`, you may notice that the console text color is still the same as whatever the last row's color happened to be. Unfortunately, there's no way to specify in the format configuration file that it should be set back to its original value after the last object is displayed. There is, however, a workaround using `out-default`.

The `out-default` cmdlet is what actually is invoked when no `format-*` cmdlet is specified. It is possible to customize the behavior of `out-default` by defining a function of the same name. The function will be invoked because command discovery will try to match a command string to functions before cmdlets. Therefore, use the following text from a script and dot-source the script to ensure that it is defined in the current session. Here, the `out-default` function will set the foreground text to gray after displaying the objects:

```
function out-default
{
# BeginProcessing()
#begin{}

# ProcessRecord()
# process {}

#EndProcessing()
end
  {
     $input | &(Get-Command -Type Cmdlet Out-Default)
     $host.UI.RawUI.ForegroundColor="Gray"
  }
}
```

Be aware that using this function will not display any objects until all objects have been streamed through the pipeline. The `out-default` cmdlet displays them as they're streamed. This is only noticeable if the number of objects being displayed is large. Defining this function and using the cmdlet-style syntax enables you to include custom script code before and after objects are displayed to the screen.

Summary

It is hoped that this chapter has provided enough detail for you to start creating your own format configurations files. Described in this chapter were the four different view types: table, list, wide, and custom. You also saw examples of how to use the `format-*` cmdlets to override the default formatting behavior. Finally, you examined each part of the XML format configuration file for the different view types, and used `update-formatdata` to add formatting files to the current session. Keep in mind that the ordering of the views is important when determining the default view for an object, as well as the view used for each different view type.

The sample format files should serve as a good baseline for creating your own custom formatting. It is recommended that you examine the format configuration files included with PowerShell, as they may spark ideas for your own custom formatting.

A

Cmdlet Verb Naming Guidelines

Windows PowerShell uses a verb-noun pair format to name cmdlets. When you are naming your cmdlets, you should specify the verb part of the name using one of the predefined verb names provided in the following tables. By using one of these predefined verbs, you ensure consistency between the cmdlets you create and those provided by Windows PowerShell and others.

The following lists of verbs are officially recommended by Microsoft. For the latest information, please refer to documents in the PowerShell SDK.

Common Verbs

Windows PowerShell uses the `VerbsCommon` class in the `System.Management.Automation` namespace to define verbs that are common in nature. The verbs defined in this class are described in the following table.

The "Common parameters" section in the Comment column contains a list of parameters commonly defined for this kind of cmdlet. The "Do not use" section of the Comment column contains verbs whose meaning overlaps with the common verb, and which should not be used. The "Use with" section of the Comment column contains a list of verbs that can be used for related cmdlets.

Verb Name	Description	Comment
Add	Add, append, or attach an element	**Common parameters:** At, After, Before, Create, Filter, ID, Name, Value **Do not use:** Append, Attach, Concatenate, Insert **Use with:** Remove
Clear	Remove all elements or content of a container	**Do not use:** Flush, Erase, Release, Unmark, Unset, Nullify
Copy	Copy a resource to another name or another container	**Common parameters:** Acl, Overwrite, Recurse, Strict, WhatIf **Do not use:** Duplicate, Clone, Replicate
Get	Get the contents, object, children, properties, relations, and so on, of a resource	**Common parameters:** All, As, Compatible, Continuous, Count, Encoding, Exclude, Filter, Include, ID, Interval, Name, Path, Property, Recurse, Scope, SortBy **Do not use:** Read, Open, Cat, Type, Dir, Obtain, Dump, Acquire, Examine, Find, Search **Use with**: Set
Lock	Lock a resource	**Use with**: Unlock
Move	Move a resource	**Do not use**: Transfer, Name, Migrate
New	Create a new resource	**Common parameters:** Description, ID, Name, Value **Do not use:** Create, Generate, Build, Make, Allocate **Use with:** Remove
Remove	Remove a resource from a container	**Common parameters:** (Get), Drain, Erase, Force, WhatIf **Do not use:** Delete, Disconnect, Detach, Drop, Purge, Flush, Erase, Release **Use with:** Add, New
Rename	Give a resource a new name	
Set	Set the contents, object, properties, relations, and so on, of a resource	**Common parameters:** PassThru **Do not use:** Write, Reset, Assign, Configure **Use with:** Get
Join	Join, or unite, so as to form one unit	**Use with:** Split
Split	Split an object into portions, parts, or fragments	**Use with:** Join
Select	Choose from among several; pick out	
Unlock	Unlock a resource	**Use with:** Lock

Data Verbs

Windows PowerShell uses the `VerbsData` class in the `System.Management.Automation` namespace to define the verbs commonly used when the cmdlet manipulates data. The verbs defined in this class are described in the following table.

Verb Name	Description	Comment
Backup	Backs up data	
Checkpoint	Creates a snapshot of the current state of the data or its configuration so that the state can be restored later	**Use with:** Restore
Compare	Compares the current resource with another resource and produces a set of differences	**Do not use:** Diff
Convert	Converts one encoding to another or from one unit to another (such as converting from feet to meters)	
ConvertFrom	Changes data from one format or encoding to another, where the source format is described by the noun name of the cmdlet. If data is being copied from a persistent data store, use Import.	**Use with:** ConvertTo, Convert
ConvertTo	Changes data from one format or encoding to another, where the destination format is described by the noun name of the cmdlet. If data is being copied to a persistent data store, use Export.	**Use with:** ConvertFrom, Convert
Dismount	Detaches an entity from a pathname location	
Export	Copies a set of resources to a persistent data store. If there is no persistent data store, use Convert, ConvertFrom, or ConvertTo.	**Do not use:** Extract, Backup
Import	Creates a set of resources from data in a persistent data store, such as a file. If there is no persistent data store, use Convert, ConvertFrom, or ConvertTo.	**Do not use:** Bulkload, Load
Initialize	Assigns a beginning value to a resource so that it is ready for use	**Do not use:** Erase, Renew, Rebuild, Reinitialize, Setup
Limit	Limits the consumption of a resource or applies a constraint to a resource	**Do not use:** Quota
Merge	Creates a single data instance from multiple instances	
Mount	Attaches an entity to a pathname location	**Use with:** Dismount
Restore	Rolls back the data state to a predefined set of conditions	**Use with:** Checkpoint
Update	Updates a resource with new elements	**Do not use:** Refresh, Renew, Recalculate, Re-index
Out	Sends data out of the environment	

Communication Verbs

Windows PowerShell uses the `VerbsCommunications` class in the `System.Management.Automation` namespace to define the verbs commonly used in communications. The verbs defined in this class are described in the following table.

Verb Name	Description	Comment
Connect	Associates an activity with a resource	**Use with:** Disconnect
Disconnect	Disassociates an activity from a resource	**Use with:** Connect
Read	Reads from a target	**Use with:** Write
Receive	Acquires elements from a source	**Use with:** Send **Do not use:** Read, Accept, Peek
Send	Sends elements to a destination	**Use with:** Receive **Do not use:** Put, Broadcast, Mail, Fax
Write	Writes to a target	**Use with:** Read

Diagnostic Verbs

Windows PowerShell uses the `VerbsDiagnostic` class in the `System.Management.Automation` namespace to define the verbs commonly used for diagnostics. The verbs defined in this class are described in the following table.

Verb Name	Description	Comment
Debug	Interacts with a resource or activity for the purpose of finding a flaw or a better understanding of what is occurring	
Measure	Identifies the resources that are consumed by a specified operation or retrieves statistics about a resource	
Ping	Determines whether a resource is active and responding to requests	
Resolve	Maps a shorthand name to a long name	
Test	Verifies the operation or consistency of a resource	**Do not use:** Diagnose, Verify, Analyze, Salvage, Verify
Trace	Tracks the activities that are performed by a specified operation	

Lifecycle Verbs

Windows PowerShell uses the `VerbsLifeCycle` class in the `System.Management.Automation` namespace to define the verbs commonly used for lifecycle management. The verbs defined in this class are described in the following table.

Verb Name	Description	Comment
Disable	Stops an activity of the cmdlet, or configures an item to be unavailable so that it cannot start again	**Use with:** Enable
Enable	Configures something to be available (for example, configures something so that it is able to start)	**Use with:** Disable
Install	Places a resource in the indicated location and optionally initializes it. Use with Uninstall.	**Do not use:** Setup
Restart	Terminates existing activity and starts it again with the same configuration. It uses a checkpoint to determine the configuration.	**Do not use:** Recycle
Resume	Starts an activity again after it has been suspended	**Use with:** Suspend
Start	Starts an activity	**Use with:** Stop **Do not use:** Launch, Initiate, Boot
Stop	Discontinues an activity	**Use with:** Start **Do not use:** End, Kill, Terminate, Cancel
Suspend	Pauses an activity	**Use with:** Resume **Do not use:** Verbs such as Pause
Uninstall	Removes a resource from an indicated location	**Use with:** Install

Security Verbs

Windows PowerShell uses the `VerbsSecurity` class in the `System.Management.Automation` namespace to define the verbs commonly used for security-related tasks. The verbs defined in this class are described in the following table.

Verb Name	Description	Comment
Block	Prevents access to a resource	**Use with:** Unblock
Grant	Grants access to a resource	**Use with:** Revoke
Revoke	Revokes access to a resource	**Use with:** Grant
Unblock	Permits access to a resource	**Use with:** Block

B

Cmdlet Parameter Naming Guidelines

Parameter names should be consistent across different cmdlets. Windows PowerShell defines and recommends the parameter names provided in this appendix. Cmdlet developers should choose from this list when possible. The tables presented here list recommended parameters from the following categories:

- Ubiquitous parameters
- Activity parameters
- Date/Time parameters
- Format parameters
- Property parameters
- Quantity parameters
- Resource parameters
- Security parameters

Ubiquitous Parameters

Parameter Name	Type	Description
Debug	Boolean	Enables debugging
ErrorAction	Enum	Tells the command what to do on error (e.g., stop, inquire)
ErrorVariable	String	Identifies a variable in which to place the command's error object

Parameter Name	Type	Description
Verbose	Boolean	Progress of the operation is displayed on the progress stream
Confirm	Boolean	Asks the user before the action is performed. This parameter is used for cmdlets that support `shouldprocess` only.
WhatIf	Boolean	This parameter is used for cmdlets that support `shouldprocess` only.

Activity Parameters

Parameter Name	Type	Description
CaseSensitive	Boolean	true = case sensitive, false = ignore case
Command	String	What command should be run
Compatible	String	Identifies what semantics to be compatible with (used for backward compatibility when changing semantics)
Compress	Boolean	
Compress	Keyword	
Confirm	Boolean	Asks the user before an action is performed
Continuous	Boolean	Keeps getting more information
Create	Boolean	Determines whether to create a resource if one does not already exist
Delete	Boolean	Deletes resources when done
Drain	Boolean	
Erase	Int32	Specifies the number of times a resource should be erased when it is deleted
Errors	String	Name of the variable in which error records will be stored
ErrorLevel	Int32	Level of problem to report
ErrorLimit	Int32	Maximum number of errors that should occur before the command is cancelled
Exclude	String	
Exclude	Keyword	
Fast	Boolean	
Filter	String	
Follow	Boolean	Tracks progress of an activity

Parameter Name	Type	Description
Force	Boolean	
Ignore	Array of keywords	
Incremental	Boolean	
Insert	Boolean	
Interactive	Boolean	
Interval	Hashtable of keyword/ values	For example, /interval {resumescan < = 15, retry < = 3}
Log	Boolean	Progress of operation is displayed on the progress stream
Migrate	Boolean	
Notify	Boolean	Indicates completion of an operation
Notify	Email address	Indicates completion of an operation
Overwrite	Boolean	
PassThru	Boolean	
Prompt	String	
Quiet	Boolean	
ReadOnly	Boolean	
Recurse	Boolean	
Repair	Boolean or string	
Retry	Int32	
Select	Array of keywords	List of items to select
SortBy	String	
Strict	Boolean	Considers any error a terminating error
Temp	Pathname	Location for temporary data
Temp	Boolean	Changes are temporary
TimeOut	Seconds	
Trace	Boolean	Internal operations are displayed on the progress stream
Truncate	Boolean	
Update	Boolean	Same as VERB

Parameter Name	Type	Description
Verbose	Boolean	Controls the quantity of data to retrieve/display
Verify	Boolean	Performs a test to ensure that an action occurred
Wait	Int32	Number of seconds the command will wait for required resources to become available
Wait	Boolean	Waits for user input before continuing
Warning	Boolean	Controls whether optional warning messages are displayed
Whatif	Boolean	Shows what would occur if the command actually ran (e.g., logs activities that would take place)
Write	Boolean	vs /Readonly

Date/Time Parameters

Parameter Name	Type	Description
Accessed	Boolean	Specifies which time /Before or /Since refers to. Incompatible with /Modified or /Created.
After	DateTimeExpression	
Before	DateTimeExpression	
Created	Boolean	Specifies which time /Before or /Since refers to. Incompatible with /Modified or /Accessed.
Modified	Boolean	Specifies which time /Before or /Since refers to. Incompatible with /Created or /Accessed.
Since	DateTimeExpression	
TimeStamp	Boolean	Sets or gets Timestamp

Format Parameters

Parameter Name	Type	Description
As	Keyword	Text, script
AsScript	Boolean	Outputs results as an msh script
AsText	CodePage	Treats binary elements as text using the specified codepage

Parameter Name	Type	Description
Binary	Boolean	
Char	Int32	
Elapsed	Boolean	Shows elapsed time
Encoding	Keyword	Ascii, UTF8, Unicode, UTF7
Exact	Boolean	
Format	String	
NewLine	Boolean	
Shortname	Boolean	Uses short names (e.g., 8.3 for filesystem)
Width	Int32	
Wrap	Boolean	

Property Parameters

Parameter Name	Type	Description
Cache	Keyword	
Count	Int32	
Default	Boolean	
Description	UserDescriptionString	
From	ResourceName	Reference object to get information from
Id	Int32	
Input	FileSpec	
LineCount	Int32	
Logname	String	
Location	String	Reference object to get information from
Name	String	
Output	FileSpec	
Owner	String	
Parameter	Hashtable	Mechanism to pass attribute/values through a common command
Password	Password	

Parameter Name	Type	Description
Priority	Int32	
Property	String	Property name
Reason	UserDescriptionString	Explanation for occurrence
Regex	Boolean	Use regex instead of wildcarding for this command
Statistic	Keyword	
Size	Int32	
Speed	Pair of int32	Baud rate (input, output)
State	Array of keywords	Named state (e.g., `KEYDOWN`)
Value	Object	
Version	VersionSpecifier	

Quantity Parameters

Parameter Name	Type	Description
All	Boolean	
Allocation	Int32	Number of items to allocate
BlockCount	Int64	
Count	Int64	
Most	Boolean	Sensible subset of all
Scope	Keyword	

Resource Parameters

Parameter Name	Type	Description
Assembly	String	
Application	String	
Attribute	String	FileSystem attributes
Class	Classname	For example, type

Parameter Name	Type	Description
Cluster	Clustername	
Directory	String	Directory or namespace location to perform an activity. When null, it specifies that the directory (not its contents) should be used.
Domain	String	Domain name
Drive	String	Drive name, e.g., C:
Event	String	Event name
FileName	Pathname	
Interface	Interface-Name	Network interface name
IpAddress	IpAddress	
Job	String	
Mac	MacAddress	
NodeName	Array of nodenames	Node to operate on
ParentID	Int32	
Port	String	Int for networking, but string for other types of port (e.g., biztalk)
Printer	PrinterName	
Size	Int32	
TID	String	Transaction ID
Type	String	Type of resource to operate on
URL	String	
User	Username	

Security Parameters

Parameter Name	Type	Description
ACL		
CertFile	FileName	A file containing a Base64 or DER-encoded x.509 certificate or a PKCS#12 file containing at least one certificate and key
CertIssuerName	String	A string indicating the issuer of a certificate, or a substring

Parameter Name	Type	Description
CertRequestFile	FileName	A file containing a Base64 or DER-encoded PKCS#10 certificate request
CertSerialNumber	String	Serial number issued by a cert authority
CertStoreLocation	String	Location of the certificate store. Typically, a file path.
CertSubjectName	String	A string indicating the issuer of a certificate, or a substring
CertUsage	String	A string representing the enhanced key usage or key usage. Can be represented as a bit bask, a bit, an OID, or a string.
CSPName	String	Name of the certificate service provider (CSP)
CSPType	Integer	Type of CSP
Group	String	A collection of principals
KeyAlgorithm	String	Key generation algorithm
KeyContainerName	String	Name of the key container
KeyLength	Int	Key length, in number of bits
Operation	String	An action that can be performed on a protected object
Principal	String	Unique identifiable entity
Privilege	Array of Privs	
Privilege	String	The ability to perform an operation
Role	String	Group of operations
SaveCred	Boolean	Use save credentials
Scope	String	Group of protected objects
SID	String	Unique identifier representing a principal
Trusted	Boolean	
TrustLevel	Keywords (Internet, intranet, fulltrust, etc.)	

C

Metadata

A key mechanism that enables the off-the-shelf parameter binding available to cmdlet developers is PowerShell's cmdlet metadata. Cmdlet metadata is a set of .NET custom attribute types that are applied to cmdlet classes and their members, and which provide the PowerShell execution engine with information necessary to run the cmdlets. Along with derivation from the cmdlet base classes, cmdlet metadata is what makes a .NET class a cmdlet.

The metadata attributes can be grouped into three general sets: the `CmdletAttribute` class, which is applied to the cmdlet class itself; the `Parameter` and `Alias` attributes, which are used to indicate that public properties and fields are cmdlet parameters; and the validation and transformation attributes, which enable a cmdlet developer to set restrictions on incoming data. One of the validation attributes, `ValidateArgumentsAttribute`, is not applied to parameters directly, but can be inherited and extended for custom validation and transformation.

Besides being directly applied to cmdlet parameters in code, the parameter metadata attributes can also be created at runtime and applied to dynamically created pseudo-parameters of cmdlets, and to the `Attributes` collection of PowerShell session-state variables.

This appendix serves as a reference describing the cmdlet metadata attribute classes, and provides examples of their use.

CmdletAttribute

The `CmdletAttribute` metadata is used to label a .NET class as a cmdlet class. In order to be recognized as a cmdlet, a class must derive from one of the cmdlet base classes and be marked with a `Cmdlet` attribute.

The `CmdletAttribute` metadata can be applied to classes that derive from one of the cmdlet base classes.

	Properties	
String	NounName	The noun part of the cmdlet's name
String	VerbName	The verb part of the cmdlet's name
String	DefaultParameterSetName	The name of the cmdlet's default parameter set
bool	SupportsShouldProcess	Boolean indicating whether the cmdlet implements the `ShouldProcess` mechanism
enum	ConfirmImpact	Indicates the risk level of data loss associated with running this cmdlet. Possible levels are High, Medium, Low, and None. The `remove-item` cmdlet, for example, would have a level of High.

Cmdlet Attribute Example

```
[Cmdlet("get", "widget", SupportsShouldProcess = false)]
public class GetWidgetCmdlet : Cmdlet
{...}
```

ParameterAttribute

The `ParameterAttribute` metadata is used to label properties and fields of cmdlet classes as parameters. During the parameter binding stage of cmdlet execution, data from the command line and from the incoming object stream is dynamically bound to the cmdlet parameter properties and fields, using the information in `ParameterAttribute` as a guide.

The `ParameterAttribute` metadata can be applied to public properties and fields.

	Properties	
Int	Position	For positional parameter binding, a zero-based index of this parameter's position on the command line
String	ParameterSetName	The name of the parameter set to which this parameter belongs
bool	Mandatory	Indicates whether this parameter must always be specified
bool	ValueFromPipeline	Indicates that this parameter takes its value from the incoming object stream
bool	ValueFromPipeline-ByPropertyName	Indicates that this parameter takes its value from a named property on objects in the incoming object stream
bool	ValueFromRemaining-Arguments	Indicates that this parameter takes its value from any command-line arguments that cannot be bound to other parameters
String	HelpMessage	A tooltip-like help message
String	HelpMessageBaseName	The resource base name for a localizable help message
String	HelpMessageResourceId	The resource identifier for a localizable help message

ParameterAttribute Example

```
[Parameter(Position = 0, ParameterSetName = "FileOperations",
           Mandatory = true)]
public string FileName
{...}

[Parameter(ParameterSetName = "FileOperations",
           ValueFromPipeline = true)]
public string WidgetName
{...}

[Parameter(ParameterSetName = ParameterAttribute.AllParameterSets,
           ValueFromRemainingArguments = true)]
public string[] ExtraArguments
{...}
```

- The `HelpMessage`, `HelpMessageBaseName`, and `HelpMessageResourceId` properties are present in PowerShell 1.0, but they are never used by the default host or cmdlets. These properties are intended for use by graphical hosts.
- The `ParameterAttribute` class also has a static string field named `AllParameterSets`, which can be used to indicate that a parameter applies to all parameter sets.
- Multiple `Parameter` attributes for different parameter sets can be applied to one property or field in the cmdlet class.

AliasAttribute

The `AliasAttribute` metadata enables the cmdlet developer to give a parameter multiple names without duplicating all of the information in the `ParameterAttribute` class. It is applied to properties and fields that also bear `ParameterAttribute` metadata.

The `AliasAttribute` can be applied to public properties and fields marked with `ParameterAttribute`.

	Properties	
String[]	AliasNames	The set of alternative names for this parameter

AliasAttribute Example

```
[Parameter()]
[Alias("FullFilePath", "SomethingElse")]
public string FileName
{...}
```

Argument Validation Attributes

The argument validation attributes can be further subdivided into attributes that limit incoming data to a set, pattern, length, count, or range of values; attributes that allow or disallow special values, such as null; and customizable attributes that validate or transform the incoming data.

ValidateSetAttribute

The `ValidateSetAttribute` metadata enables the developer to specify a set of valid values for a parameter. If a cmdlet is executed and an attempt is made to bind to the parameter a value that doesn't fall within the specified set, a parameter binding error will occur and the cmdlet will not execute.

The `ValidateSetAttribute` metadata can be applied to public properties and fields marked with `ParameterAttribute`.

	Properties	
IList<String>	ValidValues	The set of valid values for this parameter
bool	IgnoreCase	Indicates whether the set should be matched in a non-case-sensitive way. The default value is `true`.

ValidateSetAttribute Example

```
[Parameter(Position = 0, Mandatory = true)]
[ValidateSet("Visa", "Discover", "MasterCard")]
public string CardType
{...}
```

ValidatePatternAttribute

The `ValidatePatternAttribute` metadata is used to restrict a parameter's value based on whether or not the incoming data matches a regular expression pattern.

The `ValidatePatternAttribute` metadata can be applied to public properties and fields marked with `ParameterAttribute`.

	Properties	
String	RegExPattern	The pattern to be used for the match
RegExOptions	RegExOptions	A set of flags that control the behavior of .NET's regular expression implementation

ValidatePatternAttribute Example

```
[Parameter(Position = 0, Mandatory = true)]
[ValidatePattern("[0..9][0..9][0..9] [A..Z][A..Z][A..Z]")]
public string LicensePlate
{...}
```

ValidateLengthAttribute

The `ValidateLengthAttribute` metadata is used to restrict a parameter's value based on the length of an incoming string.

The ValidateLengthAttribute metadata can be applied to public properties and fields marked with ParameterAttribute.

	Properties	
Int32	MinLength	The minimum length of the incoming string
Int32	MaxLength	The maximum length of the incoming string

ValidateLengthAttribute Example

```
[Parameter(Position = 0, Mandatory = true)]
[ValidateLength(4, 10)]
public string PartCode
{...}
```

ValidateCountAttribute

The ValidateCountAttribute metadata is used to restrict a collection parameter's value based on the number of elements in the collection.

The ValidateCountAttribute metadata can be applied to public properties and fields marked with ParameterAttribute.

	Properties	
Int32	MinLength	The minimum number of elements to be bound to the parameter
Int32	MaxLength	The maximum number of elements to be bound to the parameter

ValidateCountAttribute Example

```
[Parameter(Position = 0, Mandatory = true)]
[ValidateCount(2, 4)]
public string[] DaysOfTheWeek
{...}
```

ValidateRangeAttribute

The ValidateRangeAttribute metadata is used to restrict a parameter's value based on a range of possible values, which are specified as objects of a type that implements IComparable.

The ValidateRangeAttribute metadata can be applied to public properties and fields marked with ParameterAttribute.

	Properties	
Object	MinRange	The minimum value in the range
Object	MaxRange	The maximum value in the range

ValidateRangeAttribute Example

```
[Parameter(Position = 0, Mandatory = true)]
[ValidateRange("charlie", "whiskey")]
public string AlphaBravoCode
{...}
```

When used as a hard-coded custom attribute, the input values are limited to objects that can be expressed as literals in code. However, an instance of this attribute can be created at runtime and applied to a pseudo-parameter of a cmdlet. In this case, the range objects can be anything you can create at runtime.

Allow and Disallow Attributes

AllowNullAttribute

The `AllowNullAttribute` metadata is used to indicate that a parameter can accept a null value.

The `AllowNullAttribute` metadata can be applied to public properties and fields of `reference` types, marked with `ParameterAttribute`.

AllowNullAttribute Example

```
[Parameter(Position = 0, Mandatory = true)]
[AllowNull()]
public string Name
{...}
```

AllowEmptyStringAttribute

The `AllowEmptyStringAttribute` metadata is used to indicate that a string parameter can accept an empty value. By default, a parameter binding exception will be thrown if an empty string is passed to a string parameter.

The `AllowEmptyStringAttribute` metadata can be applied to public properties and fields of type `string`, marked with `ParameterAttribute`.

AllowEmptyStringAttribute Example

```
[Parameter(Position = 0, Mandatory = true)]
[AllowEmptyString()]
public string Name
{...}
```

AllowEmptyCollectionAttribute

The `AllowEmptyCollectionAttribute` metadata is used to indicate that a `collection` parameter can accept an empty value.

The `AllowEmptyCollectionAttribute` metadata can be applied to public properties and fields of `collection` types, marked with `ParameterAttribute`.

AllowEmptyCollectionAttribute Example

```
[Parameter(Position = 0, Mandatory = true)]
[AllowEmptyCollection()]
public string[] Names
{...}
```

ValidateNotNullAttribute

The `ValidateNotNullAttribute` metadata is used to indicate that a `reference` type parameter cannot accept a null value.

The `ValidateNotNullAttribute` metadata can be applied to public properties and fields of `reference` types, marked with `ParameterAttribute`.

ValidateNotNullAttribute Example

```
[Parameter(Position = 0, Mandatory = true)]
public Process Job
{...}
```

ValidateNotNullOrEmptyAttribute

The `ValidateNotNullOrEmptyAttribute` metadata is used to indicate that a `collection` type parameter cannot accept a null or empty value. It also validates that none of the members of an incoming collection are null.

The `ValidateNotNullOrEmptyAttribute` can be applied to public properties and fields of `collection` or `string` types, marked with `ParameterAttribute`.

ValidateNotNullOrEmptyAttribute Example

```
[Parameter(Position = 0, Mandatory = true)]
[ValidateNotNullOrEmpty()]
public Process[] Jobs
{...}
```

CredentialAttribute

The `CredentialAttribute` metadata type is derived from the `ArgumentTransformationAttribute` class described in the next section. It transforms incoming objects into `PSCredential` objects.

The `CredentialAttribute` metadata can be applied to public properties and fields marked with `ParameterAttribute`.

CredentialAttribute Example

```
[Parameter(Position = 0, Mandatory = true)]
[Credential()]
public String Username
{...}
```

Extending Parameter Metadata Attributes

PowerShell provides three inheritable classes for creating custom parameter metadata attributes. Two of these can be used for validation, and the third can be used to dynamically modify or replace objects before they are bound to the cmdlet's parameters.

ValidateArgumentsAttribute

The `ValidateArgumentsAttribute` type is a base class for custom parameter validation attributes that validate an argument as a single object. It can be applied to nothing; you must first derive from it.

ValidateArgumentsAttribute Example

```
public class ValidateIsInMyAssemblyAttribute :
             ValidateArgumentsAttribute
{
    protected override void Validate(object arguments,
              EngineIntrinsics engineIntrinsics)
    {
        if (!arguments.GetType().Assembly == this.GetType().Assembly)
        {
            throw new ParameterBindingException(
                      string.Format("'{0}' isn't in my assembly.",
                      arguments.GetType().Name));
        }
    }
}
```

To create a custom validation attribute from the `ValidateArgumentsAttribute` class:

- Create a public class that derives from `ValidateArgumentsAttribute`.
- Override the `Validate()` method and add logic that throws a `ParameterBindingException` if your custom condition is false.

Collections passed to a parameter marked with this metadata will be passed to `Validate` as a single object without first being enumerated.

ValidateEnumeratedArgumentsAttribute

The `ValidateEnumeratedArgumentsAttribute` type is a base class for custom parameter validation attributes that validate the individual elements in a `collection` object. It can be applied to nothing; you must first derive from it.

ValidateEnumeratedArgumentsAttribute Example

```
public class ValidateAllInMyAssemblyAttribute : ValidateEnumeratedArgumentsAttribute
{
    protected override void ValidateElement(object element)
    {
        if (!element.GetType().Assembly == this.GetType().Assembly)
        {
            throw new ParameterBindingException(
                      string.Format("'{0}' isn't in my assembly.",
                      element.GetType().Name));
        }
    }
}
```

To create a custom validation attribute from the `ValidateEnumeratedArgumentsAttribute` class:

- Create a public class that derives from `ValidateEnumeratedArgumentsAttribute`.
- Override the `ValidateElement()` method and add logic that throws a `ParameterBindingException` if your custom condition is false.

Collections passed to a parameter marked with this metadata will be enumerated and each element of the collection will be passed to `ValidateElement` individually.

ArgumentTransformationAttribute

The `ArgumentTransformationAttribute` type is a base class for custom parameter validation attributes that perform transformations on incoming objects. It can be applied to nothing; you must first derive from it.

ArgumentTransformationAttribute Example

```
public class TurnBeansIntoPeasAttribute :
          ArgumentTransformationAttribute
{
    public override object Transform(EngineIntrinsics engineIntrinsics,
                                     object inputData)
    {
        if (inputData.ToString().ToLower() == "bean")
        {
            return "pea";
        }
        return inputData;
    }
}
```

To create a custom validation attribute from the `ArgumentTransformationAttribute` class:

- Create a public class that derives from `ArgumentTransformationAttribute`.
- Override the `Transform()` method and add logic that returns a possibly transformed version of the input object.

Collections passed to a parameter marked with this metadata will be passed to `Transform` as a single object without first being enumerated.

Adding Attributes to Dynamic Parameters at Runtime

Typically, parameter metadata of PowerShell cmdlets is defined in source code as .NET custom attributes. It's possible, however, for a cmdlet to enumerate its parameters at runtime, by implementing the `IDynamicParameters` interface. If the `IDynamicParameters` implementation returns a `RuntimeDefined-ParameterDictionary`, then the attribute classes must be created dynamically at runtime and added to the `Attributes` collection of each parameter. The following code demonstrates how you can add a `ValidateRangeAttribute` to a dynamic parameter at runtime:

```
[Cmdlet("filter", "name")]
public class FilterNameCmdlet : Cmdlet, IDynamicParameters
{
    RuntimeDefinedParameter firstName = new RuntimeDefinedParameter();

    protected override void ProcessRecord()
    {
        WriteObject(firstName.Value);
    }

    public object GetDynamicParameters()
    {
        RuntimeDefinedParameterDictionary parameters = new RuntimeDefined-
ParameterDictionary();

        // Set the name and type of the parameter
        firstName.Name = "FirstName";
        firstName.ParameterType = typeof(string);

        // Add a parameter attribute and a range attribute
        firstName.Attributes.Add(new ParameterAttribute());
        firstName.Attributes.Add(new ValidateRangeAttribute("Erin", "Jonathan"));

        // Add the parameter to the collection and return it
        parameters.Add(firstName.Name, firstName);
        return parameters;
    }
}
```

ValidateScriptAttribute

The PowerShell public API defines one more attribute class we haven't mentioned, and which is not documented in the SDK. The `ValidateScriptAttribute` metadata takes a PowerShell script block as its sole parameter, and therefore is not definable at compile time in the C# language. `ValidateScriptAttribute` can, however, be instantiated at runtime and applied to dynamic parameters or session-state variables.

D

Provider Base Classes and Overrides/Interfaces

This appendix lists cmdlet provider base classes and interfaces that you may derive from to implement a PowerShell provider. A brief description is provided along with each method and property.

CmdletProvider

`CmdletProvider` is a base class for all derived Windows PowerShell provider classes. It is possible for derive a class from this base class, but in most cases you would derive your classes from some derived classes such as the following:

- **ItemCmdLetProvider:** Derive from this class to expose an item as a PowerShell path and to support provider cmdlets such as `Get-PSProvider`.
- **ContainerCmdletProvider:** Derive from this class to support provider core cmdlets such as rename, move, and copy.
- **NavigationCmdletProvider:** Derive from this class to support navigation against a data store that has multiple levels.

Here is the prototype for the `CmdletProvider` base class:

```
namespace System.Management.Automation.Provider
{
    public abstract class CmdletProvider
    {
        //The credential used to run an operation
        public PSCredential Credential { get; }
```

```
//Wildcard patterns to determine which items are excluded
//when performing an action.
public Collection<string> Exclude { get; }


//The provider-specific filter supplied by the caller
public string Filter { get; }


//Whether to try vigorously to perform an operation
public SwitchParameter Force { get; }


//The host interaction APIs
public PSHost Host { get; }


//Wildcard patterns to determine which items are included
//when performing an action.
public Collection<string> Include { get; }


//Get the command invocation API for the current runspace
public CommandInvocationIntrinsics InvokeCommand { get; }


//Get the provider interface APIs for the current runspace
public ProviderIntrinsics InvokeProvider { get; }


//Get the session state for the current runspace
public SessionState SessionState { get; }


//Whether a stop request has been made on the provider.
public bool Stopping { get; }


//Get the dynamic parameters specified by the user.
protected Object DynamicParameters { get; }


//Get information about the current PowerShell provider.
protected internal ProviderInfo ProviderInfo { get; }


//Get the drive for the current operation
protected PSDriveInfo PSDriveInfo { get; }


//Query user to confirm whether PowerShell should proceed
//with an operation.
//
//Both should-process and should-continue can be used to
//confirm an operation with the user.  While the behavior of
```

```
//ShouldProcess can be affected by preference settings and
//command-line parameters that can specify whether the query
//is displayed to the user, the behavior of ShouldContinue
//is not affected by preference settings or command-line
//parameters.
public bool ShouldContinue(
    string query,
    string caption
    );
public bool ShouldContinue(string query,
    string caption,
    ref bool yesToAll,
    ref bool noToAll
    );


//Query user to confirm an operation before making changes
//to the system.
//
//Both should-process and should-continue can be used to
//confirm an operation with the user.  While the behavior of
//ShouldProcess can be affected by preference settings and
//command-line parameters that can specify whether the query
//is displayed to the user, the behavior of ShouldContinue
//is not affected by preference settings or command-line
//parameters.
public bool ShouldProcess(string target);
public bool ShouldProcess(
    string target,
    string action
);
public bool ShouldProcess(
    string verboseDescription,
    string verboseWarning,
    string caption
);
public bool ShouldProcess(
    string verboseDescription,
    string verboseWarning,
    string caption,
    out ShouldProcessReason shouldProcessReason
);


//PowerShell provider should call this method when encounter
//a fatal error.  Call WriteError method for nonfatal error.
public void ThrowTerminatingError(
    ErrorRecord errorRecord
);


//Writes a debug message to the host.
public void WriteDebug(
    string text
);
```

```
//Call this method write a error record to the pipeline
//and the provider will continue to perform more operations.
public void WriteError(
    ErrorRecord errorRecord
);


//Write an item to the output as a PSObject object
public void WriteItemObject(
    Object item,
    string path,
    bool isContainer
);


//Write a progress record to the host.  This method is called
//to display the progress of a PowerShell provider for a long
//running operation.  The behavior of progress status can be
//configured through the ProgressPreference variable.
public void WriteProgress(
    ProgressRecord progressRecord
);


//Write a property object to the output
public void WritePropertyObject(
    Object propertyValue,
    string path
);


//Writes a security descriptor object to the output
public void WriteSecurityDescriptorObject(
    ObjectSecurity securityDescriptor,
    string path
);


//Write a message to the host for informational purpose
public void WriteVerbose(
    string text
);


//Write a warning message to the host.  The behavior of
//Warning messages can be configured through the
//WarningPreference variable or the Verbose and Debug
//command-line options.
public void WriteWarning(
    string text
);
```

```
            //Get the resource string from the current assembly that
            //corresponds to the specified base name and resource
            //identifier.  Override this method if a different behavior
            //is required.
            public virtual string GetResourceString(
                string baseName,
                string resourceId
            );


            //PowerShell runtime call this method to initialize the
            //provider when the provider is loaded into a session.
            //The default implementation of this method returns the object
            //specified in the providerInfo parameter.  Provider should
            //override this method if it needs to initialize the provider
            //with additional information.
            protected virtual ProviderInfo Start(
                ProviderInfo providerInfo
            );


            //Call this method to add more parameters to the Start method
            //implemented by a PowerShell provider.
            protected virtual Object StartDynamicParameters();


            //The PowerShell runtime calls this method before it removes
            //a provider.  A PowerShell provider should override this
            //method to free any resources before the provider is removed
            //by the PowerShell runtime.
            protected virtual void Stop();


            //The PowerShell runtime call this method when the user
            //cancels an opertion.
            protected internal virtual void StopProcessing();
        }
    }
```

DriveCmdletProvider

The `DriveCmdletProvider` class defines a Windows PowerShell drive provider that supports operations for adding new drives, removing existing drives, and initializing default drives. For example, the `FileSystem` provider provided by Windows PowerShell initializes drives for all volumes that are mounted, such as hard drives and CD/DVD device drives.

The methods of this class must be overridden to provide the ability to create drives, initialize default drives (those that the specific provider should supply, given the user environment), as well as to remove drives.

Although it is possible to derive from this class, this class does not define the methods needed to get or change the data (referred to as "item") in the data store. In most cases, developers should derive from one of the following classes to implement their own Windows PowerShell providers:

- **ItemCmdletProvider:** This base class defines methods that can get, set, and clear the items of a data store.
- **ContainerCmdletProvider:** This base class defines methods that can get the child items (or just their names) of the data store, as well as methods that create, copy, rename, and remove items of a data store.
- **NavigationCmdletProvider:** This serves as the base class for Windows PowerShell providers that perform operations against items in a multi-level store.

This class derives from the `CmdletProvider` base class. The class prototype is as follows:

```
namespace System.Management.Automation.Provider
{
    public abstract class DriveCmdletProvider : CmdletProvider
    {
        //The provider override this method to map drives after
        //initialization.  All providers should mount a root drive
        //to increase discoverability. This root drive might contain
        //a set of locations that would be interesting as roots for
        //other mounted drives.
        protected virtual Collection<PSDriveInfo>
        InitializeDefaultDrives();

        //Use this method to associate provider-specific data
        //with a drive by deriving a new class from PSDriveInfo.
        protected virtual PSDriveInfo NewDrive(
            PSDriveInfo drive
        );


        //Use this method to add more parameters to the
        //New-Drive cmdlet for the provider.
        protected virtual Object NewDriveDynamicParameters();


        //Use this method to clean up any provider-specific data
        //before the drive is removed.
        protected virtual PSDriveInfo RemoveDrive(
            PSDriveInfo drive
        );
    }
}
```

ItemCmdletProvider

This class derives from the `DriveCmdletProvider` base class. It is a base class for cmdlet providers that expose an item as a PowerShell path. Deriving a class from `ItemCmdletProvider` allows the PowerShell engine to support a core set of cmdlets for getting and setting data items; however, it does not provide any container or navigation capabilities.

The `ItemCmdletProvider` prototype is as follows:

```
namespace System.Management.Automation.Provider
{
    public abstract class ItemCmdletProvider : DriveCmdletProvider
    {
        //Override this method to give the user access to the provider
        //objects using the get-item and get-childitem cmdlets.
        //Nothing is returned and all objects should be written
        //using the WriteItemObject method.
        //
        //Provider should not write objects that are generally hidden
        //from the user unless the Force property is set to true.
        protected virtual void GetItem(string path);


        //Use this method to add additional custom paramaters to
        //the Get-Item cmdlet.
        protected virtual object GetItemDynamicParameters(
            string path
        );


        //Override this method to allow the user to modify
        //provider objects using the set-item cmdlet.
        //
        //Provider should not write objects that are generally hidden
        //from the user unless the Force property is set to true.
        protected virtual void SetItem(
            string path,
            object value
        );


        //Use this method to add additional custom paramaters to
        //the Set-Item cmdlet.
        protected virtual object SetItemDynamicParameters(
            string path,
            object value
        );


        //Override this method to allow the user to clear
        //provider objects using the Clear-Item cmdlet.
        //
        //Provider should not clear or write objects that are
        //generally hidden from the user unless the Force property
        //is set to true.
        protected virtual void ClearItem(string path);


        //Use this method to add additional custom paramaters to
        //the Clear-Item cmdlet.
```

```
            protected virtual object ClearItemDynamicParameters(
                string path
            );


            //Override this method to allow the user to invoke
            //provider objects using the Invoke-Item cmdlet. The default
            //action for the path will be performed.
            //
            //Provider should not invoke objects that are generally
            //hidden from the user unless the Force property
            //is set to true.
            protected virtual void InvokeDefaultAction(
                string path
            );


            //Use this method to add additional custom paramaters to
            //the Invoke-Item cmdlet.  It retrieves the dynamic parameters
            //for the item at the indicated path
            protected virtual object InvokeDefaultActionDynamicParameters(
                string path
            );


            //Use this method to add additional custom paramaters to
            //the Test-Path cmdlet.
            protected virtual object ItemExistsDynamicParameters(
                string path
            );

        }
    }
```

ContainerCmdletProvider

The `ContainerCmdletProvider` base class defines a Windows PowerShell container provider that exposes a container of items to the user. Note that the Windows PowerShell container provider can be used only when there is one container with items in it. You must implement a Windows PowerShell navigation provider to support nested containers.

The `ContainerCmdletProvider` derives from the `ItemCmdletProvider` base class. By deriving from `ContainerCmdletProvider`, a provider gets all the functionality of the `ItemCmdletProvider` base class, plus the following set of core provider cmdlets:

- Get-ChildItem
- Rename-Item
- New-Item
- Remove-Item

- Set-Location
- Push-Location
- Pop-Location
- Get-Location -stack

The prototype of `ContainerCmdletProvider` is as follows:

```
namespace System.Management.Automation.Provider
{
//Base class for Cmdlet providers that expose a single
//level container of items.
    public abstract class ContainerCmdletProvider : ItemCmdletProvider
    {
        //Get the children of the item specifed by the path.
        //all objects should be written to the WriteItemObject method.
        //
        //Providers override this method to allow the user access
        //to data objects using the Get-ChildItem cmdlet.
        //
        //The value for recurse should only be true for classes
        //derived from NavigationCmdletProvider.
        //
        //The provider implementation should prevent infinite
        //recursion when there are circular links and the like.
        //
        //Provider should not get objects that are generally
        //hidden from the user unless the Force property
        //is set to true.
        protected virtual void GetChildItems(
            string path,
            bool recurse
        );

        //Use this method to add additional custom paramaters to
        //the Get-ChildItem cmdlet.
         protected virtual object GetChildItemsDynamicParameters(
            string path,
            bool recurse
        );


        //Get names of the children of the specified path.  All
        //objects should be written to the WriteItemObject method.
        //
        //Providers override this method to give the user access
        //to data objects using the get-childitem -name cmdlet.
        //
        //The provider implementation should prevent infinite
        //recursion when there are circular links and the like.
        //
        //Provider should not get objects that are generally
        //hidden from the user unless the Force property
        //is set to true.
```

```
protected virtual void GetChildNames(
    string path,
    ReturnContainers returnContainers
);

//Use this method to add additional custom paramaters to
//the Get-ChildItem -name cmdlet.
protected virtual object GetChildNamesDynamicParameters(
   string path);


//Rename the item to the new name.  The renamed items
//should be written using WriteItemObject.
//
//Providers override this method to support the ability
//to rename objects using the rename-item cmdlet.
//
//Provider should not allow renaming objects that are
//generally hidden from the user unless the Force property
//is set to true.
//
//RanameItem does not support moving the object from one
//location to another.  Use MoveItem instead for that purpose.
protected virtual void RenameItem(
    string path,
    string newName
);

//Use this method to add additional custom paramaters to
//the Rename-Item cmdlet.
protected virtual object RenameItemDynamicParameters(
    string path,
    string newName
);

//Create a new item of the specified type at the
//specified path.
//
//Providers override this method to support the ability
//to create new objects using the new-item cmdlet.
//
//itemTypeName is provider specific.
protected virtual void NewItem(
    string path,
    string itemTypeName,
    object newItemValue
);

//Use this method to add additional custom paramaters to
//the New-Item cmdlet.
protected virtual object NewItemDynamicParameters(
    string path,
    string itemTypeName,
    object newItemValue
);
```

```
//Remove the item specified by the path
//
//recurse is a boolean value used to determine if all children
//in a subtree should be removed.  This parameter should only
//be true for NavigationCmdletProvider derived classes.
//
//Providers override this method to support the ability
//to remove objects using the remove-item cmdlet.
//
//Provider should not allow removing objects that are
//generally hidden from the user unless the Force property
//is set to true.
protected virtual void RemoveItem(
    string path,
    bool recurse
);


//Override this method to add additional custom paramaters to
//the Remove-Item cmdlet.
protected virtual object RemoveItemDynamicParameters(
    string path,
    bool recurse
);


//Determines if the item specified by the path has children.
//
//Providers override this method to give the provider
//infrastructure the ability to determine if a particular
//provider object has children without having to retrieve
//all the child items.
protected virtual bool HasChildItems(string path);


//Copy an item to a new path.  The boolean value of recurse
//tells the provider whether to recurse sub-containers
//when copying, and it should only be true for
//NavigationCmdletProvider derived providers.
//
//Providers override this method to support the ability to
//copy objects using the copy-item cmdlet.
//
//By default overrides of this method should not copy objects
//over existing items unless the Force property is set to
//true.
//
//If recurse is true, the provider implementation should
//prevent infinite recursion when there are circular links
//and the like.
protected virtual void CopyItem(
    string path,
    string copyPath,
    bool recurse
);
```

```
            //Use this method to add additional custom paramaters to
            //the Copy-Item cmdlet.
            protected virtual Object CopyItemDynamicParameters(
                string path,
                string destination,
                bool recurse
            );
        }
    }
```

NavigationCmdletProvider

The `NavigationCmdletProvider` class defines a Windows PowerShell navigation provider that performs operations for items that use more than one container. Deriving from this class enables users to work with nested containers using path and recursive commands. The `NavigationCmdletProvider` class derives from the `ContainerCmdletProvider` base class.

Here's the definition of the `NavigationCmdletProvider` class:

```
    namespace System.Management.Automation.Provider
    {
    public abstract class NavigationCmdletProvider :
                                 ContainerCmdletProvider
        {
            //Join two path segments with a path separator character.
            protected virtual string MakePath(
                string parent,
                string child
            );


            //Get and return the remaining parent segment of the path.
            protected virtual string GetParentPath(
                string path,
                string root
            );

            //Return the normalized path relative to the basePath.
            protected virtual string NormalizeRelativePath(
                string path,
                string basePath
            );


            //Return the child segment of the path
            protected virtual string GetChildName(string path);
```

```
        //Return true if the path is a container.
        //
        //Providers supporting ExpandWildcards, Filter, Include, or
        //Exclude should ensure that the path passed meets those
        //requirements.
        protected virtual bool IsItemContainer(string path);


        //Move the item specified by path to the destination path.
        //All the objects that were moved should be written using
        //WriteItemObject method.  Implementing this methods allows
        //the provider to support the Move-Item cmdlet.
        //
        //By default overrides of this method should not move objects
        //over existing items unless the Force property is set to
        //true.
        protected virtual void MoveItem(
            string path,
            string destination
        );


        //Use this method to add additional custom paramaters to
        //the Move-Item cmdlet.
        protected virtual object MoveItemDynamicParameters(
            string path,
            string destination
        );
    }
}
```

IContentCmdletProvider

The `IContentCmdletProvider` interface defines a content provider that performs operations on the content of a data item. Use `IContentReader` to read contents from an item, and `IContentWrite` to write contents to an item.

The interface definition of `IContentCmdletProvider` is as follows:

```
namespace System.Management.Automation.Provider
{
//Only classes that derive from CmdletProvider or its
//derived classes should implement this interface.
    public interface IContentCmdletProvider
    {
        //Get the content reader for the item.
        //
```

```
            //By default overrides of this method should not return
            //a content reader for hidden objects unless the Force
            //property is set to true.
            IContentReader GetContentReader(string path);

            //Use this method to add additional custom paramaters to
            //the Get-Content cmdlet.
            object GetContentReaderDynamicParameters(string path);

            //Get the content writer for the item.
            //
            //By default overrides of this method should not return
            //a content writer for hidden objects unless the Force
            //property is set to true.
            IContentWriter GetContentWriter(string path);

            //Use this method to add additional custom paramaters to
            //the Set-Content and Add-Content cmdlets.
            object GetContentWriterDynamicParameters(string path);

            //Clear the content from the item.
            //
            //By default overrides of this method should not clear
            //hidden objects unless the Force property is set to true.
            void ClearContent(string path);

            //Use this method to add additional custom paramaters to
            //the Clear-Content cmdlet.
            object ClearContentDynamicParameters(string path);
        }
    }
```

IContentReader

The `IContectReader` interface defines the methods used to implement a content reader. The interface definition is as follows:

```
namespace System.Management.Automation.Provider
{
    public interface IContentReader : IDisposable
    {
        //Read an array of blocks of data from the item.
        //What makes a "block" is provider specific.
        IList Read(long readCount);

        //Set the position from where data will be read next time.
        void Seek(long offset, SeekOrigin origin);

        //Closes the reader and resources held by the reader.
        void Close();
    }
}
```

IContentWriter

The IContectWrite interface defines the methods used to implement a content writer. The interface definition is as follows:

```
namespace System.Management.Automation.Provider
{
    public interface IContentWriter : IDisposable
    {
        //Write an array of blocks of data to the item.
        //What makes a "block" is provider specific.
        IList Write(IList content);

        //Set the position from where data will be written next time.
        void Seek(long offset, SeekOrigin origin);

        //Closes the writer and resources held by the writer.
        void Close();
    }
}
```

IPropertyCmdletProvider

The IPropertyCmdletProvider interface is used by PowerShell providers to expose properties of an item in the data store. Implementing this interface enables the provider to support the following ItemProperty-related cmdlets:

- Clear-ItemProperty
- Get-ItemProperty
- Set-ItemProperty

Following is the IPropertyCmdletProvider interface definition:

```
namespace System.Management.Automation.Provider
{
    public interface IPropertyCmdletProvider
    {
        //Providers implement this method to support the
        //Get-Itemproperty cmdlet.
        //
        //By default overrides of this method should not retrieve
        // properties from hidden objects unless the Force property
        //is set to true.
        void GetProperty(
            string path,
            Collection<string> providerSpecificPickList
        );


        //Use this method to add additional custom paramaters to
        //the Get-Itemproperty cmdlet.
```

```
        object GetPropertyDynamicParameters(
            string path,
            Collection<string> providerSpecificPickList
        );


        //Providers implement this method to support the
        //Set-Itemproperty cmdlet.
        //
        //By default overrides of this method should not set
        //properties of hidden objects unless the Force property
        //is set to true.
        void SetProperty(
            string path,
            PSObject propertyValue
        );


        //Use this method to add additional custom paramaters to
        //the Set-Itemproperty cmdlet.
        object SetPropertyDynamicParameters(
            string path,
            PSObject propertyValue);


        //Providers implement this method to support the
        //Clear-Itemproperty cmdlet.
        //
        //By default overrides of this method should not clear
        //properties of hidden objects unless the Force property
        //is set to true.
        void ClearProperty(
            string path,
            Collection<string> propertyToClear
        );


        //Use this method to add additional custom paramaters to
        //the Clear-Itemproperty cmdlet.
        object ClearPropertyDynamicParameters(
            string path,
            Collection<string> propertyToClear);
    }
}
```

IDynamicPropertyCmdletProvider

The `IDynamicPropertyCmdletProvider` interface, derived from `IPropertyCmdletProvider`, is used by PowerShell providers to manage dynamic properties of an item. Implementing this interface enables the provider to support the following `ItemProperty`-related cmdlets:

- Copy-ItemProperty
- Move-ItemProperty

- New-ItemProperty
- Remove-ItemProperty
- Rename-ItemProperty

Following is the `IDynamicPropertyCmdletProvider` interface definition:

```
namespace System.Management.Automation.Provider
{
public interface IDynamicPropertyCmdletProvider :
                       IPropertyCmdletProvider
    {
        //Providers implement this method to support the
        //New-Itemproperty cmdlet.
        //
        //By default overrides of this method should not create
        //a new property from hidden objects unless the Force property
        //is set to true.
        void NewProperty(
            string path,
            string propertyName,
            string propertyTypeName,
            object value
        );


        //Use this method to add additional custom paramaters to
        //the New-Itemproperty cmdlet.
        object NewPropertyDynamicParameters(
            string path,
            string propertyName,
            string propertyTypeName,
            object value
        );


        //Providers implement this method to support the
        //Remove-Itemproperty cmdlet.
        //
        //By default overrides of this method should not remove
        //properties from hidden objects unless the Force property
        //is set to true.
        void RemoveProperty(
            string path,
            string propertyName
        );


        //Use this method to add additional custom paramaters to
        //the Remove-Itemproperty cmdlet.
        object RemovePropertyDynamicParameters(
            string path,
            string propertyName
        );
```

```
//Providers implement this method to support the
//Rename-Itemproperty cmdlet.
//
//By default overrides of this method should not rename
//a property from hidden objects unless the Force property
//is set to true.
void RenameProperty(
    string path,
    string sourceProperty,
    string destinationProperty
);


//Use this method to add additional custom paramaters to
//the Rename-Itemproperty cmdlet.
object RenamePropertyDynamicParameters(
    string path,
    string sourceProperty,
    string destinationProperty
);


//Providers implement this method to support the
//Copy-Itemproperty cmdlet.
//
//By default overrides of this method should not copy
//properties from or to hidden objects unless the Force
//property is set to true.
void CopyProperty(
    string sourcePath,
    string sourceProperty,
    string destinationPath,
    string destinationProperty
);


//Use this method to add additional custom paramaters to
//the Copy-Itemproperty cmdlet.
object CopyPropertyDynamicParameters(
    string sourcePath,
    string sourceProperty,
    string destinationPath,
    string destinationProperty
);


//Providers implement this method to support the
//Move-Itemproperty cmdlet.
//
//By default overrides of this method should not move
//properties from hidden objects unless the Force property
//is set to true.
```

```
        void MoveProperty(
            string sourcePath,
            string sourceProperty,
            string destinationPath,
            string destinationProperty
        );


        //Use this method to add additional custom paramaters to
        //the Move-Itemproperty cmdlet.
        object MovePropertyDynamicParameters(
            string sourcePath,
            string sourceProperty,
            string destinationPath,
            string destinationProperty
        );
    }
}
```

E

Core Cmdlets for Provider Interaction

This appendix lists the cmdlets shipped with Windows PowerShell that directly interact with different provider interfaces. All these cmdlets are common cmdlets that work with any provider. The provider must, however, implement certain interfaces or derive from certain classes to take advantage of these cmdlets. The following sections describe these common cmdlets and what a provider implementation must do to take advantage of them.

Drive-Specific Cmdlets

These cmdlets support operations such as creating a new drive, removing a drive, and so on, in the context of a provider. A provider implementation must derive from `DriveCmdletProvider` in order to take advantage of these cmdlets.

Cmdlet	Description
New-PSDrive	Supports creating a new drive
Remove-PSDrive	Supports removing a drive
Get-PSDrive	Supports retrieving information about an existing drive

Item-Specific Cmdlets

These cmdlets support operations such as the getting and setting of data on one or more items in the context of a provider. A provider implementation must derive from `ItemCmdletProvider` in order to take advantage of these cmdlets.

Cmdlet	Description
Get-Item	Supports retrieving information about an existing item
Set-Item	Supports setting a value to an item
Clear-Item	Supports clearing an item. The item will not be removed, however. For example, in the context of a variable provider, the following operation clears the value of variable `TestVariable`: `PS D:\psbook> Clear-Item Variable:TestVariable`
Invoke-Item	Invokes the provider-specific default action on an item

Container-Specific Cmdlets

These cmdlets support operations such as getting children, removing an item, creating an item, and so on, in the context of a provider. A provider implementation must derive from `ContainerCmdletProvider` in order to take advantage of these cmdlets.

Cmdlet	Description
Get-ChildItem	Retrieves items and child items from a specified location
Rename-Item	Renames an existing item
New-Item	Creates a new item
Remove-Item	Removes an existing item
Copy-Item	Copies an existing item from a specified location

Property-Specific Cmdlets

These cmdlets support operations such as getting a property of an item, clearing a property of an item, and so on, in the context of a provider. A provider implementation must implement the interface `IPropertyCmdletProvider` in order to take advantage of these cmdlets.

Cmdlet	Description
Get-ItemProperty	Retrieves properties of a specified item from a specified location
Set-ItemProperty	Sets the value of a property
Clear-ItemProperty	Clears the value of a property. The property will not be removed, however.

Dynamic Property Manipulation Cmdlets

These cmdlets support operations such as renaming a property, moving a property of an item, and so on, in the context of a provider. A provider implementation must implement the interface `IDynamicPropertyCmdletProvider` in order to take advantage of these cmdlets.

Cmdlet	Description
Copy-ItemProperty	Copies a property and its value from a specified location to another location
Move-ItemProperty	Moves a property and its value from a specified location to another location
New-ItemProperty	Creates a new property of an item
Remove-ItemProperty	Removes a property of an item
Rename-ItemProperty	Renames a property of an item

Content-Related Cmdlets

These cmdlets are designed to manage the contents of an item. They support operations such as clearing content, retrieving content, and so on. A provider implementation must implement the interfaces `IContentbreak CmdletProvider`, `IContentReader`, and `IContentWriter` in order to take advantage of these cmdlets.

Cmdlet	Description
Add-Content	Adds content to a specified item
Clear-Content	Clears the content of a specified item
Get-Content	Retrieves the content of a specified item
Set-Content	Sets the content of a specified item

Security Descriptor–Related Cmdlets

These cmdlets are designed to manage the security descriptors of a provider store. A provider implementation must implement the interface `ISecurityDescriptorCmdletProvider` in order to take advantage of these cmdlets.

Cmdlet	Description
Get-Acl	Gets the security descriptor for an item
Set-Acl	Sets the security descriptor for an item

Index

SYMBOLS

A

B

C

D

Q

R